What people are saying about …

REIMAGINING CHURCH

"Dissent is a gift to the church. It is the imagination of the prophets that continually call us back to our identity as the peculiar people of God. May Viola's words challenge us to become the change that we want to see in the church … and not to settle for anything less than God's dream for Her."

Shane Claiborne, author, activist, and recovering sinner
(thesimpleway.org)

"True to form, this book contains a thoroughly consistent critique of prevailing forms of church. However, in *Reimagining Church,* Frank Viola also presents a positive vision of what the church can become if we truly reembraced more organic, and less institutional, forms of church. This is a no-holds-barred prophetic vision for the church in the twenty-first century."

Alan Hirsch, author of *The Forgotten Ways* and
The Shaping of Things to Come

"Frank not only pulls fresh insights out of well-known concepts, but also keeps challenging us to go back to basics and focus on Christ Himself. Thank you, Frank! This practical book will identify what church can look like when it is focused on Jesus."

Tony Dale, author and editor of *House2House* magazine
and founder of The Karis Group

"*Reimagining Church* is a valuable addition to the resources being produced on the subject of organic churches. Written from the perspective of a long-time practitioner, Frank conveys these concepts with his usual clarity and insight and covers many of the practical aspects of starting a church. I recommend this book to anyone interested in organic church."

Felicity Dale, author of *An Army of Ordinary People* and *Getting Started: A Practical Guide to House Church Plantings*

"Reimagining Church will be certain to disturb the comfortable and comfort the disturbed at the same time. Frank Viola cuts through the fog by putting his finger on the problems of man-made churchianity, while providing a solidly biblical, practical, and strategic vision for a powerful New Testament expression of the body of Christ."

Rad Zdero, PhD, author of *The Global House Church Movement* and editor of *Nexus: The World House Church Movement Reader*

"Reimagining Church is a readable (and livable!) description of organic, New Testament–rooted church life for the twenty-first century. Avoiding the weeds of both wooden fundamentalism and unreflective over-contextualization, Frank Viola paints a winsome and attractive portrait of a gospel people, inhabited by the Holy Spirit with God in Christ as their energetic center. Frank helps us learn from the peculiar genius of Jesus and His earliest followers, planting seeds for authentic, deeply rooted life together."

Mike Morrell, Graduate Fellow in Emergent Studies, MA in Strategic Foresight, Regent University (zoecarnate.com)

"What if the word *church* in ordinary conversation called to mind 'uncontrived,' 'joy,' or 'where God has His way' instead of pews, parking lots, and preachers? What if church people had no idea what a 'sinner's prayer' or 'tithing' meant, but were instead joyfully repentant, generous without hesitation, and innately compelled by love? What if church were not a place to learn religion but the best tangible proof of God's existence? *Reimagining Church* hazards a dream while pulling together the best rational arguments for church as it could be."

Charles J. Wilhelm, author of *Biblical Dyslexia: Overcoming the Barriers to Understanding Scripture*

"For those who are not threatened by the idea that church must change, *Reimagining Church* is an absolutely timely and much-needed perspective, delivering a solid biblical vision for the body of Christ. Using the entire scope of New Testament church life, Frank Viola lays out the core values and the essential principles that must form the foundation of life together as the body of Christ. The book delivers an exceptionally hopeful, visionary picture of all that church can and should be."

Grace, blogging at Kingdomgrace.wordpress.com

"The body of Christ has been stifled by human traditions for far too long. *Reimagining Church* charts a fresh course for the church that recovers the simplicity of Christ and listens seriously to what the voice of the Great Shepherd is saying to His people."

Jon Zens, editor of *Searching Together* and author of *A Church Building Every ½ Mile: What Makes American Christianity Tick?*

"If *Pagan Christianity* exposes the reality that much of our current church practice has little basis in the Bible, *Reimagining Church* takes the next step to establish what truly biblical church life looks like. With the inner life of the Trinity as the starting point, Viola paints an amazing picture of organic church life."

John White, community facilitator at LK10: A Community of Practice for Church Planters

"If we are indeed at the cusp of the next major reformation of the church, as many suggest, then Frank Viola is one of the significant voices we all should lend our ears to. Frank's humble heart and bold keyboard have once again delivered a book to be read by those who desire to take an honest look at the state of the contemporary church. *Reimagining Church* calls us to first remember the church from the original blueprint of Scripture."

Lance Ford, cofounder of Shapevine.com

"Whether you agree with all that Frank Viola writes in this book or not, I'm sure its contents will challenge you to rethink the way church is done. It will cause you to reconsider why we do many of the things we do and the way in which we do them. If you, like me, believe we are living in one of the greatest shifts in Christendom that we have ever known, then this book is a valuable tool to help you ask the right questions as you journey."

Tony Fitzgerald, apostolic team leader and international speaker

PURSUING THE DREAM OF
ORGANIC CHRISTIANITY
REIMAGINING
CHURCH
FRANK VIOLA

David C Cook®
transforming lives together

REIMAGINING CHURCH
Published by David C. Cook
4050 Lee Vance View
Colorado Springs, CO 80918 U.S.A.

David C. Cook Distribution Canada
55 Woodslee Avenue, Paris, Ontario, Canada N3L 3E5

David C. Cook U.K., Kingsway Communications
Eastbourne, East Sussex BN23 6NT, England

David C. Cook and the graphic circle C logo
are registered trademarks of Cook Communications Ministries.

The Web site addresses recommended throughout this book are offered as a
resource to you. These Web sites are not intended in any way to be or imply an
endorsement on the part of David C. Cook, nor do we vouch for their content.

Unless otherwise noted, Scripture quotations are taken from the *Holy Bible, New International Version®. NIV®*. Copyright © 1973, 1978, 1984 by International Bible Society. Used by permission of Zondervan. Scripture quotations marked NKJV are taken from the New King James Version. Copyright © 1982 by Thomas Nelson, Inc. Used by permission. All rights reserved; NLT are taken from the *Holy Bible, New Living Translation*, copyright © 1996. Used by permission of Tyndale House Publishers, Inc. Wheaton, Illinois 60189. All rights reserved; KJV are taken from the King James Version of the Bible. (Public domain.); NASB are taken from the *New American Standard Bible*, Copyright © 1960, 1995 by The Lockman Foundation. Used by permission; YLT is from Young's Literal Translation of the Bible. (Public Domain.); DARBY is from the Darby Translatioin. (Public Domain.) Italics in Scripture are added by the author for emphasis.

ISBN 978-1-4347-6875-9
LCCN 2008928481

Published in association with the literary agency of Daniel Literary
Group, 1701 Kingsbury Dr., Ste. 100, Nashville, TN 37215

The Team: Don Pape, John Blase, Amy Kiechlin, Jaci Schneider, and Karen Athen
Cover/Interior Design: Disciple Design
Cover Photo: Image Source

Printed in the United States of America
First Edition 2008

1 2 3 4 5 6 7 8 9 10

022608

To every Christian who has reimagined church

Other Books by Frank Viola

Pagan Christianity

The Untold Story of the New Testament Church

Rethinking the Will of God

Bethany

For these titles and more, visit **www.ptmin.org.**

To correspond with the author, e-mail him at **Violabooks@aol.com.**

To subscribe to Frank's free monthly eNewsletter, go to **http://www.ptmin.org/network.html.**

CONTENTS

PREFACE

After thirteen years of attending scores of churches and para-church organizations, I took the daring step of leaving the institutional church. That was in 1988. Since that time, I've never returned to institutional Christianity. Instead, I've been meeting in what I call "organic churches."

Why did I leave the institutional church? To begin with, I became painfully bored with Sunday-morning church services. That was true across the board—no matter what denomination (or nondenomination) I attended. I also saw very little spiritual transformation in the people who attended these churches. And the spiritual growth that I myself experienced seemed to occur *outside* of traditional church settings.

In addition, something deep within me longed for an experience of church that mapped to what I read about in my New Testament. And I couldn't seem to find it in any traditional church I attended. In fact, the more I read the Bible, the more I became convinced that the contemporary church had departed far from its biblical roots. The result was that I pulled the rip cord on institutional Christianity, and I began meeting with a group of Christians in an organic way.

After I took that step, friends and acquaintances would often ask me, "So where do you go to church?" Giving an answer was always a study in awkwardness. "I belong to a church that doesn't have a pastor or a church building; we meet very much like the early Christians did, and we are consumed with Jesus Christ" was my standard reply. But as soon as those words left my mouth, the person asking would typically look at me as though I had come from Planet 10!

Today, I'm still asked the question, "So where do you go to church?" But I have a better way of articulating an answer than I did twenty years ago (though I admit that my answer is still clumsy and imperfect).

Herein lies the purpose of this book: to articulate a biblical, spiritual, theological, and practical answer to the question, Is there a viable way of doing church outside the institutional church experience, and if so, what does it look like?

If the past twenty years have taught me anything, they have taught me this: There will be two major responses to this book. One will sound something like this: "Thank goodness, I'm not crazy! I thought I lost my mind. I'm grateful that there are others who feel the same way I do about church. This book has given language to feelings and beliefs I've had for years. And it's given me hope that there really is a church life experience beyond what's commonly known and accepted."

The other will sound something like this: "How dare you challenge our church practices! God loves the church. What right do you have to criticize it!? And who gives you the right to say that *your* way of doing church is the *only* valid way!?"

I'll be the first to admit that I am not beyond correction in my views. I'm still growing and learning. However, the problem with this particular objection is that it exposes the very problem that this book sets out to address. Namely, we Christians are very confused about what the church is. By no means am I criticizing the church. In fact, I'm writing this volume because I love the church very much. And it's because of that love that I wish to see the body of Christ express itself in ways that I believe God originally intended. The church, therefore, should not be confused with an organization, a denomination, a movement, or a leadership structure. The church is the people of God, the very bride of Jesus Christ. And as I will argue in this book, God has not been silent on how the church naturally expresses herself on the earth. Therefore, it's the *present practices* of the church that I'm seeking to reimagine, not the church itself.

In addition, I would never claim that there is one "right" way of doing church. And I certainly do not claim that I've found it. This book reimagines church in some fresh ways—ways that I believe are in harmony with the teachings of Jesus and the apostles. And for me and scores of other believers, we have found these ways to match our deepest longings as Christians.

Two books precede this one. The first is titled *The Untold Story of the New Testament Church*. In *The Untold Story*, I rehearse the entire saga of the first-century church in chronological order. The book of Acts and the Epistles are blended together to create an unbroken narrative of the early church. *Reimagining Church* is based on that free-flowing story. The difference is that *Reimagining* takes certain frames from that beautiful narrative and divides them up into specific categories. Together, both books paint a compelling portrait of New Testament church life.

The second book, titled *Pagan Christianity*, historically demonstrates that the contemporary church has strayed far from its original roots. The church as we know it today evolved (or more accurately, devolved) from a living, breathing, vibrant, organic expression of Jesus Christ into a top-heavy, hierarchical organization whose basic structure is patterned after the ancient Roman Empire. Tellingly, most churches today still hold that structure.

This book is divided into two parts. The first part is titled "Community and Gatherings." In it, I explore how the early church lived its life and how it gathered together. I then compare and contrast these elements with the practices of the contemporary church.

The second part of the book is titled "Leadership and Accountability." In it, I introduce a fresh model for understanding leadership, authority, and accountability. This model is countercultural as well as rooted in biblical principle. But it's also practical. I've watched it work over the past twenty years. I've also designed an appendix to give answers to common objections.

Please note that my aim in writing is constructive rather than controversial. Nevertheless, because many of the ideas I present are so radically different from traditional understanding, they will probably raise eyebrows and, in some cases, hostility.

My hope is that you will bear with me and consider each of my arguments in the light of Scripture and under the scrutiny of your own conscience. My attitude in writing is best described by C. S. Lewis: "Think of me as a fellow-patient in the same hospital who, having been admitted a little earlier, could give some advice." My heart's desire is to see God's people set free from the tyranny of the status quo as well as oppressive leadership structures. All for one reason—so that Jesus Christ can be made central and supreme in His church again.

Frank Viola
Gainesville, Florida
October 2007

INTRODUCTION
TOWARD A NEW KIND OF CHURCH

*We are living in an age hopelessly below the New Testament pattern—
content with a neat little religion.* —Martyn Lloyd-Jones

*Most professing Christians do not realize that the central concepts and prac-
tices associated with what we call "church" are not rooted in the New Testament, but in patterns established in the post-apostolic age.* —Jon Zens

A revolution in both the theology and practice of the church is upon us. Countless Christians, including theologians, ministers, and scholars, are seeking new ways to renew and reform the church. Others have given up on the traditional concept of church altogether. They have come to the conviction that the institutional church as we know it today is not only ineffective, but it's also without biblical merit. For this reason, they feel it would be a mistake to reform or renew the present church structure. Because the structure is the root problem.

I came to this unnerving conclusion twenty years ago, when few people I knew dared to question the practices of the institutional church. For that reason, I felt quite alone. And on some days, I honestly wondered if I had lost my mind.

Things have changed. Today, the number of those who are questioning the institutional church is growing.[1] Their tribe is increasing every year. A large number of them have stepped out of the institutional church. And they are in quest for a church experience that better fits the deepest longings of their hearts.

Indeed, a revolution is brewing today. And that revolution goes beyond church reform and renewal. Instead, it goes straight to the root of the practice and theology of the church itself. Perhaps a historical example will help explain this phenomenon.

For centuries, astronomers in the West sought to understand the rotation of the stars and planets. Yet no matter how many times they sought to tweak the data they possessed, they couldn't make their calculations work. The reason was simple. Their point of reference was flawed. They were working with a geocentric model of the universe. They believed that the stars and planets rotated around a stationary earth. And upon that premise, they built their entire understanding of the universe.

An iconoclast named Copernicus came along and questioned that premise. He postulated the revolutionary idea that the planets and stars rotate around the sun. Copernicus's heliocentric view of the universe was vehemently challenged at first. But no one could dispute the fact that this new model made the data work far better than the geocentric view. For that reason, the heliocentric point of reference was eventually accepted.[2]

In the same spirit, this book is a hearty attempt to present a new paradigm for the church. One that's built on the New Testament concept that the church of Jesus Christ is a spiritual organism, not an institutional organization.

I have met few Christians who would question that last sentence. In fact, I've met countless believers who have said, "The church is an organism, not an organization." Yet as they formed those very words, they continued to be devout members of churches that were organized along the lines of General Motors and Microsoft.

In this book, I will be raising some pointed questions on that score. Namely, what does the phrase "the church is an organism" really mean? And how does an "organic church" operate and function in the twenty-first century?

Throughout the book, I will be using the terms "New Testament church," "early church," and "first-century church" as synonyms. All of these terms refer to the early church of Century One as it is portrayed in the New Testament.

I will also be referring to those churches with which most people are familiar as "institutional churches." I could have just as easily called them "establishment churches," "basilica churches," "traditional churches," "organized churches," "clergy-dominated churches," "contemporary churches," "audience churches," "spectator churches," "auditorium churches," "inherited churches," "legacy churches," or "program-based churches." All are inadequate linguistic tools. Yet to my mind, "institutional church" best captures the essence of most churches today.

Please keep in mind that when I use the term "institutional church" I am *not* speaking about God's people. I'm speaking about a *system*. The "institutional church" is a system—a way of *doing* "church." It's not the people who populate it. This distinction is important, and it's one that must be kept in mind as you read this book.

A sociologist may object to my use of the word "institutional." Sociologically speaking, an institution is any patterned human activity. Therefore, a handshake and a greeting hug are institutions. I readily admit that all churches (even organic churches) assume *some* institutions.

But I'm using the phrase "institutional church" in a much narrower sense. Namely, I am referring to those churches that operate primarily as institutions that exist above, beyond, and independent of the members that populate them. These churches are constructed on programs and rituals more than relationships. They are highly structured, typically building-centered organizations regulated by set-apart professionals ("ministers" and "clergy") who are aided by volunteers (laity). They require staff, building, salaries, and administration. In the institutional church, congregants watch a religious performance once or twice a week led principally by one person (the pastor or minister), and then retreat home to live their individual Christian lives.

By contrast, I'm using "organic church" to refer to those churches that operate according to the same spiritual principles as the church that we read about in our New Testament. The New Testament church was first and foremost organic, as are all churches that stand in its lineage. T. Austin-Sparks is the man who deserves credit for the term "organic church." He writes,

> God's way and law of fullness is that of organic life. In the Divine order, life produces its own organism, whether it be a vegetable, animal, human or spiritual. This means that everything comes from the inside. Function, order and fruit issue from this law of life within. It was solely on this principle that what we have in the New Testament came into being. Organized Christianity has entirely reversed this order.[3]

Taking this idea further, my friend Hal Miller brilliantly compares the institutional church with the organic church using a simple metaphor. He writes,

Institutional churches are a lot like trains. They are going in a certain direction, and they will continue in that direction for a good long time even if all hands try to make them stop. As with trains, the options for turning the direction of institutional churches are limited at best. If a switch or siding is available, the train could turn. Otherwise, it just follows its tracks. So everyone aboard had best hope that he is on the right train headed in the right direction.

Organic churches, like those in the New Testament, are different. They are not trains, but groups of people out for a walk. These groups move much more slowly than trains—only several miles per hour at the fastest. But they can turn at a moment's notice. More importantly, they can be genuinely attentive to their world, to their Lord, and to each other.

Like trains, institutional churches are easy to find. The smoke and noise are unmistakable. Organic churches are a bit more subtle. Because they do not announce their presence with flashing lights at every intersection, some believe that churches like those in the New Testament died out long ago. But nothing could be further from the truth. Organic churches are everywhere. I personally have been part of one for more than twenty years. Still, groups like ours are quietly walking together, not bothering to call undue attention to ourselves. We are simply pilgrims together.

Once you learn how to spot an organic church, you will soon discover groups of people everywhere meeting just like the New Testament church—as bodies, families, and brides, rather than as institutions.

Organic churches are groups of people walking with God. The trains pass them by all the time. Sometimes the people on board wave. Sometimes they cannot because the train is moving so fast that people going a few miles per hour just look like a blur. If you are in one of the groups of people now walking around as an organic church, Reimagining Church *will give you a new appreciation of your roots in the New Testament. If you are on one of the trains whizzing by, it may be a bit surprising to find out that some of those blurred patches of color outside your window are groups of people walking with God. That thing you just passed was an organic church.*

It's important for you to know that reimagining the church as a living organism isn't a pipe dream. The church actually can express herself organically just as she did in the first century. That said, the following letters were written by various people who have experienced organic church life in recent years. These are their impressions:

LETTER 1

I never planned on leaving the old way of doing church. I wasn't looking for a new church and couldn't even conceive of what an organic church would look like when I was first invited to visit one. But I visited and what I found was unlike anything I had ever seen. This church wasn't a Bible study, a prayer group, a healing/soaking prayer session, or a worship service.

Instead, this church focused on Jesus Christ. And everyone sang about Him, shared about Him, and worshipped Him. These Christians had been captivated by the beauty of the Lord Jesus Christ and, quite honestly, they didn't desire to spend time doing anything else when they met, but sing to/with/about Him, share Him, and love one another through Him.

It was their intimacy I noticed first. I had never met people with such an intimate life with the Lord. These people needed Him and were sustained by His life. In my previous church experience, I had seen dedicated people, passionate people, and loving people. But I had never met Christians before who seemed to know the very heart of God.

Long ago I learned that the Lord is in His people, but this church was the first one I had ever seen where Christians really put this into practice. They all shared Christ in their meetings one by one so that He was brought right before my eyes. I learned through them that He is our food and our drink. I came to see who He really is in our gatherings and in our life together, and I fell in love with Him as a result.

The intimacy I saw had drawn me in, but it was the freedom that these Christians lived in that kept my attention and made me decide to keep coming back to their meetings and become part of their community life. When I saw something in the Lord that might be an encouragement, I could speak it out and they would say "Amen" or "Praise the Lord." Their verbal encouragement made me realize that I had freedom to share, but more so, that Christ had freedom to be known in His people—including me.

It was the first time I had seen such freedom among Christians. I began to see what it looked like when Christ has the first place in the lives and meetings of His people, which brought incredible unity. For almost two years, I saw Christ fill every meeting with the truth about Himself. He never ran dry. I cannot imagine fully mining the depths of Jesus Christ. But in this church, with the combined love of my brothers and sisters, I began to discover just how glorious He really is.

(A female schoolteacher)

LETTER 2

The whole experience of organic church life has changed my life in so many ways. The church was planted through a conference. The messages that were shared at that conference were amazing. The Lord was showing me His plan and purpose for the church, His bride. My vision was being lifted to one that was heavenly and truly Christ-centered in nature. But that was just the beginning.

After the church was planted, I was experiencing Christ with my brothers and sisters as I never had before. I knew this was "it" for me. I had finally come home. God knew what my husband and I needed. The revelation I received began to grow and unfold before my very eyes. I saw a beautiful and radiant bride filled with passion for her Lord. I saw a community of believers being built together as a dwelling place. I saw brothers and sisters from different backgrounds who had never met before begin to love one another.

As we loved Christ together our hearts were knit with each other. True change was being made in our lives as we were learning of the Lord's eternal purpose. I saw that the church really is Christ's body, and He is the Head. Only as we allow Him to have His rightful place will we experience His life as we were meant to. Church life in this way is the Christian's natural habitat where we grow and flourish, being nourished by all the riches of Christ. I could go on and on because there is so much more!

All that I have seen and experienced has forever changed my life and my husband's as well. We prayed long ago for the Lord to reveal His heart and His dreams to us, and I believe He has answered that prayer. It is so exciting to know we will get to spend the rest of our lives seeing Christ revealed in His church!

(An ex-minister's wife)

LETTER 3

I was raised in a Christian home and attended church every time the doors were open. I knew how to live and behave like a Christian should. You might say I was the poster child.

Late in high school and early college, I met some Christians who sparked a passion in me that I never knew was possible. I saw their passion to know Christ in deep ways, and more than that, they actually seemed to know Christ much more deeply than I. In meeting them, I discovered that my own faith and knowledge of Christ was very shallow. You see, I realized that although I enjoyed going to church to be with my family and friends, I really viewed church as an obligation to endure in order to "hang out" with them before and after Sunday school, services, or youth group meetings.

I quietly sat through sermon after sermon hoping it would hurry up so we could go to the restaurant afterwards. Minutes after the sermons I couldn't actually remember what was said. I already heard that I needed to go to church more, I needed to tithe more, I needed to read my Bible more, and I needed to witness more. It wasn't until I met these other Christians that I realized that all of the previous churches that I was a member of didn't fulfill my thirst for Jesus. They gave me rules and regulations instead of something that gave life. Instead of growing in Christ, I was "dying on the vine," filled with fear, shame, and inadequacy. I didn't actually enjoy talking about the Lord. Nor was I near as bold to share Jesus with nonbelievers.

I would ask myself, If I was such a good Christian like I thought I was, why do I feel so far behind the curve? *The more I was with these believers, the more I wanted to know Christ like they did. I was drawn to Christ like a moth to a streetlight. I gradually began to spend more time with them and started going to their meetings. Their meetings were free and open. There was no liturgy. There were no clergy. They didn't actually need them. There were plenty of believers who had encountered the Lord and had encouraging things to share with the others.*

They didn't need someone to give them permission to speak. They didn't need someone to bury them in rules and lifeless duties. They wrote many of their own songs. They prayed together, taking turns talking to Jesus unrehearsed and from the heart. They met together as if Jesus was actually in the room. They treated each other like a family that loved each other.

After just a short while, I realized that this organic experience of Christ was exactly what was missing from my own experience. I began to crave gathering with these believers. I would go to their meetings and see a much bigger Lord than just someone who died for my sins. I would see Him in much deeper ways.

I was no longer satisfied with watching a performance. In this organic meeting, I began to want to share with my brothers and sisters what I had seen of the Lord. Instead of being passive, I now thought it was easy to function and contribute. Every one of our meetings was free to be different. Sometimes we sang for hours. Sometimes the believers were bursting at the seams to share what Jesus had done in their lives that week. Sometimes we revered the Lord's awesomeness in silence. No one had to tell us to do these things. The Spirit was moving in these ways and they just spontaneously happened. We often ate together as one family. Sometimes we shared scriptures with each other. Other times we enacted scenes and stories from the Bible that shed light on Christ.

We met all throughout the week. In the mornings, the brothers would find another brother or two, and the sisters would get together with sisters. And we would pursue the Lord in prayer and contemplate Scripture together. We would start our day with Christ. In the evenings, some of the members would open up their homes and share Christ over dinner. We had brothers and sisters meetings where we would collectively decide on matters relating to the church. And we would share responsibilities for caring for one another.

If there were no pressing needs, we would just sing to the Lord and pursue His presence together. If there was a member in need, we would think of ways to help them. Sometimes we would just plan ways to bless each other for the fun of it. Sometimes the single people would babysit for the parents and give them a night out on the town. Sometimes when one of the brothers or sisters went away on a long trip, the whole church would show up at the airport to greet them. And we would have a church meeting right in the airport.

There was always something happening where you could share Christ and love the Lord together. We would also have spontaneous times of outreach to the lost. Everything we did, the Spirit was free to move and change the direction of the event. When we did get together, I saw a Christ glorified and magnified. We were constantly making new discoveries in Him. Every time I saw Him in a new way, I wanted to see more. The feeling of guilt, shame, and unworthiness was gone. I had a passion to know Christ in deeper ways.

I am through with dying on the vine. I have now seen the freedom that Christians can really have in meeting together organically, just like the early church did.

(A male international marketing and business consultant)

In short, this book reimagines a vision of church that's organic in its construction; relational in its functioning; scriptural in its form; Christ-centered in its operation; Trinitarian in its shape; communitarian in its lifestyle; nonelitist in its attitude; and nonsectarian in its expression.

Stated simply, the purpose of this book is to discover afresh what it means to *be* church from God's standpoint. So with the New Testament as our starting point, let's reimagine church together.

I HAVE A DREAM

I have a dream that one day the church of Jesus Christ will rise up to her God-given calling and begin to live out the true meaning of her identity—which is, the very heartthrob of God Almighty—the fiancée of the King of all Kings.

I have a dream that Jesus Christ will one day be Head of His church again. Not in pious rhetoric, but in reality.

I have a dream that groups of Christians everywhere will begin to flesh out the New Testament reality that the church is a living organism and not an institutional organization.

I have a dream that the clergy/laity divide will someday be an antique of church history, and the Lord Jesus Himself will replace the moss-laden system of human hierarchy that has usurped His authority among His people.

I have a dream that multitudes of God's people will no longer tolerate those man-made systems that have put them in religious bondage and under a pile of guilt, duty, condemnation, making them slaves to authoritarian systems and leaders.

I have a dream that the centrality and supremacy of Jesus Christ will be the focus, the mainstay, and the pursuit of every Christian and every church. And that God's dear people will no longer be obsessed with spiritual and religious things to the point of division. But that their obsession and pursuit would be a person—the Lord Jesus Christ.

I have a dream that countless churches will be transformed from high-powered business organizations into spiritual families—authentic Christ-centered communities—where the members know one another intimately, love one another unconditionally, bleed for one another deeply, and rejoice with one another unfailingly.

I have a dream today....[4]

PART ONE
COMMUNITY AND GATHERINGS

CHAPTER 1
REIMAGINING THE CHURCH AS AN ORGANISM

A truth's initial commotion is directly proportional to how deeply the lie was believed. It wasn't the world being round that agitated people, but that the world wasn't flat. When a well-packaged web of lies has been sold gradually to the masses over generations, the truth will seem utterly preposterous and its speaker a raving lunatic. —Dresden James

The ministry of the Holy Spirit has ever been to reveal Jesus Christ, and revealing Him, to conform everything to Him. No human genius can do this. We cannot obtain anything in our New Testament as the result of human study, research, or reason. It is all the Holy Spirit's revelation of Jesus Christ. Ours is to seek continually to see Him by the Spirit, and we shall know that He—not a paper-pattern—is the Pattern, the Order, the Form. It is all a Person who is the sum of all purpose and ways. Everything [in the early church] then was the free and spontaneous movement of the Holy Spirit, and He did it in full view of the Pattern—God's Son. —T. Austin-Sparks

The New Testament uses many images to depict the church. Significantly, all of these images are living entities: a body, a bride, a family, one new man, a living temple made up of living stones, a vineyard, a field, an army, a city, etc.

Each image teaches us that the church is a living organism rather than an institutional organization. Few Christians today would disagree with that statement. But what does it mean in practice? And do we *really* believe it?

The church we read about in the New Testament was "organic." By that I mean it was born from and sustained by spiritual life instead of constructed by human institutions, controlled by human hierarchy, shaped by lifeless rituals, and held together by religious programs.

To use an illustration, if I try to create an orange in a laboratory, the lab-created orange would not be organic. But if I planted an orange seed into the ground and it produced an orange tree, the tree would be organic.

In the same way, whenever we sin-scarred mortals try to create a church the same way we would start a business corporation, we are defying the organic principle of church life. An organic church is one that is *naturally* produced when a group of people have encountered Jesus Christ in reality (external ecclesiastical props being unnecessary), and the DNA of the church is free to work without hindrance.

To put it in a sentence, organic church life is not a theater with a script; it's a gathered community that lives by divine life. By contrast, the modern institutional church operates on the same organizational principles that run corporate America.

The DNA of the Church   *perichorēsis*

All life forms have a DNA—a genetic code. DNA gives each life form a specific expression. For example, the instructions to build your physical body are encoded in your DNA. Your DNA largely determines your physical and psychological traits.

If the church is truly organic, that means that it, too, has a DNA—a spiritual DNA. Where do we discover the DNA of the church? I submit that we can learn a great deal about it by looking into God Himself.

We Christians uniquely proclaim a triune God.[1] In the words of the Athanasian Creed, "The Father is God, the Son is God, and the Holy Spirit is God, yet there are not three gods, but one God." Classic Christianity teaches that God is a fellowship of three persons: Father, Son, and Spirit. The Godhead is a Community of three, or a "Trinity" as theologians call it. Theologian Stanley Grenz writes,

God's triune nature means that God is social or relational—God is the "social Trinity." And for this reason, we can say that God is "community." God is the community of the Father, Son, and Spirit, who enjoy perfect and eternal fellowship.[2]

For many years, I heard precise teachings on the doctrine of the Trinity. But they never had any practical application in my life. I found them highly abstract and impractical.

Later, I discovered that understanding the activity within the triune God was the key to grasping everything in the Christian life—including the church.[3] As Eugene Peterson has said, "Trinity is the most comprehensive and integrative framework that we have for understanding and participating in the Christian life."[4]

Other theologians agree. Catherine LaCunga says, "The doctrine of the Trinity is ultimately a practical doctrine with radical consequences for the Christian life."[5]

In the same vein, Miroslav Volf writes, "The triune God stands at the beginning and at the end of the Christian pilgrimage and, therefore, at the center of Christian faith."[6]

The biblical teaching of the Trinity is not an exposition about the abstract design of God. Instead, it teaches us about God's nature and how it operates in Christian community. As such, it shouldn't be relegated to an endnote to the gospel. Rather, it should shape the Christian life and inform the practice of the church.[7]

Throughout the gospel of John, Jesus makes many statements that give us insight into His relationship with His Father. He says, "Father ... you loved me before the creation of the world" (John 17:24). He also said, "The world must learn that I love the Father" (John 14:31). From these two texts alone, we learn that there was a mutual love flowing within the Godhead before the foundation of the world.

In the opening chapters of Genesis, we discover that there is also fellowship within the Godhead: "Let *us* make man in *our* image, in *our* likeness" (Gen. 1:26). Here we see the triune God taking counsel and planning.

The gospel of John teaches us further about the nature of the Godhead. Namely, that the Son lives by the life of the Father (5:26; 6:57). The Son shares and expresses the glory of the Father (13:31–32; 17:4–5). The Son lives within the Father and the Father lives within the Son (1:18; 14:10). The Son lives in complete dependence upon the Father (5:19). The Son reflects the Father in His words and deeds (12:49; 14:9). The Father glorifies the Son (1:14; 8:50, 54; 12:23; 16:14; 17:1, 5, 22, 24), and the Son exalts the Father (7:18; 14:13; 17:1, 4; 20:17)

Within the triune God we discover mutual love, mutual fellowship, mutual dependence, mutual honor, mutual submission, mutual dwelling, and authentic community. In the Godhead there exists an eternal, complementary, and reciprocal interchange of divine life, divine love, and divine fellowship.

Amazingly, this same relationship has been transposed from the divine key into the human key. The passage has moved from the Father to the Son, from the Son to the church (John 6:57; 15:9; 20:21). It has moved from the eternal God in the heavenlies to the church on earth, the body of the Lord Jesus Christ.

The church is an organic extension of the triune God. It was conceived in Christ before time (Eph. 1:4–5) and born on the day of Pentecost (Acts 2:1ff.).

Properly conceived, the church is the gathered community that shares God's life and expresses it in the earth. Put another way, the church is the earthly image of the triune God (Eph. 1:22–23).

Because the church is organic, it has a natural expression. Accordingly, when a group of Christians follows their spiritual DNA, they will gather in a way that matches the DNA of the triune God—for they possess the same life that God Himself possesses. (While we Christians are by no means divine, we have been privileged to be "partakers of the divine nature"—2 Peter 1:4 NASB.)

Consequently, the DNA of the church is marked by the very traits that we find in the triune God. Particularly, mutual love, mutual fellowship, mutual dependence, mutual honor, mutual submission, mutual dwelling, and authentic community. Put another way, the headwaters of the church are found in the Godhead. It is for this reason that Stanley Grenz could say, "The ultimate basis for our understanding of the church lies in its relationship to the nature of the triune God Himself."[8]

Theologian Kevin Giles echoes this thought when he says that the Trinity is the "model on which ecclesiology should be formulated. On this premise, the inner life of the divine Trinity provides a pattern, a model, an echo, or an icon of the Christian communal existence in the world."[9]

Simply put, the Trinity is the paradigm for the church's native expression. Beloved theologian Shirley Guthrie unfolds this concept by describing the relational nature of the Godhead:

> *The oneness of God is not the oneness of a distinct, self-contained individual; it is the unity of a community of persons who love each other and live together in harmony.... They are what they are only in relationship with one another.... There is no solitary person separated from the others; no above and below; no first, second, third in importance; no ruling and controlling and being ruled and controlled; no position of privilege to be maintained over against others; no question of conflict concerning who is in charge; no need to assert independence and authority of one at the expense of the others. Now there is only fellowship and communion of equals who share all that they are and have in their communion with each other, each living with and for the others in mutual openness, self-giving love, and support; each free not from but for the others. That is how Father, Son, and Holy Spirit are related in the inner circle of the Godhead.[10]*

Look again at the triune God. And notice what's absent. There's an absence of command-style leadership. There's an absence of hierarchical structures.[11] There's an absence of passive spectatorship. There's an absence of one-upmanship. And there's an absence of religious rituals and programs.

(Some have suggested that there is a graded hierarchy within the Trinity. But this view is scripturally and historically untenable. See pages 295-96 for details.)

Command-style relationships, hierarchy, passive spectatorship, one-upmanship, religious programs, etc. were created by fallen humans. And they run contrary to the DNA of the triune God as well as the DNA of the church. Sadly, however, after the death of the apostles, these practices were adopted, baptized, and brought into the Christian family.[12] Today, they have become the central features of the institutional church.

Four Paradigms for Church Restoration

There are four chief paradigms for reimagining the church today. They are as follows:

Biblical Blueprintism. Those who advocate this paradigm champion the idea that the New Testament contains a meticulous blueprint for church practice. To their minds, we simply need to tease out of the Bible the proper blueprint and mimic it. But as I shall argue in this book, the New Testament contains no such blueprint for church practice. Neither does it contain a list of rules and regulations for Christians to follow.[13] As New Testament scholar F. F. Bruce puts it, "In applying the New Testament text to our own situation, we need not treat it as the scribes of our Lord's day treated the Old Testament. We should not turn what were meant to be guiding lines for worshippers in one situation into laws binding for all time."[14]

Cultural Adaptability. Those who advocate this paradigm are quick to point out that human culture changes over time. The church of the first century adapted to its culture. Today, the culture is very different. So the church must adapt to its present culture. Champions of this view say that in every age the church reinvents itself to adapt to the current culture.

This paradigm is based on the idea of "contextualization." Contextualization is the theological method that tries to translate the biblical message into different cultural settings.

Contextualization is certainly needed when we apply Scripture. It's because of contextualization that we don't wear sandals, togas, speak Greek, and use horses for transportation.

However, some people wave the contextualization flag to the point of *overcontextualizing* the Scriptures until they have no present relevance at all. Overcontextualization eats up the biblical text to where it disappears entirely. And we are left to create the church after our own image.

F. F. Bruce warns against the dangers of extreme contextualization, saying,

> *The restatement of the gospel in a new idiom is necessary in every generation—as necessary as its translation into new languages. [But] in too much that passes for restatement of the gospel, the gospel itself disappears, and the resultant product is what Paul would have called 'another gospel which in fact is no gospel at all' (Gal. 1:6f.). When the Christian message is so thoroughly accommodated to the prevalent climate of opinion that it becomes one more expression of that climate of opinion, it is no longer the Christian message.*[15]

I've met many advocates of the cultural adaptability paradigm. And I've been fascinated to discover that every one of them believes that there *are* normative church practices that transcend time and culture. For instance, most Christians who hold to the cultural adaptability paradigm would find the suggestion that we should abandon water baptism and change the Lord's Supper from bread and wine to french fries and mugs of root beer to be offensive. (Those under ten years old may be the exception!)

The critical question then becomes which practices of the New Testament church are solely descriptive and which are normative? Or to put it another way, which are tied to the culture of the first century and which are reflections of the unchanging nature and identity of the church?

The dangers of overcontextualization are real, and not a few Christian leaders have been unwittingly guilty of it. We must be careful not to hold to biblical principles unconsciously when they suit our purposes, but abandon them in the name of "contextualization" when they do not.

The fact of the matter is, virtually all Christians derive their ideas of the Christian life and church life from the Bible. (Ironically, those who claim that they do not nearly always end up turning to the teachings of Jesus or Paul to support or condemn a particular idea or practice.) The early church was not perfect. If you doubt that, just read 1 Corinthians. So romanticizing the early Christians as if they were flawless is a mistake.

On the other hand, the first-century church was the church that Jesus and the apostles founded. And insofar as the first-century communities were fleshing out the teachings of Jesus and the apostles, they can teach us a great deal. To ignore them as irrelevant for our time is a gross mistake. In the words of J. B. Phillips,

> *The great difference between present-day Christianity and that of which we read in these [the New Testament] letters is that to us it is primarily a performance; to them it was a real experience. We are apt to reduce the Christian religion to a code, or at best a rule of heart and life. To these*

*men it is quite plainly the invasion of their lives by a new quality of life
altogether.*[16]

Postchurch Christianity. This paradigm is rooted in the attempt to
practice Christianity without belonging to an identifiable community
that regularly meets for worship, prayer, fellowship, and mutual edification. Advocates claim that spontaneous social interaction (like having
coffee at Starbucks whenever they wish) and personal friendships embody
the New Testament meaning of "church." Those who hold to this paradigm believe in an amorphous, nebulous, phantom church.

Such a concept is disconnected with what we find in the New Testament.
The first-century churches were locatable, identifiable, visitable communities that met regularly in a particular locale. For this reason, Paul could write
a letter to these identifiable communities (local churches) with some definite
idea of who would be present to hear it (Rom. 16). He would also have a
good idea of when they gathered (Acts 20:7; 1 Cor. 14) and the struggles
they experienced in their life together (Rom. 12—14; 1 Cor. 1–8). While
unbiblical in its viewpoint, the postchurch paradigm appears to be an expression of the contemporary desire for intimacy without commitment.

Organic Expression. Throughout this book, I will argue for this particular paradigm. I believe that the New Testament is a record of the church's
DNA at work. When we read the book of Acts and the Epistles, we are
watching the genetics of the church of Jesus Christ expressing itself in various cultures during the first century. Because the church is truly a spiritual
organism, its DNA never changes. It's the same biological entity yesterday,
today, and tomorrow. As such, the DNA of the church will always reflect
these four elements:

1. It will always express the headship of Jesus Christ in His church as opposed to the headship of a human being. (I'm using the term "headship" to refer to the idea that Christ is both the authority and the source of the church.)[17]

2. It will always allow for and encourage the every-member functioning of the body.

3. It will always map to the theology that's contained in the New Testament, giving it visible expression on the earth.

4. It will always be grounded in the fellowship of the triune God.

The Trinity is the paradigm informing us on how the church should function. It shows us that the church is a loving, egalitarian, reciprocal, cooperative, nonhierarchical community.

F. F. Bruce once said, "*Development* is the unfolding of what is there already, even if only implicitly; *departure* involves the abandonment of one principle or basis in favor of another."[18]

All that enables the church to reflect the triune God is development; all that hinders it from doing so is departure.

As George Barna and I have argued in our book, *Pagan Christianity*, very little of what is practiced in the modern institutional church has its roots in the New Testament. Instead, human-invented practices that were spawned centuries ago have both shaped and redefined the church. Such practices undermine the headship of Christ, hamper the every-member functioning of Christ's body, violate New Testament theology, and disaffirm the fellowship of the triune God. As Emil Brunner puts it, "The delicate structure of the fellowship founded by Jesus, and anchored by the Holy Spirit, could not be replaced by an institutional organization without the whole character of the *ecclesia* being fundamentally changed."[19]

Yet despite this fact, many of these practices are justified by Christians even though they lack biblical merit. Why? Because of the incredible power of religious tradition. Consider the following texts:

The grass withers and the flowers fall, but the word of our God stands forever. (Isa. 40:8)

For the word of God is living and active. Sharper than any double-edged sword, it penetrates even to dividing soul and spirit, joints and marrow; it judges the thoughts and attitudes of the heart. (Heb. 4:12)

As the rain and the snow come down from heaven, and do not return to it without watering the earth and making it bud and flourish, so that it yields seed for the sower and bread for the eater, so is my word that goes out from my mouth: It will not return to me empty, but will accomplish what I desire and achieve the purpose for which I sent it. (Isa. 55:10–11)

These texts inform us about the enormous power of God's Word. The Word of God stands forever. The Word of God will accomplish whatever God desires. The Word of God will achieve the purpose to which God has sent it. The Word of God will not return void.

Yet despite the incredible power of God's Word, there is one thing that can stop it dead in its tracks. That one thing is religious tradition. Note the words of Jesus, the incarnate Word:

Thus you nullify the word of God for the sake of your tradition. (Matt. 15:6)

And again:

Neglecting the commandment of God, you hold to the tradition of men....
You are experts at setting aside the commandment of God in order to keep
your tradition. (Mark 7:8–9 NASB)

In so many ways, religious tradition has shaped our minds. It's captured our hearts. It's framed our vocabulary. So much so that whenever we open our Bibles, we automatically read our current church practices back into the text.

Whenever we see the word *pastor* in the Bible, we typically think of a man who preaches sermons on Sunday mornings.[20] Whenever we see the word *church*, we typically think of a building or a Sunday-morning service. Whenever we see the word *elder*, we typically think of someone on a church board or committee.

This raises an important question: How can we read our present church practices back into the New Testament so easily? One of the reasons is because we have inherited a "cut-and-paste" approach to Bible study. In this approach, out-of-context "proof-texts" are pieced together to support man-made doctrines and practices. This process is largely unconscious. And two things make it very easy. First, the New Testament letters aren't arranged in chronological order. Second, the New Testament letters are divided into chapters and verses.[21]

Philosopher John Locke articulated the problem well when he wrote, "The Scriptures are chopped and minced, and, as they are now printed, stand so broken and divided, that not only the common people take the verses usually for distinct aphorisms [rules]; but even men of more advanced knowledge, in reading them, lose very much of the strength and force of the coherence, and the light that depends on it."[22]

By contrast, when the New Testament is read in chronological order, without chapters and verses, a beautiful narrative emerges. A story materializes. When we read the New Testament as it's presently arranged, however, we encounter that story in fragments. And we miss the fluid narrative.

In Greek mythology, a man named Procrustes was reputed to possess a magical bed that had the unique property of matching the size of the persons who lay upon it. But behind the "magic" was a crude method for creating a "one-size-fits-all" bed. If the person lying on it was too small, Procrustes would stretch the person's limbs out to fit the bed. If the person was too large, Procrustes would chop off his limbs to make him fit!

The modern concept of church is a Procrustean bed. Scriptures that do not fit the shape of the institutional church are either chopped off (dismissed) or they are stretched to fit its mold. The cut-and-paste method of Bible study makes this rather easy to pull off (no pun intended). We lift various verses out of their chronological and historical setting and then paste them together to create a doctrine or support a practice. By contrast, the chronological narrative provides a control on our interpretation of Scripture. It prevents us from cutting and pasting verses together to make the Bible fit our preconceived ideas.

The fact is, many of our present-day church practices are without scriptural merit. They are human-invented practices that are at odds with the organic nature of the church. They do not reflect the desire of Jesus Christ, nor do they express His headship nor His glorious personality (the very things that the church is called to bear). Instead, they reflect the enthronement of man's ideas and traditions. And as a result, they smother the church's native expression. Yet we justify them by our cut-and-paste hermeneutic.

Violating the Church's DNA

Some Christians have tried to justify a slew of unbiblical church practices by suggesting that the church is different in every culture, and it adapts to the world in which it lives. It is thought, therefore, that God now approves of the clergy system, hierarchical leadership, the performance-spectator order of worship, the single leader model, the concept of "going to church," and a host of other practices that were created around the fourth century as a result of Christians borrowing from the Greco-Roman customs of their day.

But is the church really different in every culture? And if it is, does that mean that we are free to adopt any practice we like into our corporate worship? Or is it possible that the church has overadapted to modern Western culture in both its theology and its practice?

Speaking of the problem of overcontextualization, Richard Halverson writes, "When the Greeks got the gospel, they turned it into a philosophy; when the Romans got it, they turned it into a government; when the Europeans got it, they turned it into a culture; and when the Americans got it, they turned it into a business."[23]

I will borrow from Paul when he said, "Does not nature teach you?"

The New Testament is clear that the church is a biological entity (Eph. 2:15; Gal. 3:28; 1 Cor. 10:32; Col. 3:11; 2 Cor. 5:17). This biological entity is produced when the living seed of the gospel is planted into the hearts of women and men and they are permitted to gather together naturally.

The DNA of the church produces certain identifiable features. Some of them are the experience of authentic community, a familial love and devotion of its members to one another, the centrality of Jesus Christ, the native instinct to gather together without static ritual, the innate desire to form deep-seated relationships that are centered on Christ, the internal drive for open-participatory gatherings, and the loving impulse to display Jesus to a fallen world.

While the seed of the gospel will naturally produce these particular features, *how* they are expressed may look slightly different from culture to culture. For instance, I once planted an organic church in the country of Chile. The songs they wrote, the way they interacted with each other, the way they sat, what they did with their children, all looked different from organic churches born in Europe and the United States.

However, the same basic features that reside in the DNA of the church were all present. Never did any of these churches produce a clergy system, a sole pastor, a hierarchical leadership structure, or an order of worship that rendered the majority passive.

In nature, there's a flowering shrub called the bigleaf hydrangea. If you take the seed of that shrub and plant it in the soil of Indiana, it will yield pink flowers when it blooms. But if you take that same seed and plant it in the soil of Brazil or Poland, it will produce blue flowers. Even more interesting, if you take the same seed and plant it in another type of soil, it will yield purple flowers.[24]

The bigleaf hydrangea, however, will *never* produce thorns or thistles. It will never bear oranges or apples. And it will never grow tall like a pine tree. Why? Because these features are not within the DNA of the seed.

In the same way, the church of Jesus Christ—when planted properly and left on its own without human control and institutional interference—will produce certain features by virtue of its DNA. Like the bigleaf hydrangea, the church may look different from culture to culture, but it will have the same basic expression wherever it's allowed to flourish.

On the other hand, when we humans introduce our fallen systems into this living organism, the church loses her organic features and produces a foreign expression that runs contrary to her DNA. To put it bluntly, it's possible to distort the organic growth of the church and violate its DNA.

Let me tell a tragic story that illustrates this principle. On November 4, 1970, a very unusual thirteen-year-old girl was discovered. From early childhood, she had lived in a state of intense sensory and social deprivation. Genie, as she came to be called, wasn't taught to speak. And she was denied normal human interaction.

Genie was tied to a potty-chair and left to sit alone day after day. In the evenings, she was tied into a sleeping bag, which restrained movement of her arms. She was also beaten for making noises—including forming words.

The result: Her natural traits were permanently distorted. Genie had a strange bunny-like walk. She constantly held her hands up in front of her body like paws. She couldn't chew solid food, and she could hardly swallow. She also spat constantly, sniffled often, and couldn't focus her eyes beyond twelve feet. Genie's speech was limited to short, high-pitched squeaks that were barely understandable.

After years of being removed from her abysmal home life, Genie's vocabulary grew significantly. Yet she wasn't capable of stringing words together into meaningful sentences. What happened? Some scientists concluded that her normal DNA was altered because she was deprived of proper nutrition and stimulation.

Let's apply this story to the spiritual realm. Like the bigleaf hydrangea, the culture in which an organic church is born may influence its expression. At the same time, like Genie's tragic experience, the culture can also distort the church's expression by interrupting its organic growth. In my opinion, that's exactly what has happened with the church historically.

Hence, what passes for "church" today is not what God had in mind from the beginning.

The church is organic. If her natural growth is not tampered with, she will grow up to be a beautiful girl—a living witness to the glories of her Bridegroom, Jesus Christ. She will not grow up to be an organization like General Motors or Microsoft. She will be something wholly different—completely unique to this planet. Just as unique as Jesus Christ was when He walked this earth. For after all, the church is His very body, and its nature is identical to God's.

That said, this book is an effort to reimagine church in the image of the triune God. It seeks to anchor the practice of the church in the eternal Godhead rather than in the shifting sands of cultural fads, the muddied bottom of biblical blueprintism, or the polluted waters of religious tradition.

Questions That Must Be Faced

- Do you think the New Testament offers any guidance for our church life and practices today, or should we discard it as being completely irrelevant? Explain.
- Consider the churches you have been a part of in the past. In what ways did they or did they not reflect the relationship of the triune God?
- What does it mean to be faithful to the Word of God with respect to our church life and practices? How about our individual life and practices? Explain.
- On what basis do we determine what is normative and timeless in the New Testament from what is merely descriptive and tied to first-century culture? Explain.

CHAPTER 2
REIMAGINING THE CHURCH MEETING

Some institutions are allowed to grow so old and venerable that the idea of scrapping them is unthinkably sacrilegious. —F. F. Bruce

The whole concern of Reformation theology was to justify restructuring the organized church without shaking its foundations. —John Howard Yoder

It's commonplace for Christians to speak about "going to church." By this, they mean attending a religious (church) service.

Interestingly, neither "going to church" nor "church services" appear in the New Testament. Both of these terms emerged long after the death of the apostles. The reason is simple: The early Christians had no such concept. They didn't view church as a place to go. Neither did they see their gatherings as "services."

As we read the New Testament with an eye for understanding how the early Christians gathered, it becomes clear that they had four main types of meetings. They were

- *Apostolic Meetings.* These were special meetings where apostolic workers preached to an interactive audience. Their goal was either to plant a church from scratch or to encourage an existing one. The twelve apostles held such meetings in the temple courts in Jerusalem during the birth of the church in Jerusalem (Acts 5:40–42). Paul held the same kind of meetings in the hall of Tyrannus when he planted the church in Ephesus (Acts 19:9–10; 20:27, 31). There are two chief characteristics of the apostolic meeting. One is that an apostolic worker does most of the ministry. The other is that such meetings are never permanent. They are temporary and have a long-range goal. Namely, to equip a local body of believers to function under the headship of Jesus Christ without the presence of a human head (Eph. 4:11–16; 1 Cor. 14:26). For this reason, an apostle always ends up leaving the church on its own.[1]

- *Evangelistic Meetings.* In the first century, evangelism commonly occurred *outside* the regular meetings of the church. The apostles preached the gospel in those places where unbelievers frequented. The synagogue (for the Jews) and the marketplace (for the Gentiles) were among their favorite places to evangelize (Acts 14:1; 17:1–33; 18:4,19). Evangelistic meetings were designed to plant a new church or to numerically build an existing church. These meetings were done "in season." They weren't a permanent fixture of the church. Philip's trip to Samaria is an example of this kind of meeting (Acts 8:5ff.).

- *Decision-Making Meetings.* Sometimes a church needed to assemble together to make an important decision. The meeting in Jerusalem described in Acts 15 was such a meeting. The chief feature of this meeting is that everyone participated in the decision-making process, and the apostles and elders played a helpful role. (See chapter 10 for details.)

- *Church Meetings.* These were the regular gatherings of the church.

They would be the first-century equivalent of our Sunday-morning "church service." Yet they were radically different.

The first-century church meeting was primarily a *believers* meeting. The context of 1 Corinthians 11—14 makes this plain. While unbelievers were sometimes present, they were not the focus of the meeting. (In 1 Corinthians 14:23–25, Paul fleetingly mentions the presence of unbelievers in the gathering.)

Unlike today's practice, this was not a meeting where a pastor preached a sermon and everyone else passively listened. The notion of a sermon-focused, pulpit-to-pew, audience-styled "church service" was alien to the early Christians.

Mutual Edification

Today, the weekly "church service" is designed for worship, the hearing of a sermon, and in some cases, evangelism. But in the first-century church, the governing purpose of the church meeting was quite different. The purpose was *mutual edification.* Consider the following texts:

What is the outcome then, brethren? When you assemble, each one has a psalm, has a teaching, has a revelation, has a tongue, has an interpretation. Let all things be done for edification. (1 Cor. 14:26 NASB)[2]

And let us consider one another in order to stir up love and good works, not forsaking the assembling of ourselves together, as is the manner of some, but exhorting one another, and so much the more as you see the Day approaching. (Heb. 10:24–25 NKJV)

The regular meetings of the church envisioned in Scripture allowed for *every member* to participate in the building up of the body of Christ (Eph. 4:16). There was no "up-front" leadership. No one took center stage.

Unlike today's practice, the teaching in the church meeting was not delivered by the same person week after week. Instead, every member had the right, the privilege, and the responsibility to minister in the gathering. Mutual encouragement was the hallmark of this meeting. "Every one of you" was its outstanding characteristic.

In addition, while the early Christians worshipped God through song, they didn't confine their singing to the leadership of a group of professional musicians. Instead, the meeting allowed for "each one" to lead a song. Or in the words of Paul, "each of you has a psalm" in the gathering (1 Cor. 14:26 NKJV). Even the songs themselves were marked by an element of mutuality. Consider Paul's exhortation:

Let the word of Christ richly dwell within you, with all wisdom teaching and admonishing one another with psalms and hymns and spiritual songs, singing with thankfulness in your hearts to God. (Col. 3:16 NASB)

Speak to one another with psalms, hymns and spiritual songs. Sing and make music in your heart to the Lord. (Eph. 5:19)

Again, "one-anothering" was the dominant ingredient of the early church gathering. In such an open format, the early Christians regularly composed their own songs and sang them in the meetings.[3]

In like manner, each Christian who was given something to say by the Holy Spirit had the liberty to supply it through his or her unique gift.

"For you can all prophesy in turn so that everyone may be instructed and encouraged," says Paul (1 Cor. 14:31).

As Paul pulls back the curtain of the first-century church gathering in 1 Corinthians 11—14, we see a meeting where every member is actively involved. Freedom, openness, and spontaneity are the chief marks of this meeting. "One another" is its dominant feature—mutual edification its primary goal.

Christ, the Director of the New Testament Gathering

The New Testament church meeting depended entirely upon the headship of Jesus Christ. Christ was fully preeminent. He was its center and its circumference. He set the agenda and directed what took place. Although His leading was invisible to the naked eye, He was clearly the guiding agent.

In this gathering, the Lord Jesus was free to speak through whomever He chose and in whatever capacity He saw fit. There was no fixed liturgy to tie His hands or box Him in.

The church meeting was based upon the "round-table" principle. That is, every member was encouraged to function and participate. By contrast, the institutional church service is built on the "pulpit-pew" principle. It divides the members into the active few and the passive many. For this reason, some people call it the "audience church."

In the first-century gathering, neither the sermon nor "the preacher" was the center of attention. Instead, congregational participation was the divine rule. The meeting was nonliturgical, nonritualistic, and nonsacral. Nothing was perfunctory. Everything came out of the living presence of Christ.

The meeting reflected a flexible spontaneity where the Spirit of God was in utter control. He was free to move through any member of the body as He willed (1 Cor. 14:26, 31). And if He was allowed to lead the entire meeting, everything would be done in an orderly fashion (1 Cor. 14:40).

The Holy Spirit so governed the gathering that if a person received an insight while another was sharing, the second speaker was free to interject his or her thought (1 Cor. 14:29–30). Accordingly, interruptions were a common part of the gathering (1 Cor. 14:27–40). Such a meeting is unthinkable in today's institutional church. (Just imagine what would happen if you interrupted the pastor with a word of insight while he was delivering his sermon.)

Nowhere in the New Testament do we find grounds for a church meeting that is dominated or directed by a human being. Neither do we find any biblical merit for a gathering that's centered on a pulpit and focused upon one man.[4]

Consider the words of John Howard Yoder:

There are few more reliable constants running through all human society than the special place every human community makes for the professional religionist.... But if we were to ask whether any of the N.T. literature makes the assumptions listed—Is there one particular office in which there should be only one or a few individuals for whom it provides a livelihood, unique in character due to ordination, central to the definition of the church and the key to her functioning? Then the answer from the biblical material is a resounding negation.... Let us then ask first not whether there is a clear, solid concept of preaching, but whether there was in the N.T. one particular preaching office, identifiable as distinctly as the other ministries. Neither in the most varied picture (Corinthians) nor in the least varied (Pastoral Epistles) is there one particular ministry thus defined.[5]

Perhaps the most startling characteristic of the early church meeting was the absence of any human officiation. Jesus Christ led the gatherings by the medium of the Holy Spirit through the believing community. The result? The spirit of "one-anothering" pervaded the entire meeting. It's no wonder that the New Testament uses the phrase *one another* nearly sixty times. Each member came to the meeting knowing that he or she had the privilege and the responsibility to contribute something of Christ. (Incidentally, women had both the right and the privilege to participate in the meetings of the church. See endnote for details.)[6]

Some may object and say, "But in my church, I'm allowed to do some ministry." My question is, are you allowed to carry out such ministry in the major gatherings of the church when all the members are present? Are you free to stand up at any time and give a word of testimony, a teaching, an exhortation, a song, or whatever else the Lord has laid on your heart? More importantly, are you *encouraged* to do this?

Let's be honest. The idea of mutual ministry envisioned in the New Testament is a far cry from the pinched definition of "lay ministry" that's promoted in the typical institutional church. Most organized churches offer a surplus of volunteer positions for "laypeople" to fill. Positions like cutting the lawn of the parsonage, ushering the aisles, shaking hands at the sanctuary door, passing out bulletins, teaching Sunday school, singing in the choir, participating on the worship team (if you make the cut), flipping transparencies, turning PowerPoint slides, etc.

But these restricted "ministry" positions are light-years away from the free and open exercise of spiritual gifts that was afforded to every believer in the early church gathering. An exercise that benefited the entire church when it gathered together.

The Necessity of a Functioning Priesthood

So why did the early church meet in this way? Was it just a passing cultural tradition? Did it, as some say, represent the early church's infancy, ignorance, and immaturity? I'm unconvinced. The first-century church meeting is deeply rooted in biblical theology. It made real and practical the New Testament doctrine of the priesthood of all believers—a doctrine that all evangelicals affirm with their lips.

And what is that doctrine? In the words of Peter, it is the doctrine that *all* believers in Christ are spiritual priests called to offer up "spiritual sacrifices" unto their Lord. In Paul's language, it's the idea that all Christians are *functioning* members of Christ's body.

In addition, the open-participatory meeting envisioned in the New Testament is native to our spiritual nature. Every Christian has an innate spiritual instinct to gather together with other Christians and share their Lord in an open atmosphere that's free of ritual and human control. To pour out of their hearts what God has poured into them.

Consider the revivals of the past. If you've ever studied the history of past revivals, you'll discover that they shifted the entire terrain of the traditional church service for a time. Preachers would stop giving sermons for months. Instead, God's people would gather and sing, testify, and share about the Lord for hours. Such meetings were spontaneous, open, and full of participation. There was no human control.

Why did this happen? Because God's people were yielding to their spiritual instincts, and no one could stop the flood tides of the Holy Spirit who was moving within them. Unfortunately, after the revival waters receded, the five-hundred-year-old Protestant order of worship was quickly reerected and open meetings vanished in most places.

At bottom, the first-century church gathering was a reflection of the self-emptying exchange of life, love, and fellowship that has been going on in the triune God from before time. By means of the Holy Spirit, the Father eternally pours Himself into His Son, and the Son eternally pours Himself into the Father. The mutual fellowship and sharing of life that marked the early church meeting was an earthly expression of this divine interchange.

Add to that, the early church meeting was the God-created environment that produced spiritual growth—both corporately and individually (Eph. 4:11–16). We grow into God's fullness when the different parts of His body minister Christ to us (Eph. 3:16–19). But we also grow when we function (Mark 4:24–25).

By contrast, in the typical institutional church, the spiritual nourishment of the believer is limited to and dependent on the spiritual and academic preparation of one or two people: the pastor and the Sunday school teacher. Could this be one of the reasons why there is so little transformation happening in the modern institutional church?[7]

Speaking of the normative nature of the every-member ministry of the body of Christ, John Howard Yoder remarks, "The conclusion is inescapable that the multiplicity of ministries is not a mere *adiaphoron,* a happenstance of only superficial significance, but a specific work of grace and a standard for the church."[8] Granted, Christians can and should function outside of church meetings. But the gatherings of the church are especially designed for every believer to express Christ through his or her gift (1 Cor. 11—14; Heb. 10:24–25). Unfortunately, the institutional church commonly pushes "one-anothering" exclusively outside the church service. And this retards the spiritual growth of the believing community.

The Reformation recovered the truth of the priesthood of all believers. But it failed to restore the organic practices that embody this teaching. The Reformation view of the priesthood of all believers was individualistic, not corporate. It was restricted to soteriology (salvation) and didn't involve ecclesiology (the church). The Reformers claimed the ground of a believing priesthood, but they failed to occupy that ground. In the typical Protestant church, the doctrine of the priesthood of all believers is no more than a sterile truth. It would better be described as the "priesthood of some believers."

Truthfully, there are few things more conducive to the culture of spiritual life than the open-participatory church meeting that's depicted in the New Testament. God established open-participatory meetings to incarnate the glorious reality of expressing Christ through a fully employed priesthood.

The writer of Hebrews amply demonstrates that mutual participation in the body is vital for the spiritual formation of every member. He teaches that mutual exhortation is the divine *antidote* for preventing apostasy, the divine *requirement* for ensuring perseverance, and the divine *means* for cultivating individual spiritual life:

> *Take heed, brethren, lest there be in any of you an evil heart of unbelief, in departing from the living God. But exhort one another daily, while it is called Today; lest any of you be hardened through the deceitfulness of sin. (Heb. 3:12–13 KJV)*

Here we are told that mutual exhortation is the remedy for a hardened, unbelieving heart and a deceived mind. In like manner, the New Testament presents mutual exhortation to be the divine safeguard against willful sin:

> *And let us consider one another in order to stir up love and good works, not forsaking the assembling of ourselves together, as is the manner of some, but exhorting one another, and so much the more as you see the Day approaching. For if we sin willfully ... (Heb. 10:24–26 NKJV)*

While multitudes of clergy have made common use of this text to stress the importance of "attending church," they have blissfully ignored the rest of the passage. The passage says that *mutual exhortation* (not hearing a pulpit sermon) is the primary purpose of the church gathering. And mutual exhortation is the God-ordained deterrent for willful sin.

In my personal judgment, we ignore the full teaching of this passage to our own peril. The reason is simple: Our spiritual prosperity hinges upon corporate meetings that are marked by mutual, every-member functioning.

Manifesting Jesus Christ in His Fullness

The Greek word for church is *ekklesia,* and it literally means "assembly." This meshes nicely with the dominant thought in Paul's letters that the church is Christ in corporate expression (1 Cor. 12:1–27; Eph. 1:22–23; 4:1–16).

From the human perspective, the purpose of the church meeting is mutual edification. But from God's perspective, the purpose of the gathering is to express His glorious Son and make Him visible. (The church is the body, and Christ is the Head. The purpose of one's body is to express the life that's within it.)

Put another way, we gather together so that the Lord Jesus can manifest Himself in His fullness. And when that happens, the body is edified.

Note that the only way that Christ can be properly expressed is if *every* member of a church freely supplies that aspect of the Lord that he or she has received. Make no mistake about it: The Lord Jesus cannot be fully disclosed through only one member. He is far too rich for that (Eph. 3:8).

So if the hand doesn't function in the gathering, Christ will not be manifested in fullness. Likewise, if the eyes fail to function, the Lord will be limited in His self-revelation. On the other hand, when every member of a local assembly functions in the meeting, Christ is seen. He is made visible. And why? Because He is *assembled* in our midst.

Consider the analogy of a puzzle. When each puzzle piece is properly positioned in relation to the other pieces, the puzzle is assembled. The net effect? We see the entire picture. It's the same way with Christ and His church.

The highest purpose of the church meeting, then, is to make the invisible Christ visible through His body. Put another way, *we gather together to reassemble the Lord Jesus Christ on the earth.* When this happens, not only is Christ glorified in His saints, and not only is each member edified, but something is also registered in unseen realms: Principalities and powers in heavenly places are shamed!

Paul tells us that the manifold wisdom of God is made known through the church to the spiritual forces of evil in heavenly places. Through open-participatory meetings, the church demonstrates to other realms that Jesus Christ—the embodiment of God's wisdom—is alive enough to lead a fallen race who once belonged to God's enemy. This brings great glory to God. And it's a central aspect of His eternal purpose. Here's how Paul put it:

Christ the power of God and the wisdom of God. (1 Cor. 1:24)

His intent was that now, through the church, the manifold wisdom of God should be made known to the rulers and authorities in the heavenly realms, according to his eternal purpose which he accomplished [fashioned] in Christ Jesus our Lord. (Eph. 3:10–11)

For our struggle is not against flesh and blood, but against the rulers, against the authorities, against the powers of this dark world and against the spiritual forces of evil in the heavenly realms. (Eph. 6:12)

Open-participatory meetings do not preclude the idea of planning. Nor do they have to be disorderly. In 1 Corinthians 14, Paul formulates a number of broad guidelines designed to keep the meeting running in an orderly fashion.

In Paul's thought, there's no tension between an *open*-participatory meeting and an *orderly* one that edifies the church. The order of the meeting is organic. It's the by-product of each member seeking to edify the whole.

As far as content goes, the meetings were centered on Christ. Every word shared shed light on Him. Every song sung brought glory to Him. Every prayer offered brought Him into view. All the arrows of the meetings pointed to Him. As they experienced the indwelling life of Christ during the week, the early Christians came together to share that life with one another.

In this respect, the early church meeting served as an outlet. It was the venue in which the excess and overflow of spiritual life was shared and released.

Have you ever received an insight about the Lord or had an encounter with Him that filled you spiritually to the point where you felt you were going to burst if you didn't share it with others? If so, just imagine an entire church experiencing this. Therein lies a central feature of the church gathering: to allow that spiritual life to break loose whereby all could be blessed. Just as the members of the triune God selflessly pour Their life into one another, so the members of the church do the same in their gatherings.

In this regard, participating in a New Testament church meeting meant giving more than receiving. Unlike today's popular practice, the early Christians didn't attend "services" to receive from a class of religious specialists called the "clergy." They met to *serve* their sisters and brothers by ministering something of the Lord's life to them. In so doing, they sought to build up the church (Rom. 12:1–8; 1 Cor. 14:26; Heb. 10:24–25).

The Question of Sustaining Force

In the typical institutional church, the religious machinery of the church program is the force that fuels and propels the church service. Consequently, if the Spirit of God were ever to leave a typical institutional church, His absence would go unnoticed.

The "business-as-usual" program would forge ahead. The worship program would be unaffected. The liturgy would march on uninterrupted. The sermon would be preached, and the doxology would be sung. Like Samson of old, the congregation would go right along with the religious program, not knowing "that the LORD had departed" (Judg. 16:20 NASB).

By contrast, the only sustaining force of the early church gathering was the life of the Holy Spirit. The early Christians were clergyless, liturgyless, programless, and ritualless. They relied entirely on the spiritual life of the individual members to maintain the church's existence and the quality of their gatherings.

Thus if the spiritual life of the church was at a low ebb, everyone would notice it in the gathering. They couldn't overlook the cold chill of silence. What is more, if the Spirit of God left the meetings for good, the church would collapse altogether.

Stated simply, the first-century church knew no sustaining influence other than the life of the Holy Spirit. It didn't rely on a clergy-led, man-programmed, humanly planned, institutionally fueled system to preserve its momentum.

The tabernacle of Moses perfectly mirrors those churches that are held together by an institution rather than the life of God. When God's presence left the holy tent, the tent became nothing more than a hollow shell accompanied by an impressive exterior. Even though the Lord's glory had departed, worshippers continued to offer their sacrifices at the empty tabernacle, never noticing that God wasn't there (1 Chron. 16:39–40; 2 Chron. 1:3–5; Jer. 7:12–14).

In this way, the vice of the institutional church lies in its reliance upon a humanly devised, program-driven religious system that serves to scaffold the "church" structure when the Spirit of God is absent. This moss-laden system betrays the fact that when the spontaneous life of Jesus Christ has ebbed away in a Christian assembly, that assembly ceases to be operating as a church in any biblical sense—even though it may preserve the outward form.

The Clerical Objection

While the New Testament envisions the early church meetings as open, participatory, and spontaneous, many modern clergy refuse to approve of such meetings today. Clerical thinking on the subject frequently goes something like this: "If I allowed my congregation to exercise its gifts in an open meeting, there would be sheer chaos. I have no choice but to control the services—lest the people spin out of control."

Others have confessed, "I tried to have open meetings with *my* people once. And it just doesn't work."

These objections betray a gross misunderstanding of God's ecclesiology. First, the notion that a clergyman has the authority to "allow" or "forbid" his fellow brethren to function in a gathering of God's people is built on a skewed understanding of authority. (We will explore this aspect further in part 2.) No human has the right to permit or prohibit the believing priesthood in the exercise of its Spirit-endowed gifts. In addition, no one has the right to refer to God's people as "my people."

Second, the assumption that chaos would ensue if clerical control were removed betrays a lack of confidence in the Holy Spirit. It also reveals a lack of trust in God's people, something that violates the New Testament outlook (Rom. 15:14; 2 Cor. 2:3; 7:6; 8:22; Gal. 5:10; 2 Thess. 3:4; Philem. 21; Heb. 6:9).

Third, the idea that the church meeting would turn into a tumultuous free-for-all is simply not true. But it hinges upon a very important ingredient: *God's people must be properly equipped to function under Christ's headship.*

Having said that, I'll make a candid observation: If a pastor decides to implement open meetings in his church, I can well understand why it wouldn't work. The reason is simple—he probably hasn't equipped God's people to function under the headship of Jesus Christ.

Christians do not become equipped by listening to sermons week after week while sitting muted in a pew. Instead, God's people are equipped by Christian workers who are able to teach them *how* to fellowship with the Lord and *how* to function in a group setting. Such workers equip the saints (Eph. 4:11–16). And then they do something that few contemporary pastors would ever dare—*they leave the church on its own* (Acts 13—20).

Granted, open-participatory meetings may not always be as prim and proper as the traditional church service that runs flawlessly according to what is published in the weekly church bulletin. Nevertheless, they reveal much more of the fullness of Christ than any human arrangement could manufacture.

In a first-century-styled meeting, there will be times when some may bring unprofitable ministry. This is particularly true in the infancy stages of a church's life. But the antidote for this is not to put a lid on open participation. Those who over-function and give unedifying ministry should be given instruction. In the foundational stage, this largely falls on the shoulders of those who are planting the church. It will later shift to those who are older and more seasoned in the assembly. (See chapter 9.)

Recall what happened when Paul faced the frenzied morass in Corinth. The apostle didn't shut down the meetings and hand out a liturgy. Nor did he introduce human officiation. Instead, he supplied his fellow brethren with a number of broad guidelines to facilitate order and edification in the gatherings (1 Cor. 14:1ff.).

What is more, Paul was confident that the church would adhere to those guidelines. This sets forth an important principle. Every church in the first century had at its disposal an itinerant apostolic worker who helped navigate it through common problems. Sometimes the worker's help came in the form of letters. At other times, it came during personal visits from the worker himself.

Present-day workers give similar guidelines to churches that are having difficulties in their meetings. And those guidelines are designed to put the meetings back into the hands of the Holy Spirit rather than under the domain of strong personalities.

When such guidelines are given and heeded, there's no need for human officiation, fixed liturgies, or scripted services. Again, the tendency to reject the first-century-styled church meeting unearths a lack of trust in the Holy Spirit.

Forgive the personal illustration, but in all the years that I've worked with organic churches, I never once felt compelled to resort to liturgy, ritual, or human officiation. A large part of my ministry has been to equip God's people to function. That would include helping those who overparticipate to step back a bit and emboldening those who underparticipate to function more often.

In Numbers 11, we have the first appearance of clericalism in the Bible. Two servants of the Lord, Eldad and Medad, received God's Spirit and began to prophesy (vv. 26–27). In hasty response, a young zealot urged Moses to "restrain them" (v. 28 NASB). Moses reproved the young suppressor, saying that *all* God's people should receive the Spirit and prophesy.

Moses' desire was fulfilled at Pentecost (Acts 2:17–18). And it continued to find fulfillment throughout the first century (Acts 2:38–39; 1 Cor. 14:1, 31). Unfortunately, the kingdom of God does not lack those who wish to again restrain Eldad and Medad from ministering in the Lord's house.

Headship vs. Lordship

The Bible draws a careful distinction between Christ's headship and His Lordship. Throughout the New Testament, the *headship* of Christ virtually always has in view the Lord's relationship with His body (Eph. 1:22–23; 4:15; 5:23; Col. 1:18; 2:19). The *lordship* of Christ virtually always has in view His relationship with His individual disciples (Matt. 7:21–22; 10:24–25; Luke 6:46).

What lordship is to the *individual*, headship is to the *church*. Headship and lordship are two dimensions of the same thing. Headship is lordship worked out in the corporate lives of God's people.

This distinction is important to grasp because it throws light on the problem of church practice today. It's all too common for Christians to know Christ's lordship and yet know nothing of His headship. A believer may submit to the lordship of Jesus in his or her own personal life. He may obey what he understands in the Bible. He may pray fervently. He may live self-sacrificially. Yet at the same time, he may know nothing about shared ministry, mutual submission, authentic community, or corporate testimony.

In the final analysis, to be subject to the headship of Jesus means to respond to His will concerning the life and practice of the church. It means submitting ourselves to the way that God designed the church to be, and giving ourselves to that design.

Submission to the headship of Christ incarnates the New Testament reality that Jesus is not only Lord of the individual believer, He is also the functioning Head of His church.

My friend and mentor Stephen Kaung put it best when he said,

> *People believe that the Word of God shows them how to live individually before God, but they think that insofar as their corporate life is concerned, God says, "It's up to you; do whatever you like." And that's what we find today in Christianity; there is no guiding principle as to our corporate life—everyone does what is right in his own eyes. But, dear brothers and sisters, we are saved individually, but we are called corporately. There is as much teaching and example in the Word of God that governs our corporate life as there is our personal life.*[9]

For these reasons, I believe that modern evangelicalism has held the doctrine of the believing priesthood only intellectually. But it has failed to apply it practically due to the subtle entrapment of deeply entrenched traditions.

What Does It Look Like Today?

Over the past twenty years, I've been privileged to attend hundreds of open-participatory church meetings. Some of them were drop-dead glorious. Those meetings have been burned into the circuitry of my brain. Others were decent. Others were horrible. Still others were unmentionable!

While institutional "church services" are essentially flawless, organic church meetings will vary depending on the spiritual condition and preparation of each member.

Herein lies one of the tasks of an apostolic worker. It's to equip God's people to function together in a free-yet-orderly meeting that expresses Christ in His fullness.

In all the years that I've been gathering in and planting organic churches, I've discovered that there's no way to explain accurately what a meeting under the headship of Christ looks like to those who have never seen one. Nevertheless, I'll do my best to paint a picture of one meeting that will give you the flavor of what a glorious meeting can look like.

About a decade ago, a church made up of about twenty-five Christians gathered together in a home one evening. I had just spent a year and a half ministering Jesus Christ to this group in biweekly "apostolic meetings." The goal of that ministry was to equip this new church where it could function on its own—without any human headship.

The day arrived. The church was to have its first meeting on its own. I wasn't to be present. However, I snuck into the room without any-one noticing and hid behind a couch. (I felt that if I were visible in that meeting, it would have affected the way the believers functioned. This is usually the case when the person who plants the church is present during its gatherings—especially in the early years of a church's life.)

The believers gathered together and began the meeting with singing. The singing was *a capella*. A Christian sister began the meeting by starting a song. And everyone sang with her. Then prayers were offered spontane-ously one by one. Then a brother in Christ started another song. By this time, everyone was standing together. More prayers were offered. More songs were sung. During the singing, different ones would share short exhortations based upon the lyrics of the songs. The word *moving* doesn't quite say it. There was no song leader present. All were participating in offering praises to God freely and spontaneously.

After they sang for a time, everyone sat down. And immediately a sister stood up and began sharing. She spoke about how she had found Christ as her living water during the week. She read a few verses out of John 4. As she began to share from the text, two other sisters interrupted her and shared insights out of their own experience from the same passage and the same theme. Yet what they shared of Christ was different.

When the first sister was finished, a brother stood up and began to speak. He also talked about the Lord as living water, but he spoke from a passage in Revelation 22. He spoke for several minutes, and then a sister stood up and began adding to what he had shared. This went on for over an hour. One by one, without pauses, brothers and sisters in Christ stood up and shared out of their spiritual experience of the Lord Jesus Christ. They all revealed Him as living water.

Some shared poems, others shared songs, others shared stories, others shared from Scripture, others offered prayers.

As I heard all of this from behind the couch, I couldn't resist the tears. I was so touched I began to weep. That meeting was electric. It was as if a flowing river had poured into that room and it couldn't be stopped. I could sense the Lord's presence and grace. The sharing was rich, full, living, and vibrant. I wished I had a pen and pad to write down the glorious things that were being said. Many of them bristled with seminal insight. But I just listened in amazement.

The incredible thing was that no one was leading this gathering. No one was facilitating, either. (No human being, that is.) And it was incredibly Christ-centered.

The meeting finally wound down and someone stood up and began a song. The rest of the church stood up and joined in. As they sang, I slipped out of the room. Only a few people noticed me. When I met with the church the following week, I divulged to them that I had been present. The church had prepared for this gathering. They had broken up into pairs and pursued the Lord together during the week in preparation for the meeting. The result was a corporate explosion of spiritual life that displayed the Lord Jesus Christ through His every-membered body.

Please understand that this group of Christians couldn't have had a meeting like this when I first began working with them. At that time, most of them were habituated to be passive and quiet. Some, who had stronger personalities, would dominate the sharing. But after a year and a half of receiving practical and spiritual ministry, they were equipped to know the Lord together, function in a coordinated way, open their mouths, and share the living Christ in an orderly fashion. And God was magnified as a result.

I could multiply examples of this kind of meeting and the wide variety expressed within them. I trust, however, that you now have an impression of how a meeting of the church can be under the Lord's living headship in our day.

Questions That Must Be Faced

- Do our modern church services, largely built around the sermon of one man and the worship program of an established "worship team," reflect the core principles of the New Testament church—or are they at odds with them? Explain.
- Why would open-participatory meetings be good for the early Christians but somehow be unworkable for us today? Explain.
- Does your church provide any meetings where you have an outlet to

share what God has shown you with your Christian brothers and sisters in a free and open environment uncontrolled and unfacilitated by a human being? Explain.

- Is your present practice of church an expression of the complete headship of Jesus Christ or the headship of a human being? Explain.

CHAPTER 3
REIMAGINING THE LORD'S SUPPER

The most visible and profound way in which the community gives physical expression to its fellowship is the common meal. The word "deipnon" (1 Cor. 11:20), meaning "dinner," tells us that it was not a token meal (as it has become since) or part of a meal (as it is sometimes envisaged), but an entire, ordinary meal. —Robert Banks

The Lord's Supper in the New Testament is a meal. The appropriate setting for the sacrament is a table, and the appropriate posture in our western culture is sitting. —I. Howard Marshall

Consider how your church takes the Lord's Supper. (You may call it the Eucharist, Holy Communion, or the breaking of bread.) Depending on your religious background, you either take the Lord's Supper weekly, monthly, or periodically. If you are a Protestant Christian, it's typically comprised of a tiny glass of grape juice (or wine) and a bite-sized wafer or cracker.

In this chapter, we'll examine how the early Christians took the Lord's Supper and what it meant to them. It is beyond dispute that the Supper held a very special place in the life of the early church. This is reflected by the fact that they took it on a regular basis. The church in Troas took it weekly (Acts 20:7). The church in Jerusalem and the church in Corinth took it regularly (Acts 2:42; 1 Cor. 11:20–21, 33). And Jesus Himself made a strong point about not neglecting the Supper (Luke 22:19–20).

The reason why the Lord's Supper held such a significant place in the early church is because it embodies the major features of the Christian life. Let's explore some of them now.

The Broken Bread

The Lord's Supper includes the breaking of bread (Matt. 26:26; 1 Cor. 10:16). The broken bread points us to the humanity of Jesus. The Son of Glory took upon Himself the form of a servant. The Almighty lowered Himself by becoming a man.

The bread—being the most basic and lowly of all foods—points to the humility and availability of our Lord. By taking on our humanity, Jesus Christ became accessible to us all—just as bread is available to everyone, both rich and poor.

The breaking of bread also reminds us of the cross upon which our Lord's body was broken. Bread is made from the crushed wheat. Wine is made from the pressed grape. Both elements represent death.

Yet the breaking of bread not only depicts the death of Christ. It also shows forth His resurrection. The grain of wheat has gone into the ground. But it now lives to produce many grains like unto itself (John 12:24). As we eat Christ's flesh and drink His blood through the Supper, we obtain His life (John 6:53). This is the principle of resurrection—life out of death.

The revelation of the resurrected Christ is also bound up with the broken bread. When the risen Lord ate with His disciples, it was bread that

He broke with them (John 21:13). In like manner, the resurrected Christ appeared to two people on the Emmaus road. But their eyes were not opened to recognize Him until He broke the bread (Luke 24:30–32).

The testimony of the oneness of Christ's body is also embodied in the breaking of bread. Recall that there was only one loaf that the early Christians broke. Paul writes, "Because there is *one* loaf, we, who are many, are *one* body, for we all partake of the *one* loaf" (1 Cor. 10:17).

The Lord's Banquet

Contrary to today's practice, the early church took the Lord's Supper in the context of a normal meal. When Jesus instituted the Supper, it was taken as part of the Passover Feast (Luke 22:15–20). In fact, the Passover was the forerunner of the Lord's Supper.

First Corinthians 11 makes clear that the early Christians gathered to eat the Supper as a meal. Some in the church at Corinth weren't waiting for their brethren to show up to the meeting. The result: Those who ate were full and those who showed up late went hungry. In addition, the Corinthian Christians were getting drunk at the Supper (1 Cor. 11:21–22, 33–34). Now think: Is it possible to get drunk on a thimble of grape juice and satisfy one's hunger with a bite-sized cracker?

The New Testament word for "supper" literally means a dinner, a meal, or a banquet. And the Greek word for "table" refers to a table in which a full meal is spread (Luke 22:14; 1 Cor. 10:21). To the first-century Christians, the Lord's Supper was just that—a *supper*. It was a banquet—a potluck dinner that included bread and wine. It was the table communion of the saints. A family festival. A fellowship meal.

By it, the Christians who were better off monetarily showed their love and concern for their less fortunate brethren. This ran against the grain of Greco-Roman norms, where class distinctions were sharply recognized during banquets. But not so with the Christians. In the Supper, the early believers showed their unity and oneness, ignoring social distinctions of class and race. Perhaps this is why the early church referred to the Supper as the *Agape*—or "love feast" (2 Peter 2:13; Jude 12).

Regrettably, centuries of ecclesiastical tradition have made today's truncated version of the Supper an event that is far removed from what it was in the first century.[1] As eminent scholar Eduard Schweizer notes, "A practice which separates the sacrament from the brotherhood meal turns the former into a strange, almost heathen rite which totally lacks its 'bodily' expression in the context of the whole life of its participants."[2]

Consequently, the communal meaning of the breaking of bread has been largely lost to us. It's no longer the "Lord's Supper." Today's version would better be called the "Savior's Sampler," the "Nazarene Niblet," or the "Lord's Appetizer." Forgive the humor, but can we really call a cracker crumb and a shot glass of grape juice a supper?

A Covenant Meal

Shared memories are part of what make up a people. By sharing a set of memories, people groups gain a sense of identity and belonging. One of the avenues by which a group revisits its shared memories is through a shared meal. The American holiday Thanksgiving is an example. Family reunions, anniversaries, and birthdays are others. All are accompanied by a shared meal.

In the Old Testament, the Passover meal was instituted as a way for God's people to revisit their shared memory of God's faithful deliverance.

The Passover meal gave them a sense of identity and belonging. But it did something beyond that: It cemented their lives together.

You see, among the ancient Jews, a meal was seen as a sacred act that united those who shared it. Eating established sacred ties between the people who ate.

The Passover was also a covenant meal. A covenant is a binding agreement between two parties. All throughout the Old Testament, when two people cut a covenant, the covenant was sealed by the sharing of a meal.

For example, after God gave Moses the words of the Law, offerings were made and Moses sprinkled blood on the people, saying, "This is the blood of the covenant that the LORD has made with you" (Ex. 24:8). Then Moses and the seventy elders went up into a mountain and saw God. And they ate and drank in His presence (Ex. 24:9–11).

When Jesus celebrated the Passover, which was the first Lord's Supper, He offered the wine cup to His disciples with the words, "This cup is the new covenant in my blood" (Luke 22:20). By this action, the Lord was pointing out this one fact: The Supper was a covenant meal wherein His disciples revisited the common memories they shared and celebrated their new identity in the Messiah.

Today, when we celebrate the Lord's Supper as a meal, we are remembering the covenant we have with God in Christ. We are participating in the shared memory of what Jesus has done for us. And we are proclaiming our new identity in Him.

Water baptism is the scriptural mode of our *initiation* into the Christian faith. But the Lord's Supper is a *reaffirmation* of our initial commitment to Christ. Through it, we reaffirm our faith in Jesus and our identity in Him as part of the new creation.

The Wedding Feast to Come

The Supper also points to Christ's future coming in glory. At the end of the age, the heavenly Bridegroom will preside at a sumptuous wedding feast and sup with His beloved bride in His Father's kingdom (Matt. 26:29). The Lord's Supper, therefore, possesses eschatological overtones. It's a last-days feast. A figure of the messianic banquet that will occur at Christ's future coming (Matt. 22:1–14; 26:29; Luke 12:35–38; 15:22–32; Rev. 19:9).

In this connection, the Lord's Supper was never meant to be a morbid reminder of Christ's sufferings. Nor was it a somber occasion where Christians mourned over their sins. Instead, the Supper was a cheerful reminder of who Jesus Christ is and what He has done. It was a reminder and a proclamation of His glorious victory at Calvary, which will be consummated at His future coming.

The Lord's Supper, therefore, is a celebration. It's a banquet of joy marked by sharing and thanksgiving (Luke 22:17; Acts 2:46; 1 Cor. 10:16). It's a foretaste of the wedding feast to come. More specifically, the Lord's Supper is the bride's visible petition for her Bridegroom to return for her.

The Supper Transcends Time

The Lord's Supper possesses past, present, and future implications. It's a reproclamation of the Lord's sacrificial death for us in the *past*. It's a redeclaration of His ever-abiding nearness with us in the *present*. And it's a repronouncement of our hope of glory—His coming in the *future*.

Put differently, the Lord's Supper is a living testimony to the three chief virtues: faith, hope, and love. Through the Supper, we reground ourselves in that glorious salvation that is ours by *faith*. We reexpress our *love* for the brethren as we reflect on the one body. And we rejoice in the *hope* of our Lord's soon return. By observing the Supper, we "proclaim [present] the Lord's death [past] until he comes [future]" (1 Cor. 11:26).

Catholics have made the Lord's Supper literal and sacrificial. Every time they take the Eucharist, they believe that Jesus' sacrifice is being represented for our sins. Protestants have reacted to this view by making the Supper merely symbolic and commemorative.

But the Lord's Supper is neither a literal sacrifice nor an empty ritual.

The Lord's Supper is a spiritual reality. Through the Supper, the Holy Spirit reveals the living Christ to our hearts anew and afresh. By it, we reaffirm our faith in Jesus and our membership to His body. Through the Supper, we sup with Christ and His people.

A Shadow of the Triune God

As with all aspects of organic church life, the Supper was foreshadowed and previously experienced by the Trinitarian Community. A careful reading of Scripture will show that God the Father is food to God the Son (Matt 4:4; John 4:31ff.; 6:27, 57, etc.). In turn, God the Son is food to us (John 1:29; 6:27, 32–35, 53–57). He is also drink (John 4:10; 6:53; 1 Cor. 10:4; 12:13; Rev. 22:17).

Throughout eternity, the Father and the Son have coparticipated in the divine life they share. The Father is the portion of the Son, and the Son is the portion of the Father.[3] In the Godhead, each member coparticipates in the divine life that flows between them.

Not surprisingly, the image that the Bible draws for this coparticipation is that of eating and drinking. Through the Lord's Supper, we enact the divine participation in the triune God and make it visible on the earth. As theologian Stanley Grenz puts it, we are "coparticipants in the fellowship of the triune God."[4] The Supper, therefore, is rooted in an eternal activity within God Himself. And it is one way that we participate in and reflect that activity.

These are but a few precious truths bound up with the Lord's Supper. And they help explain why the early Christians made it an important part of their gatherings. Suffice it to say that the Lord Jesus Himself instituted the Supper (Matt. 26:26). And His apostles handed it down to us (1 Cor. 11:2).

A Present-Day Example

Since 1988, I have been in scores of meetings where the Lord's Supper was taken "first-century style." Some of them were rather simple. They were essentially potluck dinners where everyone brought something— including unleavened bread and grape juice or wine. Those who couldn't afford to bring food helped cook the meal. The meal usually opened with someone saying a few words about the body of the Lord Jesus. The unleavened loaf was broken and passed around. And the eating would begin.

We would all partake of the food as we communed with Christ and spoke of His riches. Near the end of the meal, someone would lift up a glass of wine (or grape juice) and say a few words about the blood of our Lord. If it was wine, the glass would be passed around the table and everyone would take a sip. If it was grape juice, the juice would be poured into individual glasses.[5] Sometimes we would toast and drink at the same time.

I've been in other Lord's Supper meetings that were far more elaborate. Several months of planning went into them. In these meetings, everyone dressed up in formal attire. The church provided a beautiful spread, often in a rented banquet hall. The table was draped with a white linen cloth. The food was prepared ahead of time, and it was spread out on the table before the majority of the church arrived. I remember one such meeting quite vividly.

This particular meeting began with everyone standing near their chairs, singing praises to God. Then, two people who were previously selected shared a few thoughts on the meaning of the bread as the rest of the church took their seats. Afterward, the bread was broken. It was passed around, and the meal began.

As everyone began eating, one by one, men and women stood and shared something about the Lord Jesus Christ. A young woman stood and shared about how the blood of Christ cleansed her conscience. All of her guilt was gone. A man stood and shared a poem on the broken bread. Another gentleman who brought a guitar sang a song on the broken body and the precious blood. Following him, a sister in Christ stood and spoke on remembering the Lord's death.

Someone then started a song on the eternal eating and drinking that has been going on in the triune God from before time began. And everyone began singing. Not a few times people would tear up. Others would rejoice. Sometimes we would clap while praising the Lord together. All the while the church was enjoying a lavish, bountiful meal. After several hours of eating, drinking, and sharing in this way, two people stood and spoke on the cup. The meal was concluded with everyone drinking from the cup and worshipping the Lord Jesus.

Questions That Must Be Faced

- Should New Testament teaching and example shape how we observe the Lord's Supper today? If not, what should shape our observation of the Supper?
- Were you stirred in any way by the description of the core elements of fellowship in the Supper? Have you ever experienced any of these elements when taking the Lord's Supper? Explain.
- Do we not do violence to the coparticipation of the triune God that the Supper was meant to depict when we strip it from a meal and turn it into a somber ritual? Explain.
- Do we really have a spiritual and biblical right to change the way the Lord's Supper is taken from the way that Jesus and the apostles originally delivered it to us? Explain.

CHAPTER 4
REIMAGINING THE GATHERING PLACE

The choice of "ekklesia" as the designation of the Christian community suggests that the New Testament believers viewed the church as neither an edifice nor an organization. They were a people—a people brought together by the Holy Spirit—a people bound to each other through Christ. —Stanley Grenz

God wants the intimacy of the "upper room" to mark the gatherings of His children, not the stiff formality of an imposing public edifice. That is why in the Word of God we find His children meeting in the family atmosphere of a private home. —Watchman Nee

So where do you go to church? This question is commonplace today. Yet it speaks volumes.

Suppose that a new employee was recently hired at your workplace. You learn that he is a Christian. Upon your asking what church he attends, he responds by saying: "I attend a church that meets in a home."

Now be honest. What are the thoughts that run through your mind? Do you think, "Well, that's strange. He must be a religious misfit of some sort." Or, "He's probably part of some cult or flaky fringe group." Or, "There must be something wrong with him. If there wasn't, he would be going to a *regular* church." Or, "He has to be a rebel of some sort—a loose cannon on the deck—unable to submit to authority. Else he would be attending a normal church—you know, the kind that meets in a building."

Unfortunately, these are the reactions of many Christians whenever the idea of a "house church" is brought to their attention. But here's the punch line: That new employee's place of meeting is identical to that of every Christian mentioned in the New Testament. In fact, the church of Jesus Christ met in the homes of its members for the first three hundred of its existence.[1]

The Witness of the Early Christians

The common meeting place for the early Christians was none other than the home. Anything else would have been the exception. And the first-century church would have looked upon it as being *out of* the ordinary. Note the following passages:

> *And breaking bread from house to house, they ate their food with gladness and simplicity of heart. (Acts 2:46 NKJV)*

> *I did not shrink from declaring to you anything that was profitable, and teaching you publicly and from house to house. (Acts 20:20 NASB)*

> *Greet Priscilla and Aquila.... Greet also the church that meets at their house. (Rom. 16:3, 5)*

> *Aquila and Priscilla greet you warmly in the Lord, and so does the church that meets at their house. (1 Cor. 16:19)*

Give my greetings to the brothers at Laodicea, and to Nympha and the church in her house. (Col. 4:15)

To Apphia our sister, to Archippus our fellow soldier and to the church that meets in your home. (Philem. 2)

The above scriptures show that the early Christians held their meetings in the hospitable homes of their fellow brethren. (See also Acts 2:2; 9:11; 10:32; 12:12; 16:15, 34, 40; 17:5; 18:7; 21:8.) Interestingly, the early church knew nothing of what would correspond to the "church" edifice of our day. Neither did it know anything about houses converted into basilicas. That is, none of the churches had hardwood pews bolted to the floor and a pulpit accompanying the living room furniture! While such oddities exist in our time, they were foreign to the early Christians.

The first-century believers assembled in ordinary, livable houses. They knew nothing of "church-houses." They only knew the "church in the house."

What did the church do when it grew too large to assemble in a single home? It certainly didn't erect a building. It simply multiplied and met in several other homes, following the "house to house" principle (Acts 2:46; 20:20).

New Testament scholarship is agreed that the early church was essentially a network of home-based meetings. So if there is such a thing as a *normal* church, it's the church that meets in the house. Or as Howard Snyder once put it, "If there is a New Testament form of the church, it is the house church."

Advocates of "church" buildings have tried to argue that the primitive Christians would have erected religious edifices if they weren't under persecution. They say that the early believers met in homes to hide from their persecutors. While this idea is popular, it's rooted in pure conjecture. And that conjecture doesn't map to actual history.

Consider these facts: The early church enjoyed peace and favor from the people (Acts 2:46–47; 9:31), and they made no secret about where they met; unbelievers could find them quite easily (Acts 8:3; 1 Cor. 14; 23). The truth is that prior to AD 250, the persecution of Christians was sporadic and highly localized. It was typically the result of mob hostility in a local area. It wasn't an exercise of the Roman Empire. (That happened much later.)

That said, if we read the New Testament with an eye for understanding how the first-century Christians related to one another, we'll quickly discover why they gathered in homes.

(1) The Home Testifies That the People Comprise God's House

The present-day notion of "church" is frequently associated with a building. (The building is commonly called the "sanctuary" or the "house of God.") According to the Bible, however, it is the community of God's people that is called the church. The believing community is said to be the "house of God"—never the brick and mortar.

One of the most striking marks of the early church was the absence of special religious buildings. In Judaism, the temple is the sanctified meeting place. In Christianity, the believing community is the temple (1 Cor. 3:16; 2 Cor. 6:16; Eph. 2:21–22). Both Judaism and paganism teach that there must be a sanctified place for divine worship. Consequently, the ancient Jews erected special buildings to carry out their spiritual functions (synagogues). So did the pagans (shrines). Not so with Christianity.

The early believers understood that God sanctifies people, not objects. In this way, the spatial location of the early Christian gathering cut sharply against the religious customs of the first century.

In fact, the early church was the only religious group in the first century that met exclusively in the homes of its members. It would have been quite natural for the Christians in Judea to pursue their Jewish heritage and erect buildings to suit their needs. But they intentionally kept from doing so. The same is true for the Gentile Christians. None of them erected "Christian" shrines or temples. Not in the first century, anyway.

Perhaps the early Christians knew the confusion that sanctified buildings would produce. So they kept from building them to preserve the testimony that the *Lord's people* comprise the living stones of God's habitation.

Just think of the massive confusion that the common practice of calling a building a "church" has created today. Christians view buildings as "the house of the Lord" and as possessing some sort of sacred element. But nothing could be further from the truth. The church of God has never been a building.

(2) The Home is the Natural Setting for One-Anothering

The apostolic instructions concerning the church meeting are best suited for a small-group setting like a home. The organic activities of the church, such as mutual participation (Heb. 10:24–25); the exercise of spiritual gifts (1 Cor. 14:26); the building together of God's people into an intentional, face-to-face community (Eph. 2:21–22); the communal meal (1 Cor. 11); the mutual love of members one toward another (Rom. 15:14; Gal. 6:1–2; James 5:16,19–20); the freedom for interactive sharing (1 Cor. 14:29–40); and the *koinonia* (shared life) of the Holy Spirit (2 Cor. 3:17; 13:14) all operate best in a small-group setting like a house.

Add to that, the fifty-eight "one-another" exhortations in the New Testament can only be fleshed out in a houselike environment.[2] For this reason, the home church meeting is highly conducive to the realization of God's ultimate purpose. A purpose that is centered upon "being built together" as *living* stones to create a house for the Lord (Eph. 2:19–22).

(3) The Home Represents the Humility of Christ

The home represents humility, naturalness, and pure simplicity—the outstanding marks of the early church (Acts 2:46; 2 Cor. 11:3). Let's face it. The home is a far more humble place than the stately religious edifices of our day with their lofty steeples and elegant decor. In this way, most modern "church" buildings reflect the boastings of this world rather than the meek and lowly Savior whose name we bear. Rodney Stark confirms the point, saying,

> *For far too long, historians have accepted the claim that the conversion of the Emperor Constantine (ca. 285–337) caused the triumph of Christianity. To the contrary, he destroyed its most attractive and dynamic aspects, turning a high-intensity, grassroots movement into an arrogant institution controlled by an elite who often managed to be both brutal and lax.... Constantine's "favor" was his decision to divert to the Christians the massive state funding on which the pagan temples had always depended. Overnight, Christianity became "the most-favoured recipient of the near*

*limitless resources of imperial favors." A faith that had been meeting in
humble structures was suddenly housed in magnificent public buildings—
the new church of Saint Peter in Rome was modeled on the basilican form
used for imperial throne halls.[3]*

In addition, the overhead costs of a religious building cost God's
people enormous financial loss. As George Barna and I point out in our
book, *Pagan Christianity,* institutional churches in the United States alone
own over $230 billion worth of real estate. And much of that money is
borrowed (debt). Christians give between $9 and $11 billion a year on
church buildings. How much freer would their hands be to support the
poor and needy as well as to spread the gospel if they didn't have to bear
such a heavy burden?

(4) The Home Reflects the Family Nature of the Church

There is a natural affinity between the home meeting and the family
motif of the church that saturates Paul's writings. Because the home is the
native environment of the family, it naturally furnishes the *ekklesia* with
a familial atmosphere—the very atmosphere that pervaded the life of the
early Christians.

In stark contrast, the artificial environment of the "church" building
promotes an impersonal climate that inhibits intimacy and participation.
The rigid formalism of the building runs contrary to the refreshing, unof-
ficial air that the home meeting breathes.

In addition, it's quite easy to "get lost" in a large building. Because of
the spacious and remote nature of the basilica "church," folks can easily
go unnoticed. Or worse, hide in their sins. But not so in a home. All our

warts show there. And rightly so. Everyone in the gathering is known, accepted, and encouraged.

In this regard, the formal manner in which things are done in the basilica "church" tends to discourage the mutual intercourse and spontaneity that characterized the early Christian gatherings. Winston Churchill wisely said, "First we shape our buildings. Thereafter, they shape us." Exegete the architecture of a typical church building and you'll quickly discover that it effectively teaches the church to be passive.

The interior structure of the building is not designed for interpersonal communication, mutual ministry, or spiritual fellowship. Instead, it's designed for a rigid one-way communication—pulpit to pew, leader to congregation.

In this way, the typical "church" edifice is unquestionably similar to a lecture hall or cinema. The congregation is carefully arranged in pews (or chairs) to see and hear the pastor (or priest) speak from the pulpit.

The people are focused on a single point—the clergy leader and his pulpit. (In liturgical churches, the table/altar takes the place of the pulpit as the central point of reference. But in both cases, the building promotes a clergy centrality and dependence.)

But that's not all. The place where the pastor and staff are seated is normally elevated above the seating of the congregation. Such an arrangement reinforces the unbiblical clergy/laity chasm. (See part 2 of this book for details.) It also feeds the spectator mentality that afflicts most of the body of Christ today.

By contrast, the early Christians conducted their meetings in the home to express the unique character of church life. They met in houses to encourage the family dimension of their worship, their fellowship, and their ministry. Home meetings naturally made the people of God feel that the church's interests were their interests. It fostered a sense of closeness between themselves and the church, rather than distancing them from it. The situation today is very different. Most contemporary Christians attend "church" as remote spectators, not as active participants.

In addition, home meetings provided a venue for God's people to demonstrate hospitality—a basic virtue of authentic church life (Rom. 12:13; 1 Tim. 3:2; Titus 1:8; 1 Peter 4:9). The house church meeting provided both the connectedness and deep-seated relationships that characterize the *ekklesia*. It furnished the Christians with a family-like atmosphere where true fellowship occurred shoulder-to-shoulder, face-to-face, and eyeball-to-eyeball. It provided a climate that fostered open communication, spiritual cohesiveness, and unreserved communion—the necessary features for the full flourishing of the *koinonia* (shared fellowship) of the Holy Spirit.

(5) The Home Models Spiritual Authenticity

The church in the home also serves as a fruitful testimony of spiritual reality and authenticity. For many, it's a refreshing witness against those religious institutions that equate glamorous buildings and multimillion-dollar budgets with success.

Equally so, many non-Christians will not attend a modern religious service held in a basilica "church" where they are expected to dress up for the show. Yet they feel unthreatened and uninhibited gathering in the natural comfort of someone's home where they can be themselves.

The unprofessional atmosphere of the home, as opposed to a clinical building, is much more inviting. Compared to a home, buildings are impersonal and nonrelational. Perhaps this is another reason why the early Christians chose to gather in homes rather than erecting shrines, sanctuaries, and synagogues, as did the other religions of their day.

In addition, the home church meeting defies the unbiblical disconnect of sacred versus secular. There is no such disconnect in Scripture. Meeting for "religious" purposes in a "religious" building merely reinforces this unscriptural mind-set. But meeting in a home demonstrates that the sacred and the secular are blended together.[4]

Consider the fellowship that exists within the triune God. There is no secular versus spiritual disconnect there. The Father is the *natural* abode of the Son, and the Son is the *natural* abode of the Father (John 10:30, 38; 14:10–11; 17:21–23). The Father, the Son, and the Spirit mutually and inseparably indwell one another. This mutual indwelling is intimate, natural, and constant. And it gives us a glimpse into the normative "home life" of God Himself. In the words of Kevin Giles, "the communion of the divine persons with each other is so complete that each could be said to be dwelling entirely in the other in a complete exchange of divine life."[5]

Meeting in the naturalness of a home for the purpose of expressing the living God better reinforces this spiritual reality. Meeting in a "sacred" building used for "sacred" events distorts it.

Ironically, many Christians believe that if a church doesn't own a building, its testimony to the world is inhibited and its growth stifled. But nothing could be further from the truth. The fact is, the Christian faith grew dramatically for the first three hundred years of its life—all without the use of "church" buildings.[6]

In all these ways, the house church meeting is fundamentally biblical. It's also spiritually practical. And it's strikingly at odds with the modern pulpit-pew-styled service where believers are forced to fellowship with the back of someone's head for an hour or two.

The Social Location of the Church

What's been said so far can be reduced to this simple but profound observation: The social location of the church meeting both expresses and influences the character of the church itself.

Put another way, the spatial setting of the church possesses theological significance. In the typical sanctuary or chapel, the pulpit, the pews (or rowed chairs), and the massive space breathe a formal air that inhibits interaction and relatedness.

The peculiar features of a home produce the opposite effects. The low-volume seating. The casual atmosphere. The convivial setting for shared meals. The family pictures on the walls. The personalized space of soft sofas and comfy couches. All of these characteristics contain a relational subtext that befits mutual ministry.

Stated simply, the early church met in the homes of its members for spiritually viable reasons. The modern institutional church undermines those reasons. Howard Snyder puts it beautifully:

> *The New Testament teaches us that the church is a community in which all are gifted and all have ministry. The church as taught in Scripture is a new social reality that models and incarnates the respect and concern for people that we see in Jesus Himself. This is our high calling. And yet the church, in fact, often betrays this calling. House churches are a big part of the way out of this betrayal and this paradox. Face-to-face community breeds mutual respect, mutual responsibility, mutual submission, and mutual ministry. The sociology of the house church fosters a sense of equality and mutual worth, though it doesn't guarantee it as the Corinthian church shows.*
>
> *The New Testament principles of the priesthood of believers, the gifts of*

*the Spirit, and mutual ministry are found most naturally in this informal
context.*

*House churches are revolutionary because they incarnate this radical
teaching that all are gifted and all are ministers. They offer some hope
for healing the body of Christ from some of its worst heresies: that some
believers are more valuable than others, that only some Christians are
ministers, and that the gifts of the Spirit are no longer to function in
our age. These heresies cannot be healed in theory or in theology only.
They must be healed in practice and relationship in the social form of
the church.[7]*

Two Kinds of Meetings

That the *normative* meeting place for the church was the home is, I
believe, beyond dispute. But does this suggest that it's *never* appropriate
for a church to gather in any other location? No, it does not.

On special occasions when it was necessary for the "whole church"
to gather together, the church in Jerusalem met in large settings such
as the open courts of the temple and Solomon's porch (Acts 2:46a;
5:12).

But such large-group gatherings didn't rival the normative location for
the regular church meeting, which was the house (Acts 2:46b). Nor did it
set a biblical precedent for Christians to erect their own buildings.

The temple courts and Solomon's portico were public, outdoor arenas
that were already in existence *before* the first Christians appeared. These
large-group settings simply accommodated the "whole church" when it
was necessary to bring it together for a particular purpose.

In the beginning days of the church's existence, the apostles used such locations to hold apostolic meetings for the vast number of believers and unbelievers in Jerusalem (Acts 3:11–26; 5:20–21, 25, 42).

Instances where we find the apostles going to the synagogues should not be confused with church meetings. These were *evangelistic* meetings designed to preach the gospel to unsaved Jews. Again, the church meeting was primarily for the edification of believers. The evangelistic meeting was primarily for the salvation of unbelievers. (See chapter 2.)

Along the same lines, Paul rented a building called the hall of Tyrannus to hold *apostolic* meetings for two years. But again, those meetings were temporary. They were designed to evangelize, plant a church, and train Christian workers (Acts 19:9–10). They didn't continue permanently. Such meetings would be akin to the special seminars, workshops, and conferences of our day.

Perhaps the Holy Spirit has led and will lead some to assemble in a building for special purposes. (Beyond spiritual ministry purposes, buildings can be used for kingdom work like feeding the poor, housing the homeless, clothing the needy, etc.) Perhaps He has and will lead some to even purchase a building for special purposes. But the Spirit will do so only if it truly suits the *Lord's* purposes.

Let it be clear that if God leads a church in this direction, it will not be driven by human zeal, tradition, or pressure to conform—nor will it cloak it over with religious rhetoric justifying the decision.

That said, should we not guard against the fleshly tendency to practice something simply because it represents the latest spiritual fad of the day? The Lord spare us from falling into the peril of ancient Israel wherein they aimlessly "went after the nations" (1 Sam. 8:5, 20; 2 Kings 17:15 NASB). And may He deliver us from mindlessly adopting the present "edifice complex" because it's the conventional thing to do.

Questions That Must Be Faced

- When you see or hear the phrase *house church* or *church in the home*, what comes to your mind? Explain.
- Should not house church meetings be more the rule than the exception due to the spiritual benefits that are bound up with them? Explain.
- After reading this chapter, isn't the question no longer, "Why do some churches meet in homes?" but rather, "Why is it that so many churches *do not* meet in homes?"
- Does it bother you at all that Christians spend $9 to $11 billion a year on church buildings, and that many of these buildings aren't owned in the clear, but instead, represent great debt? Explain.

CHAPTER 5
REIMAGINING THE FAMILY OF GOD

Community is deeply grounded in the nature of God. It flows from who God is. Because he is community, he creates community. It is his gift of himself to humans. Therefore, the making of community may not be regarded as optional for Christians. It is a compelling and irrevocable necessity, a binding divine mandate for all believers at all times. It is possible for humans to reject or alter God's commission for them to build community and to be in community. But this may happen only at the cost of forsaking the Creator of community and of betraying his image in us; this cost is enormous, since his image in us is the essential attribute that defines our humanity. —Gilbert Bilezikian

Unfortunately, the metaphor that dominates most of American Christianity doesn't help us much; we usually envision the church as a corporation. The pastor is the CEO, there are committees and boards. Evangelism is the manufacturing process by which we make our product, and sales can be charted, compared, and forecast. Of course, this manufacturing process goes on in a growth economy so that any corporation-church whose annual sales figures aren't up from last year's is in trouble. Americans are quite single-minded in their captivity to the corporation metaphor. And it isn't even biblical. —Hal Miller

Surprisingly, the Bible never defines the church. Instead, it presents it through a number of different metaphors.

One of the reasons why the New Testament gives us numerous metaphors to depict the church is because the church is too comprehensive and rich to be captured by a single definition or metaphor. Unfortunately, our tendency is to latch on to one particular metaphor and understand the *ekklesia* through it alone.

But by latching on to just one metaphor—whether it be the body, the army, the temple, the bride, the vineyard, or the city—we lose the message that the other metaphors convey. The result: Our view of the church will become limited at best or lopsided at worst.

The Chief Metaphor

Do you know what metaphor for the church dominates the New Testament?

It's the family.

The writings of Paul, Peter, and John in particular are punctuated with the language and imagery of family. Consider the following examples:

Therefore, as we have opportunity, let us do good to all people, especially to those who belong to the family of believers. (Gal. 6:10)

For those God foreknew he also predestined to be conformed to the likeness of his Son, that he might be the firstborn among many brothers. (Rom. 8:29)

Consequently, you are no longer foreigners and aliens, but fellow citizens with God's people and members of God's household. (Eph. 2:19)

*Do not rebuke an older man harshly, but exhort him as if he were your
father. Treat younger men as brothers, older women as mothers, and
younger women as sisters. (1 Tim. 5:1–2)*

*If I am delayed, you will know how people ought to conduct themselves
in God's household, which is the church of the living God, the pillar and
foundation of the truth. (1 Tim. 3:15)*

*Like newborn babies, crave pure spiritual milk, so that by it you may grow
up in your salvation. (1 Peter 2:2)*

*I write to you, dear children, because your sins have been forgiven on account
of his name. I write to you, fathers, because you have known him who is
from the beginning. I write to you, young men, because you have overcome
the evil one. I write to you, dear children, because you have known the
Father. (1 John 2:12–13)*

While the New Testament authors depict the church with a variety of
different images, their favorite image is the *family*. Familial terms like "new
birth," "children of God," "sons of God," "brethren," "fathers," "brothers," "sisters," and "household" saturate the New Testament writings.

In all of Paul's letters to the churches, he speaks to the "brethren"—
a term that includes both brothers and sisters in Christ. Paul uses this
familial term more than 130 times in his epistles. So without question,
the New Testament is filled with the language and imagery of family.

In stark contrast, the dominating metaphor that's typically constructed
for the church today is the business corporation. The pastor is the CEO.
The clergy and/or staff is upper management. Evangelism is sales and

marketing. The congregation is the clientele. And there is competition with other corporations ("churches") in the same town.

But the corporation metaphor has a major problem. Not only is it glaringly absent from the New Testament, it does violence to the spirit of Christianity. Because from God's standpoint, the church is primarily a family. *His* family, in fact.

Regrettably, present-day society is plagued by what sociologists call the "dysfunctional family." This is a family that has been profoundly broken in some way. It may be intact outwardly, but it's damaged inwardly. If the truth be told, many of our modern churches are in every sense of the word "dysfunctional families."

Most Christians have no trouble giving glib assent to the idea that the church is a family. Yet giving mental assent to the family nature of the church is vastly different from fleshing out its sober implications. It would do us well to look closely at the family metaphor and discuss the practical implications that are connected with it. Let's explore six aspects of what it means for the church to be family. As you read through each aspect, I want to challenge you to compare your church to each one. Ask yourself this question: *Is my church living in the reality of being the family of God?*

(1) The Members Take Care of One Another

Because the church is family, its members take care of one another. Think about the natural family (assuming that it's healthy). Families take care of their own. Isn't it true that you take care of your natural blood? And they take care of you? If your mother, father, brother, sister, son, or daughter has a problem, do you say, "Sorry, don't bother me," or do you take care of them?

A true family takes care of its own, does it not? A dysfunctional family doesn't. A dysfunctional family is selfish, individualistic, and profoundly independent. It's characterized by detachment and unconnectedness. The members don't take the time to know one another. Nor do they seem to care much for each other.

What good is it, my brothers, if a man claims to have faith but has no deeds? Can such faith save him? Suppose a brother or sister is without clothes and daily food. If one of you says to him, "Go, I wish you well; keep warm and well fed," but does nothing about his physical needs, what good is it? In the same way, faith by itself, if it is not accompanied by action, is dead. (James 2:14–17)

This passage puts a finger on the meaning of real faith. Real faith expresses itself in acts of love toward our brothers and sisters in Christ. To paraphrase James, "If you say you have faith, but you neglect your brother or sister who is in physical need … then your faith is dead."

The "action" James is talking about is not prayer or Bible study, but acts of love toward our fellow brothers and sisters in Christ. Consider the words of Paul:

Let him who stole steal no longer, but rather let him labor, working with his hands what is good, that he may have something to give him who has need. (Eph. 4:28 NKJV)

Notice the last sentence: "Let him labor, working with his hands." Why? "That he may have something to *give* to him who has need."

You have no doubt heard of the "Protestant work ethic." Ephesians

4:28 is the "Christian work ethic." We work not just to meet our own needs; we work to meet the needs of others. That's a very different way of looking at work, isn't it? The New Testament envisions the church as a family that takes care of its members. Not only spiritually, but physically and financially—in every way that a nuclear or extended family takes care of its own.

In fact, if you read the first six chapters of the book of Acts, you'll quickly discover that the church in Jerusalem bore the burdens of its less fortunate brothers and sisters (Acts 4:34). Why? Because they saw themselves as an extended family—a shared-life community.

The early Christians regarded each member as "their own." They saw themselves as "members one of another" (Rom. 12:5; Eph. 4:25 KJV). As a result, they took care of one another (Rom. 12:13; 1 Cor. 12:25–26; 2 Cor. 8:12–15). And why? Because the church is family.

Recall what Paul told the Galatian Christians: "Carry each other's burdens, and in this way you will fulfill the law of Christ" (Gal. 6:2). The law of Christ is the inward law of love that's written on the heart of every believer. This love is rooted in Calvary's love (John 15:12–13). And it innately moves toward our brothers and sisters in Christ. "We know that we have passed from death to life, because we love our brothers" (1 John 3:14).

All told, if you belong to a church that's not taking care of the needs of its members, then your church is not fleshing out the New Testament vision of family. Again, the church is not a business; it's a family.

(2) The Members Spend Time Together

Because the church is family, the members take time to know one another. That is, they spend time together outside of scheduled meetings.

In a dysfunctional family, the children barely know the parents. And the parents hardly know the children. The same is true for the siblings. They may live under the same roof, but they live separate lives. The only time they come together is when they have a scheduled meeting—"We all have to go to Aunt Felicia's wedding this Saturday; so the family will all be together then." But after the event, the members rarely see one another.

Question: Do the members of your church see one another only during scheduled services? Are you in contact with them during the week? Do you share meals together? Consider the organic instincts of the Jerusalem church at work:

> *They devoted themselves to the apostles' teaching and to the fellowship, to the breaking of bread and to prayer.... Every day they continued to meet together.... They broke bread in their homes and ate together with glad and sincere hearts. (Acts 2:42, 46)*

The early Christians had lives that interacted with one another. This was the church's DNA at work. If we follow our spiritual instincts, we will have an innate desire to gather together often. Why? Because the Holy Spirit serves as a kind of magnet that organically draws Christians together. The Holy Spirit puts within the hearts of all genuine believers a desire for authentic community.

As Gilbert Bilezikian says, "The passion for community is contagious. Our innate need for community is so intense that once a spark of interest is ignited and a glimpse of God's dream for community is captured, a burning passion for community can spread like wildfire."[1]

The Bible says that the Jerusalem church met daily. Interestingly, the assembly in Jerusalem wasn't the only church that gathered together on a daily basis. Some thirty years later, the writer of Hebrews exhorts the Christians to "encourage one another *daily*" (Heb. 3:13). And yet today, in most contemporary churches, the only fellowship time that one gets is two minutes when the pastor says, "Turn around and greet the people behind you."

Granted, you may grab a little more time in the parking lot as you make a beeline to your car. But can we really call that fellowship? Let's be honest: For many Christians, the church is simply an event one attends once or twice a week, and that's all.

Truthfully, some of us twenty-first-century Western Christians are afraid of intimacy. That's why many people would never be interested in a church that gathers in a home. It's far safer to hang out in a pew, inspect the back of someone's neck for two hours, and then go home.

But the church of Jesus Christ is a family. It's not a theater. And in a family—a healthy family—everyone knows what's going on in one another's lives. *Dad is having trouble with his boss at work, so we're praying for him. Sis is having problems in her calculus class. Our brother got a raise at his new job. Mom is learning how to make gourmet food.* We know what's going on in one another's lives because we spend time together outside of scheduled events. The church is an extended household, and it's profoundly relational.

By contrast, how can we truly flesh out the "one another" exhortations in the New Testament if the church to which we belong is not acting like a family? How can we walk them out in shoe leather if we don't even know the people with whom we do church?

(3) The Members Show One Another Affection

Because the church is family, its members greet one another with affection. Think about it: When you see your mother, your father, your children, or your out-of-town relatives, do you just salute them at a distance? Or do you exchange hugs and perhaps kisses?

If your family is healthy, your answer is yes to the latter. It's the same way with the church. And why? Because the members of the church are related. For this reason, the apostles encouraged the early Christians to "greet one another with a holy kiss" (1 Thess. 5:26; 1 Cor. 16:20; 2 Cor. 13:12; Rom. 16:16; 1 Peter 5:14). It seemed quite important to them that the members of each church express their love for one another visibly.

I've met some Christians who have reacted to the above by saying, "I don't feel comfortable hugging anyone from my church—I barely know them." That reaction merely strengthens the point I've been trying to underscore in this chapter. Namely, the institutional church and the organic church are two very different creatures.

Living as the family of God means knowing our fellow brethren to the point where it's instinctive to show them affection. (The specific form of affection—whether hugs, kisses on the cheek, etc.—will differ depending on one's culture.)

By contrast, a dysfunctional family shows no affection toward its members. The parents never touch the children. And the children grow up feeling unloved and unaccepted. They experience little to no verbal or nonverbal expressions of love.

(4) The Family Grows

Because the church is family, it will grow. A church grows in two ways. One way is through division and multiplication. That is, if a church grows too large, it may divide and multiply into two fellowships. Our bodies grow the same way. Cells divide and then multiply.

Another way is by addition. That is, by giving birth to spiritual children. This is the principle of reproduction.

If the Lord is at work in a church, it will grow. It may not be immediate. It may take time. But if the church is alive and healthy, it will grow—both internally (spiritually) and externally (numerically).

Churches that live as families grow. Churches that operate as business corporations typically don't keep their converts. They may make converts, but those converts rarely become disciples and functioning members of the body. The reason? Christian community is indispensable for proper spiritual formation and development. The church that's living as family will produce transformation in its members. The church that isn't, won't.

In this connection, the ghost of Protestant individualism haunts the average postwar evangelical church. And until it exorcises that spirit, it will continue to see little spiritual formation in its congregants.

Let's face it. People in our postmodern world are looking for family. They're looking for authentic community. They're looking for a group of Christians who genuinely love and care for each other. In other words, *they're looking for organic Christianity.*

Numerous people in our day have been trained by bad examples. Consequently, when they see a group of people who are truly laying their lives down for one another, who are accepting one another unconditionally, and who are loving one another freely despite their flaws—they will be drawn like a thirsty deer is to water. In this way, the church as family answers the deepest cries that lie in the human heart.

(5) The Members Share Responsibility

If you look at a human family, you will see that each member has a different role. You don't ask the toddlers to go out and earn a living, do you? You don't expect the parents to consult the infants for wisdom. Each member has a distinct role—the grandparents, the father, the mother, the children, the toddlers, and the infants. Everyone works together for the common good of the family.

The family of God is the same way. In 1 John 2:13–14, John talks to the fathers, the young men, and the children. And he charges each with different responsibilities. Looking at the church through the body metaphor, each member—the eyes, ears, hands, and feet—has a different function.

In a dysfunctional family, the members don't carry out their responsibilities very well. The parents either neglect the children or they abuse them. (In some cases, the parents worship them.) They don't train the children. Nor do they give them comfort or guidance.

In the household of God, there are spiritual fathers and mothers. These are the older men and women who have known the Lord for a long time. Their role and responsibility before God is to give guidance and provide mentoring to the younger brothers and sisters. They also contribute their wisdom to the church.

In God's family, these responsibilities are not held by position or office. Neither are they hierarchical. They are organic, and they operate by spiritual life.

But here's the tragedy: Because so many of us have been conditioned in the institutional church, we have been forced to sit in a pew and passively listen to sermons week after week. And that's why scores of Christians associate "church" with an audience that hears a weekly oration.

The result? Scores of spiritual fathers are not doing what they should be doing. Many of them have confessed to me that they see no place for their contribution in the traditional church. They feel that their long spiritual history with the Lord and the lessons they learned from it will die with them. Many feel that their spiritual experiences are being wasted.

But in a church that functions according to the organic nature of the *ekklesia*, every member functions in the church meetings. They also function outside of the meetings in community life. The spiritual fathers and mothers are very active in this form of church. The fathers mentor the young men and provide wisdom during crises. The mothers teach the younger women how to be wise and how to function as wives and mothers (Titus 2:3–4).

The young men bring excitement and strength to the church. But they need the stability of the older ones to temper them. The spiritual children inject newfound zeal into the believing community. But they need nurturing. They need the others to check up on them, feed them, change their diapers, and teach them how to walk with the Lord.

(6) The Members Reflect the Triune God in Their Relationships

As we have already established, the church envisioned in the New Testament is an ecclesial community that's modeled after the triune God. Father, Son, and Spirit are all related. Their familial fellowship is both the source and the goal of the church (1 John 1:1–3).

The Godhead lives in everlasting reciprocity with each of its members. For that reason, the church is called to be a reciprocal community above everything else. Or in other words, a family.

Because we are made in the likeness and image of God, we are only truly human when we are living in community. A church that is hierarchically structured or that relegates its fellowship to a weekly religious service violates this spiritual reality.

The Trinity, therefore, shapes our understanding of the church. Significantly, the ancient Christians described the fellowship of the Godhead as an eternal dance. The three persons of the Trinity eternally give Themselves to one another. Each divine person lives out an eternal round of self-sacrificial love. The church is called to reflect this dance of fellowship and self-giving. But more than that, it has been introduced into the dance as a new partner!

And why? Because the church is family—God's family.

Interestingly, the early Christians used the term *perichoresis* to describe the divine dance of fellowship that goes on between the Father, Son, and Spirit. (The prefix *peri* means "around," and the word *choresis* literally means "dancing.")

The final end of humanity is to be fully taken up into the Trinitarian dance, brought fully into the circle of that superabundant love that flows within the Godhead (1 Cor. 15:24–28; Eph. 1:10). The good news is that we can live in the foretaste of that future reality now. As Miroslav Volf says, "Participation in the communion of the triune God, however, is not only an object of hope for the church, but also its present experience."[2]

Tragically, because we have arranged the church according to institutional lines for so long, we've been conditioned to take some wrong steps in the dance. But seeing the church as family grounds our identity firmly in the triune God and draws us back into the circle.

Community or Corporation?

Again, the New Testament writers never use the imagery of a business corporation to depict the church. Unlike many modern "churches," the early Christians knew nothing of spending colossal figures on building programs and projects at the expense of bearing the burdens of their fellow brethren.

In this way, many contemporary churches have essentially become nothing more than high-powered enterprises that bear more resemblance to General Motors than they do to the apostolic community. A great many churches have succumbed to the intoxicating seductions of an individualistic, materialistic, business-oriented, consumer-driven, self-serving society. And when everything is boiled down, the success of the enterprise rests upon the shoulders of the CEO—the pastor.

As the famed novelist Frederick Buechner says,

The church often bears an uncomfortable resemblance to the dysfunctional family. There is the authoritarian presence of the minister—the professional who knows all of the answers and calls most of the shots—whom few ever challenge either because they don't dare to or because they feel it would do no good if they did. There is the outward camaraderie and inward loneliness of the congregation. There are the unspoken rules and hidden agendas, the doubts and disagreements that for propriety's sake are kept more or less under cover. There are people with all sorts of enthusiasms and creativities which are not often enough made use of or even recognized because the tendency is not to rock the boat but to keep on doing things the way they have always been done.[3]

In short, the church that's introduced to us in Scripture is a loving household, not a business. It's a living organism, not a static organization. It's the corporate expression of Jesus Christ, not a religious corporation. It's the community of the King, not a well-oiled hierarchical machine.

As such, when the church is functioning according to its nature, it offers

- interdependence instead of independence
- wholeness instead of fragmentation
- participation instead of spectatorship
- connectedness instead of isolation
- solidarity instead of individualism
- spontaneity instead of institutionalization
- relationship instead of programs
- servitude instead of dominance
- enrichment instead of insecurity
- freedom instead of bondage
- community instead of corporation
- bonding instead of detachment.

In the language of the apostles, the church is composed of infants, little children, young men, brothers, sisters, mothers, and fathers—the language and imagery of family (1 Cor. 4:15; 1 Tim. 5:1–2; James 2:15; 1 John 2:13–14).

The Church as Family in the Twenty-First Century

I used to belong to one of the largest Pentecostal churches in the state of Florida. It was incredibly wealthy. I was good friends with a family who attended there. They were very poor.

The following scene is seared in my mind forever. I was sitting in my friend's living room in the dark with his wife and four children. We talked over a flashlight and some candles. Why were we sitting in the dark? Because they couldn't pay their electric bill that month, and the power had been turned off.

The wealthy church to which we all belonged didn't give this man or his family a red cent. At the time, I thought that was outrageous. Funny thing is, I still do. That incident was the last nail in the coffin for me. A short time afterward I left institutional Christianity, never to return again. And I began my journey into organic church life.

As I think back on the organic churches that I've met with over the past two decades, many scenes fill my mind. I'm reminded of how faithfully the members of those churches embodied the family of God. I can think of times when one such church financially supported a couple and their children for several months because the husband was injured, had no insurance, and couldn't work for a season.

Another scene comes to mind when a sister fell ill and couldn't drive. The single brothers took turns driving her to doctor's appointments and other places to fulfill her necessary errands. The sisters made meals for her. This went on for weeks.

I can think of another occasion when one church wept and mourned with a brother who experienced a family tragedy. All the believers stood by his side for many weeks, caring for his needs.

I'm reminded of another where a sister fell into depression, and the other sisters descended on her home and cleaned it from top to bottom, entertained the children, did the laundry, cooked meals, etc. until she got back on her feet. I can think of another when the church refused to give up on an erring brother and loved him back to the

Lord. I have vivid memories of how the members of these churches saw one another many times a week—eating together, recreating together, laughing together, playing together, working together, hammering out personal issues together, and sharing their lives with one another.

Still other scenes fill my mind. Single brothers voluntarily babysitting the children of young couples in the church so that they can retreat and relax at a quiet dinner. The children in the church playing with one another at the beach, at picnics, and in the backyards of the believers. Shared meals where children eavesdropped on their parents as they talked to one another enthusiastically about the Lord—then returning home to ask their moms and dads about what they heard.

As we near the end of this chapter, however, I thought I would rehearse one particular story that reflects how an organic church can show its love for the members in some pretty creative ways. The following is a report that was given by a group of women in the first organic church I planted. They tell the story about one special Valentine's Day when the brothers in the church sought to remind them of Christ's love for them.

This Valentine's Day, the brothers put on a grand hoopla for us sisters. They told us to dress up formally and wait for them at one of the sisters' homes. This would turn out to be an elegant occasion. Three of the brothers showed up. They were dressed formally with suits and ties. They brought a vase full of white tulips. They gave each of us a white tulip to hold. They told us how we represent the tulips. The white was for the purity of Christ; the green stem was for the life of Christ in us.

Then they took a picture of all of us so we would remember this evening. They escorted us to another house. We waited outside. What would happen next was a surprise. We had no idea. They told us that there was an artist in town. And he had opened up his art gallery to us. Finally, the doors opened and we walked in. There was a tour guide who escorted us into the house. The first stop was an exhibit: a tree in a potted plant. It had on it a poem that talked about what each of us sisters represented to the Lord. The poem equated us to different parts of the tree. We found pictures of each of us sisters on the leaves. It was very moving.

At each exhibit, several of the brothers were role playing, telling each other what the exhibits were about. They stayed in character the whole time. They were in an art museum.

The next exhibit was a collage of brothers holding pieces of a sign. Each sign contained a word. The words together spelled out a romantic poem that expressed Christ's love for His church.

The next exhibit was a heart put in a frame. A big red heart. Cut out in the middle of the heart was a man and a woman holding hands. Inside the man were all the brothers' faces in the church cut out to make a collage that made up the image of the man. Inside the image of the woman were all the sisters' faces cut out to make a collage. To top it off, there were rays of color radiating out of the heart—pink, green, and blue. Pink was for the Lord's love; green was for His joy; and blue was for His life. The man and the woman represented Christ and His bride.

The last exhibit was a huge mirror. It was hanging and suspending from the ceiling. Above the mirror said "the bride." The tour guide had us all stand in front of the mirror, and he angled it so that all the sisters saw themselves in the mirror. The guide pointed out that on the mirror itself was a stain of red. It represented the stain of the blood of Christ. And the verse, "now we see in a mirror dimly, but then face to face" was placed above it. This was so very touching for us all.

Once the tour was over, we were escorted outside the home. Two brothers came out and serenaded us. One had a guitar, and they both sang a song that they had written. They redid the song, "Even though we ain't got money, I'm so in love with you, honey." They rewrote the lyrics to say how much they loved us in Christ.

They videotaped the whole event. And they sang more songs to us.

Then they invited us to come inside the house again. The room was suddenly transformed into a restaurant. They had long tables with a white cloth and elegant place settings. They used fine china with gold edging. The silverware matched. They used crystal glasses. They told us to sit every other person to leave room for them so they could sit by us later. They imported this unique organic gourmet butter that was tremendous.

The brothers had prepared a lavish meal for us, and they waited on us sisters. Then they sat down to eat with us. The brothers did all the cooking. All four courses. It was genuine gourmet food. Two different brothers serenaded us again while we ate.

That night our brothers honored us sisters. And they outdid themselves. They made us feel so special and so loved. They treated us like queens just as Christ treats His bride. We will never forget this day.

When a church is operating according to its organic nature, it demonstrates that it *really* is the family of God. And thus the words of our Savior find fulfillment: "By this all men will know that you are my disciples, if you love one another" (John 13:35).

Questions That Must Be Faced

- Did it surprise you to discover that the New Testament authors' favorite metaphor for the church is the family? What does this teach us?
- It's been suggested that the main reason why so many young people are turned off by the typical church is because it isn't functioning as a genuine family. Do you agree or disagree? Explain.
- Is it really honest to call a particular church "a family" when its members hardly know one another? Explain.
- Do you have a desire to become part of an authentic community of believers that's learning what it means to be the family of God? Explain.

CHAPTER 6
REIMAGINING CHURCH UNITY

The New Testament contains full instructions, not only about what we are to believe but what we are to do and how we are to go about doing it. Any deviation from those instructions is a denial of the Lordship of Christ. I say the answer is simple, but it is not easy for it requires that we obey God rather than man, and that brings down the wrath of the religious majority. It is not a question of knowing what to do; we can easily learn that from the Scriptures. It is a question of whether or not we have the courage to do it.

—A. W. Tozer

The one who eats is not to regard with contempt the one who does not eat, and the one who does not eat is not to judge the one who eats, for God has accepted him.... Therefore, accept one another, just as Christ also accepted us to the glory of God.

—Paul of Tarsus in Romans 14:3; 15:7 NASB

The church is the body of Jesus Christ (1 Cor. 12:12, 27 NASB). More specifically, the church is the body of Christ in a given location. Rightly understood, a local church *contains* all the members of Christ's body in a particular place.

Following this line of thought, Paul writes to the church in Rome exhorting the Christians to "accept one another, just as Christ has accepted us" (Rom. 15:7 NASB). According to Paul, the church is made up of all whom God has accepted. And whomever God accepts, we cannot refuse. Our acceptance of others doesn't make them members of the church. We accept them *because* they are already members. Therefore, if God has accepted you, then you belong to the church, and I must accept you.

The upshot is that all Christians living in your city should consider you a fellow member of the household of God. And they should welcome fellowship with you. Why? Because you share the same life as that of every other believer.

Most Christians would agree with the principle of what I've just written. However, the practice is another matter entirely. The trouble today is that scores of Christians have not made God's acceptance the basis for their fellowship. They have either added or removed something from this basic standard. Not a few contemporary "churches" have either exceeded or narrowed the biblical basis for Christian unity—which is the body of Christ. Allow me to unfold that.

Suppose a group of Christians regularly meets in your city. They call themselves "First Presbycharisbaptist Community Church." You inquire about becoming a member. And you are quickly handed their statement of faith, which lists all the church's theological beliefs. Many of the doctrines that appear on this list go far beyond the essential foundations of the faith that mark all genuine Christians (such as faith in Jesus Christ, His saving work, His bodily resurrection, etc.).

As you continue to attend "First Presbycharisbaptist," you quickly discover that in order to be fully accepted by its members, you must hold to *their* view of spiritual gifts. You must also hold to *their* view of election and the second coming of Christ. If you happen to disagree with them on any of these points, you will be made to feel that you would be happier attending elsewhere.

Do you see the problem with this? While "First Presbycharisbaptist" claims to be a church, they do not meet the biblical benchmark for a church. Wittingly or unwittingly, they have undercut the biblical basis for fellowship, which is the body of Christ *alone*. The New Testament uses a term that describes such a group. It's the word *sect*.

People are accepted by God because they have repented and trusted in the Lord Jesus Christ. Again, if a person belongs to the Lord, he or she is part of the body of Christ. And on that basis alone are we to accept them into fellowship.

If a group of Christians demands anything beyond a person's acceptance of Christ before admitting that person into fellowship, then that group isn't a church in the biblical sense of the word. It's a sect. (The exception is if a Christian is willfully sinning and refuses to repent.)[1] Repeat: All whom God has received are part of the body of Christ.

The Problem of Sectarianism

Let's consider the meaning of the word *sect* as it appears in Scripture. The Greek word translated sect is *hairesis*. It's used nine times in the New Testament, and it's translated "sect," "party," "faction," and "heresy."

A sect is a division or a schism. It refers to a body of people who have chosen to separate themselves from the larger whole to follow their own tenets. The classic example of the sin of sectarianism is found in Paul's first letter to the Corinthians:

My brothers, some from Chloe's household have informed me that there are quarrels among you. What I mean is this: One of you says, "I follow Paul"; another, "I follow Apollos"; another, "I follow Cephas"; still another, "I follow Christ." Is Christ divided? Was Paul crucified for you? Were you baptized into the name of Paul? (1 Cor. 1:11–13)

In God's thought, the Corinthian church included all the Christians who lived in the city of Corinth (1 Cor. 1:2). Yet some were drawing a circle around themselves that was smaller than the body of Christ in Corinth.

Instead of making the body of Christ their basis for Christian unity, some in Corinth were making their favorite apostolic worker the basis for their fellowship. With loving severity, Paul rebuked the church for its sectarian spirit, condemning it as a work of the flesh (1 Cor. 3:3–4; Gal. 5:19–20; Jude 19).

If Paul's rebuke hadn't been heeded, four different sects would have arisen in Corinth—all of them claiming to be churches: "the church of Peter," "the church of Apollos," "the church of Paul," and "the church of Christ." (This latter group was probably claiming, "We are the only ones who follow Christ. We don't need an apostolic worker like Paul, Peter, or Apollos to help us. We just need Jesus. We are *of Christ*.")

Please understand. Anytime a group of Christians undercuts the biblical basis for fellowship by excluding those whom God has accepted—whether explicitly or implicitly—they are a sect. They may have a sign painted on their building that says "church." They may even be incorporated with "church status." But they fall short of the biblical definition of a church. The reason? Because the members are taking a sectarian stance.

This doesn't mean that the members of a sect do not belong to the body of Christ. In most cases, they do. But it does mean that the institution that they have constructed to pose as a church falls short of the reality.

That said, Christians should never join sects, because they are inherently divisive. And God does not own them. To put it plainly, the only church we as believers can claim is the one that Jesus Christ began—His body in local expression. And that body receives and accepts all who have trusted in Jesus. While not a few Christians have *narrowed* the scope of the body of Christ, others have *exceeded* it. In their attempt to be all-inclusive, these groups have sought oneness with unbelievers. But this kind of oneness is foreign to the Bible. For only those whom Christ has accepted belong to His body. And only they make up His church.

To receive unbelievers as family members is to turn the church into something earthly and human (1 Cor. 5:6; Gal. 2:4; 2 Tim. 3:6; 2 Peter 2:1; Jude 4,12). This of course doesn't mean that Christians should forbid unbelievers from attending their *gatherings*. We shouldn't forbid them (1 Cor. 14:23–24). But it does mean that we are not to accept them as our *brethren*. The oneness of the church, then, is limited to the body of Christ. And it can't be made smaller or larger than the body.

How We Got Off Track

Interestingly, the first-century Christians couldn't conceive of having more than one church in a city. For that reason, whenever the New Testament authors refer to a particular church, they identify it by the name of the city (Acts 8:1; 13:1; 18:22; Rom. 16:1; 1 Thess. 1:1; 1 Cor. 1:2; Rev. 2:1, 8, 12, 18; 3:1, 7, 14).

If you lived in the city of Jerusalem in AD 40, you would consider yourself to be part of the church in Jerusalem—even though you may have met in a home with twenty believers (Acts 2:46). You also had a spiritual connection with the rest of the church in the city. And you gathered with them periodically (Acts 15:4ff.).

Today, the situation is very different. There are hundreds of "churches" in the same city. Each one takes a separate name to distinguish itself from the others.

An important question that's rarely asked is, how did this division occur? How did Christians move from seeing themselves as being part of the one church in the city to a countless number of sects in the same town?

I believe the division of the Christian church is rooted in the evolution of the clergy/laity class distinction. This distinction began to crystallize around the third century. The emergence of this hierarchical system, which violently ruptured the priesthood of all believers into a clergy class and a laity class, was the first major division known to the body of Christ.[2]

Once the clergy/laity fault line was created, various clergymen began to divide amongst themselves on theological matters. This spawned a self-perpetuating movement that has reproduced a raft of new sects in every generation.[3] The notable feature of these sects is that the people within them gather around their favorite leader (or doctrine) instead of around Jesus Christ alone.

Perhaps a modern analogy will help to illustrate this sad chain of events. Suppose that Bob, a so-called layman, feels called to teach Scripture. In most institutional churches, Bob will have to "go into the ministry" and establish a church himself to fulfill his calling. Perish the thought of the pastor sharing his pulpit with a layman on a continuous basis—even if that layman has the gift of teaching. (See 1 Corinthians 14:26 for the folly of this mentality.)

After going through the proper institutional channels, Bob becomes a pastor. And he begins a new church in his vicinity. In reality, Bob's "church" is nothing more than an extension of his own ministry (and very likely, his own personality, too). It's also an unneeded addition to the endless sects that already exist in his town—all of which are competing with each other to recruit members.

Herein lies the root of the problem. The institutional church Bob attended would not permit him to freely exercise his teaching gift in the church gatherings. Therefore, he saw no other alternative but to begin a congregation of his own. (By the way, I believe that many, if not most, modern churches exist to give the pastor a platform by which to exercise his teaching gift.)

In this way, the clergy/laity distinction has become the seedbed for the endless production of countless schisms in the body of Christ. For when gifted people are prevented from fulfilling their God-given callings, they feel forced to begin their own churches—even though God may have never called them to do such a thing.

This situation has not only engendered numerous sects, but it has forced thousands of gifted Christians to fulfill a job description that the New Testament nowhere envisions: the modern pastoral office. (See chapter 9.)

Let's contrast the above scenario with the way things were done in the first century. If Bob were a member of a first-century church, there would have been no need for him to venture out on his own to begin an institution that God never sanctioned. As a member of an organic church, Bob would have the freedom to function freely in his teaching gift. (See chapter 2.) The church would make decisions by consensus, so Bob would have a voice in all of the church's decisions. (See chapter 10.)

Bob would only have left the church under one of five conditions: (1) if he refused to stop committing a known sin after being corrected by the church, (2) if he moved to another city, (3) if he was ambitious to begin his own ministry independently, (4) if the church he belonged to ceased from being an authentic *ekklesia* and became a business organization or a sect, or (5) if God called him to genuine apostolic work—in which case the church would send him out. Keep in mind that first-century apostles were not sent out to build their own spiritual franchises. They established organic churches where there were none present.

In sum, modern sectarianism finds it roots in the clergy/laity class distinction. In this regard, Diotrephes—whom John described as loving to have "the preeminence"—is not alone in the history of men who hunger for center stage in the church (3 John 9–10 NKJV). Lamentably, Diotrephes is still forbidding members of Christ's body from ministering in the Lord's house.

Unity Through Organization

Most Christians agree that the church is severely divided in our day. The limbs of our Lord's body have been butchered, fragmented, sliced, and diced into denominations, movements, and parachurch organizations.

Upon seeing the problem of sectarianism, some have proposed *organizational unity* as the solution. This brand of unity envisions all of the various strands of Christendom working together and relating to one another under the banner of a unified association. This kind of ecumenism, however, typically expresses itself at the higher levels only. The pastors of various churches may meet together regularly, forming an "association of ministers" of sorts.

While such an expression of unity is good, it's inadequate. It only touches a segment of the body of Christ (the clergy) and fails to touch the root problem of sectarianism. For these reasons, it's a bit like holding hands over the fence.

While it's a noble step to accept those who are part of differing Christian traditions, doing so doesn't go far enough. Denominations are man-made divisions. They are religious organizations that meet around a common denominator other than the Lord Jesus Christ. As such, denominations undermine biblical principle and fragment the body of Christ. For this reason, the early church knew nothing about denominations. It would seem to me, then, that God's ideal would be for the "fence" to come down altogether.

The only basis for Christian fellowship is the body of Christ plus nothing. The body of Christ minus nothing. The body of Christ alone. For this reason, professor of systematic theology John Frame says, the Bible "requires the abolition of denominationalism."[4] Frame even considered calling one of his books *The Curse of Denominationalism*.[5]

Unfortunately, a large number of believers today, especially a growing number of clergy, are not willing to touch that sore spot. It's far easier on our flesh to remain in close fellowship with those whose beliefs tally with our own. It's far more difficult to live with those who differ in doctrine, personality, worship style, spiritual practice, and the like.

While many Christians are willing to leave their comfort zones up to a point, a half-baked expression of unity is as far as most of us will go. The result is that the *good* often becomes the enemy of the *best*.

This reminds me of the kings of Israel who cleansed the temple but left the high places untouched. True oneness requires the power of the cross to work deeply in our lives. For this reason, Paul lovingly charged the church in Ephesus to be "longsuffering, forbearing one another in love; endeavoring to keep the unity of the Spirit in the bond of peace, [for] there is one body" (Eph. 4:2–4 KJV).

Such an exhortation makes little sense if those to whom Paul wrote divided themselves into sects and only fellowshipped with each other when it was convenient. On the contrary, the church that's envisioned in the New Testament knew nothing of separating Christians according to denominational camps, Christian franchises, religious partisans, and spiritual tribal units. Neither did it know anything about forming an association of clergy.

Rather, every member of the body of Christ in a given locale belonged to the same church. Not just in spirit, but in practical expression. Each believer saw his or her fellow Christians as organs in the same body. Bricks in the same building. Siblings in the same family. Soldiers in the same army.

As John W. Kennedy says,

> A scattered pile of bricks is not a house, although they may be united in appearance; one brick looks very much like another. Similarly, a scattered company of regenerated people all claiming that they are one in Christ is not a church. They must be "fitly framed together," each one contributing his particular place in the spiritual building, and conscious of the bond of life and mutual responsibility which binds all of them together.[6]

This being the case, a Christian may leave a sect or a religious organization that calls itself a "church." This is not the same as leaving a church that meets on the ground of Christ alone.

Unity Through Doctrine

Doctrinal unity is another idea that some have offered as a solution to mend the divisions in the church. Christians who endorse this type of unity talk much about the need for "doctrinal purity." But making doctrinal purity the basis for fellowship typically ends up splintering the body of Christ even further.

I'll put the problem in the form of a question: Whose doctrines are you willing to divide the body of Christ over? If you say, "the doctrines of the Bible," the question then becomes, which doctrines and whose interpretation of them?

Remember: Repentance and faith in Jesus Christ is what brings God's acceptance.

In my observation, those who stress doctrinal unity often go through life extremely suspicious of their brothers and sisters in Christ from other traditions. I believe that spiritual discernment is one of the most pressing needs among Christians today. But it's fundamentally unbiblical and profoundly unchristian to go about scrutinizing our fellow brethren with a critical eye.

The Bible warns against those who are ruled by a prideful, fault-finding spirit. This is the very spirit that marks the accuser of the brethren—the master divider of Christ's body (Jude 16; Rev. 12:10). If we make the Lord our sole pursuit, He will show us when falsehood is present. But if we're always seeking to smell the whiff of error in others, we'll be sure to miss the Lord when He is speaking through one of His little ones.

So rather than actively looking to floodlight the misconceptions of other Christians, I suggest we seek to find something of Christ whenever a brother or sister opens his or her mouth. Again, incorrect interpretations of the Bible are no grounds for dividing Christ's body. If Jesus Christ has accepted you, I must also—despite how lacking in light you may be or how incorrect your views of the Bible are. And you must accept me on the same basis.

If the perfect interpretation of the Bible were the standard for Christian fellowship, then I would have had to disfellowship myself fifteen years ago! I'm still learning, thank God, and my interpretations of Scripture are maturing. None of us has a corner on the truth. And if a person thinks he does, he's deluded. In the words of Paul, "We know in part" (1 Cor. 13:9).

In that connection, I have to wonder what will happen when Jesus returns. I can imagine all the Christians who specialized in perfect doctrine passing out after they discover who made it into the kingdom. Angels will be running around all over the place with smelling salts to wake them up!

Unity Through Organism

If we begin with the Trinitarian Community, then we can conclude that the anatomy of Christian unity is neither organizational nor doctrinal. *It's organic.* The crucial issue regarding fellowship and oneness is that of the life of Christ.

Therefore, the core questions that ought to govern our fellowship are simply these: Has God accepted this person? Does the life of Christ reside in him or her? Has the individual called on the name of the Lord that saves (Rom. 10:12–13)? Is he or she part of the body of Christ?

The indwelling life of Jesus Christ is the only requirement for the unity of the Spirit. And amazingly, we Christians can detect that shared

Spirit whenever we meet one another. There's an instant sense of kinship that testifies that we have the same Father.

Certainly, those who have been born of the Spirit will live in a way that is consistent with this fact. Yet they may not be clear on many spiritual things. Their personality may conflict with ours. Their worship style may be distasteful to us. They may be immature and have struggles in areas that we've surpassed. They may be painfully eccentric. Their understanding of the Bible may be poverty stricken. They may make mistakes that they regret. And they just might hold to some false ideas. Yet the fact that Christ dwells in them obligates us to accept them as family members. Not only "in word or in tongue, but in deed and in truth" (1 John 3:18 NKJV).

Restoring Our Common Oneness

Today the practical expression of the church's oneness is severely marred. God's people have splintered themselves into masses of disjointed, unconnected congregations all operating independently of one another. While the Lord works through His people regardless of their divisions, I don't believe that He approves of them.

During the New Testament era, each church was completely unified. All the believers in a specific locale lived as members of one family. For example, if you and I lived in the city of Jerusalem, we belonged to the same church, even though we may have met in different homes throughout the city. (Interestingly, the early church always took the name of the city. They had no other name—Acts 8:1; 13:1; 18:22; Rom. 16:1; etc.)

If I entertained thoughts of making my favorite apostle the basis of unity and ventured to meet with others of like mind to form the "church of Paul," I would be corrected for my sectarian tendency (1 Cor. 3:3–4).

Ironically, we make the same partisan distinctions without wincing when we say, "I'm a Baptist," "I'm a Pentecostal," "I'm a Charismatic," "I'm a Calvinist," "I'm a Presbyterian," etc. We conveniently forget that Paul leveled a stern rebuke to the Corinthians when they began to denominate themselves in the same way (1 Cor. 1:11–13).

To be quite candid, the modern denominational system runs contrary to the organic nature of the church of Jesus Christ. That nature moves toward the complete oneness of His people—just as the Father, the Son, and the Spirit are one in the Godhead.

In the words of Leonardo Boff, "In this life, the church lives on the communion of the Trinity; its unity derives from the *perichoresis* [inter-penetration] that exists between the three divine Persons." Note again our Lord's prayer in the gospel of John:

> *My prayer is not for them alone. I pray also for those who will believe in me through their message, that all of them may be one, Father, just as you are in me and I am in you. May they also be in us so that the world may believe that you have sent me. I have given them the glory that you gave me, that they may be one as we are one: I in them and you in me. May they be brought to complete unity to let the world know that you sent me and have loved them even as you have loved me. (John 17:20–23)*

There is a unified diversity in the triune God—a plurality in one-ness. God is one Being in three persons—all of whom are diverse, but not separate.

The Greek word *koinonia*—which means fellowship—takes us to the heart of New Testament ecclesiology. *Koinonia* reflects the unified diversity inherent in the Trinity. And it is what characterized the first-century church. As Kevin Giles puts it, "This fellowship does not aim to overcome all diversity, but rather to embrace it in a dynamic, relational, and growing bond of love and understanding."[7] Because there's a unified diversity in the Godhead, there's a unified diversity in the church. Denominationalism ruptures this spiritual reality. And it makes division in the body of Christ acceptable.

A Modern-Day Example

Perhaps you are wondering if I believe that the denominational system will one day disappear, and Christians everywhere will begin to practically express their oneness in Christ. Unfortunately, I don't see a day like that coming in my lifetime. But I do hope that those of you who read this book will apply its message to your own life and act accordingly.

Personally, I never knew the degree to which Christian unity was possible until I stepped outside the institutional church. Since then, I have been privileged to be part of a number of organic churches that were united around Jesus Christ *alone*.

Imagine a church where the members are incredibly close, yet they aren't overly concerned about one another's political affiliations. Imagine a church where the members don't know one another's views on the rapture. Imagine a church where the members don't know one another's theories on the millennium—and really don't care to know them. Imagine a church that has only one pursuit, one obsession, one goal, and one grand purpose: *to know and love the Lord Jesus Christ.*

This doesn't mean that various topics are off-limits for discussion. But it does mean that they will not become the focus of the church, nor will they constitute a basis for dividing God's people.

Let me rehearse a true story on this score. In 1992, I watched two very different groups of Christians come together and express the oneness of the body of Christ. One group had a charismatic background. The other, a Church of Christ background. (I was part of the group that had the charismatic background.)

After a few joint meetings, both groups decided to do what was humanly impossible. We resolved to meet together as one church. Not long after that decision was made, the sparks began to fly.

I remember those days graphically. We met in homes. Our meetings were open and participatory. Yet every meeting we had was like walking through a minefield. The environment was emotionally laden and highly flammable. The tenseness of coming to a gathering where half the group was used to functioning one way (in spiritual gifts), and the other half another way, was almost intolerable.

I could rant on about the war-story details, but I'll spare you. Let me just say that a few months after we merged together, we witnessed a church split. And our strained efforts at preemptive peacemaking and spiritual finessing couldn't prevent it.

Before the split, we had some rather intense discussions over our differences. But none of them brought a resolution. Most of those discussions degraded into noise. The only thing they increased was the blood pressure.

Consequently, some left the group. But with our garments still smoking, those of us who remained together received illumination from the Lord. A proposal was presented and all agreed upon it. To my mind, our decision proved to be worth its weight in gold.

What was the decision? It was this: that all of us lay down our view of spiritual gifts at the foot of the cross. So we did. Each one of us agreed to drop whatever we thought or experienced about the working of the Holy Spirit. We died to it completely. We gave it up. And we asked the Lord to teach us all over again as little children (Matt. 18:3).

From that point on, our entire focus shifted from what we thought we knew about the Holy Spirit to the Lord Jesus Christ Himself. We resolved to strip down to Christ alone, and we set our eyes exclusively on Him.

After about a year, something miraculous occurred. There rose up—out of death, out of the grave in the newness of life—the gifts of the Spirit. But they didn't look like anything we had seen in the Pentecostal/charismatic movement. And they certainly didn't look like anything in the Church of Christ tradition. (All things look different in resurrection.)

Those of us who remained and committed to toughing out the storm were genuinely built together. And I experienced something I had only read about in the Bible—I saw two very diverse groups of Christians love one another through their differences. The result was what Paul declared to the Corinthians: "I appeal to you, brothers, in the name of our Lord Jesus Christ, that all of you agree with one another so that there may be no divisions among you and that you may be perfectly united in mind and thought" (1 Cor. 1:10). This experience, while bloody at first, proved to me in living color that the unity of the faith is more than a pious ideal.

Healthy organic church life is nonsectarian, nonelitist, and nonexclusive. Such churches meet on the ground of Christ alone. Therefore, if Christians in organic churches are willing to go to the cross and refuse to divide from one another over doctrinal differences, God can knit their hearts and minds together.

It may involve much long-suffering, forbearance, and dying a thousand deaths. But that's exactly what Paul said the price would be for preserving the unity of the Spirit: "With all lowliness and gentleness, with longsuffering, bearing with one another in love, endeavoring to keep the unity of the Spirit in the bond of peace" (Eph. 4:2–3 NKJV).

Questions That Must Be Faced

- Are we really taking seriously the Lord's prayer for the unity of His people when we divide over theological beliefs, eschatology, politics, race, Bible versions, children's education, and other such things? Can you add some other dividing lines to this list?
- In light of 1 Corinthians 1:12–13, do you agree or disagree with the statement that denominationalism has made division in the body of Christ acceptable? Explain.
- Can you reimagine a church where every member is centered on Christ alone rather than the scores of peripheral issues that create schism among believers? Explain.

CHAPTER 7
CHURCH PRACTICE AND GOD'S ETERNAL PURPOSE

Viewed within the context of the triune God himself, the church is community. Ultimately, the community which is to characterize the church results from our communion with the Spirit. To understand this, we must review the grand sweep of God's eternal purpose as it relates to his own triune nature. The Father sent the Son in order to realize God's eternal design to draw humankind and creation to participate in his own life. Only in our Spirit-produced corporateness do we truly reflect to all creation the grand dynamic that lies at the heart of the triune God. Our fellowship is nothing more than our common participation in the divine communion between the Father and the Son mediated by the Holy Spirit.
—Stanley Grenz

Americans see the isolated individual as the source of all moral virtue and society as nothing more than a collection of these individuals. Evangelicalism implicitly agreed. It spoke eloquently of saving individuals; but it did not take seriously what these individuals were saved into. They preached the gospel of the individuals rightly enough; but as true Americans, they did not see that God might intend to go further and make a people out of these persons. Evangelicalism sought to transform people and so transform the world. They did not see that something might be missing from this vision,

*something their assumption of American individualism would hide from
them. The true Christian vision is to transform people, transforming them
into a people, and so transform the world. The evangelicals missed that
middle term. They could not see the church as a foretaste of the new society; it was a club for the new individuals. The evangelicals simply dressed
American individualism in Christian clothing. They ended up with the
new isolated individuals, but in the old society.* —Hal Miller

Over the years, a number of people have asked me, "Frank, the church really doesn't matter, does it? The Christian life is the primary thing; the church is secondary, right?"

My response to that question has been "The church matters very much, because it matters so much to God. And it should never be separated from the Christian life."

Consequently, behind the practice of the church stands an enormous and incredible purpose. Paul calls it the "eternal purpose" (Eph. 3:11).[1]

The Mission of God

Throughout the book of Ephesians, Paul spills a great deal of ink trying to unveil the eternal purpose of God to the Christians in Asia Minor. The entire letter is a breathtaking unfolding of the divine purpose. In it, Paul puts the most sublime truths into human words. In Ephesians, the ultimate purpose and passion that God has had in His heart from ages past is richly set forth.

Ephesians teaches us that the purpose of God stands far outside the reaches of redemption. In eternity past, God the Father has been after a bride and a body for His Son and a house and a family for Himself. These four images—the bride, the body, the house, and the family—comprise the grand narrative of the entire Bible.[2] And they lie at the center of God's beating heart. They are His ultimate passion, His eternal purpose, and His governing intention. To put it another way, God's eternal purpose is intimately wrapped up with the church.

As I write this book, there's a great deal of talk about the *Missio Dei* (God's Mission) in Christian circles. I think this can be a healthy emphasis. But exactly what is God's mission? I suggest that it's nothing other than God's eternal purpose.

As long as I've been a Christian, I have made this simple observation: Our modern gospel is entirely centered on human needs. The plotline of that gospel is one of a benevolent God whose main purpose is blessing and healing a fallen world. Thus our gospel is centered on saving man's spirit/soul (evangelism) and/or saving his body (healing the sick, delivering the captives, helping the poor, standing with the oppressed, caring for the earth, etc.). In short, the gospel that's commonly preached today is "human centered." It's focused on the needs of humanity, be they spiritual or physical.

But there is a purpose in God that is *for* God. That purpose was formed in Christ before the fall ever occurred. The meeting of human needs is a by-product, a spontaneous outflow, of that purpose. It's not the prime product.

Tellingly, God didn't create humans in need of salvation. Go back to the creation project in Genesis 1 and 2, and you will discover that God's purpose preceded the fall. That should lead us to ask a very incisive question: What was God going to do with human beings if they had never fallen?

Throughout my years as a Christian, I've been involved in movements that majored in evangelism, others that majored in social activism, and others that majored in spiritual gifts. All of these things were made "ends in themselves." None of them were integrated into God's ultimate purpose. In fact, "the eternal purpose" was never mentioned. The result was that those activities, though good and noble, failed to satisfy the beating heart of God.

Let me explain the last paragraph by giving an illustration. Imagine that a general contractor purchases twenty acres of land by which to build a housing complex. After the houses are built, he wishes to have a landscape garden at the entrance of the complex. This is his goal. So he hires someone to plant beautiful trees. He hires another to lay large rocks. He hires another to plant beautiful flowers. And he hires another to plant shrubs and bushes.

The person who plants the trees plants them randomly throughout the complex. The person who lays the rocks does the same. So does the person who plants the flowers. The person who plants the shrubs and bushes does the same.

When the contractor observes what they have all done, he's very disappointed. His goal was a landscape garden. Instead, he sees that the flowers, rocks, trees, shrubs, and bushes are all disconnected and scattered about the complex haphazardly.

Is it good to plant trees? Yes. Is the planting of flowers a positive thing? Certainly. But these things "in themselves" were not the contractor's goal. *He wanted a landscape garden.*

That describes the kingdom of God today. Many good deeds, but an overwhelming disconnection from God's ultimate goal—which happens to be from Him, through Him, and to Him (Rom. 11:36; Col. 1:16–18; Eph. 1:5).

Overshooting the Main Point

Why is it that so many of us Christians have shot past the main point? Why have we not seen the greater purpose of God amid all of our books, magazines, Web sites, blogs, CDs, DVDs, conferences, and seminars?

If I knew the answer to that, I would be twofold a Solomon. I'll make an educated guess, however. I think part of the reason is that evangelical Christians have built their theology mostly on Romans and Galatians. And many nonevangelical Christians have built it on the Gospels (particularly the Synoptics—Matthew, Mark, and Luke). And for both groups, Ephesians and Colossians have been but footnotes.

But what if we began, not with the needs of humans, but with the intent and purpose of God? What if we took as our point of departure, not the earth after the fall, but the eternal activity in God Himself before the constraints of physical time?

In other words, what if we built our theology on Ephesians and Colossians and allowed the other New Testament books to follow suit? Why Ephesians and Colossians? Because Ephesians and Colossians give us the clearest look at Paul's gospel with which Christ commissioned him. These two letters begin, not with the needs of postfall humans, but with God's timeless purpose before creation. They also introduce us to Christ in His preincarnate state.

I assert that if we did this, the Gospels, and the rest of the New Testament (let alone the entire Old Testament), would fall into a very different place for us. And the centrality and supremacy of Jesus Christ and His counterpart, the church, would dominate our understanding of everything spiritual and physical.

Contrary to popular opinion, the Gospels are not the beginning point of the Christian faith. Neither is the Old Testament. Both give us the middle of the story. Ephesians, Colossians, and the gospel of John are the introduction and the opening chapters of that story. Those writings give us a glimpse into Christ before time and what His mission is all about. His earthly life that's portrayed in Matthew, Mark, and Luke must be understood against that backdrop.

In this regard, we can liken the gospel that most of us heard to watching *Star Wars* Episodes IV, V, and VI first (which is the way they came out in the theaters). But for us to really understand what's going on in that drama, we must begin at the right place with Episodes I, II, and III.

Again, human beings didn't come into this world in need of salvation. Saving souls, feeding the poor, and alleviating the suffering of humanity was not part of God's first motion in eternity past because the fall had not yet occurred.

Please don't misunderstand. I'm not against any of these things. On the contrary, I'm strongly for them. But God has a purpose—an *eternal* purpose—that humans were to fulfill before sin entered the scene. And He has never let go of it. Everything else is and should be related to it. As DeVern Fromke says,

> *This which we see in Ephesians is what the Father intended to realize in His Son, and it has never been affected by sin, the fall, or time. It was this purpose which had previously been a mystery, that the Apostle Paul was now unveiling. For the Father from eternity had a wonderful purpose for Himself which of course included man. Redemption is not the end, but only a recovery program. It is but a parenthesis incorporated into the main theme.[3]*

Truthfully, it would require another book to unfold the eternal purpose of God adequately. (I'm in the process of writing such a book. It's called *From Eternity to Here: Rediscovering the Ageless Purpose of God.*)[4] In this chapter, I will briefly introduce some of its major elements.

Tracing an Unbroken Thread

One of the easiest places in which to discover God's eternal purpose is in the first two chapters of the Bible (Genesis 1 and 2) and the last two chapters of the Bible (Revelation 21 and 22). The reason is because these four chapters are the only chapters in Holy Writ that are untouched by sin. Let me explain.

Genesis 1 and 2 have to do with events *before* the fall. Revelation 21 and 22 have to do with events *after* the fall has been erased. The fall begins immediately when Genesis 2 closes, and it ends right before Revelation 21. Genesis 3 opens with the Devil deceiving Eve. Revelation 20 ends with the Devil being thrown into the lake of fire.

Because of their uniqueness, Genesis 1 and 2 and Revelation 21 and 22 teach us a great deal about God's eternal purpose. All four chapters are filled with many glorious themes that can be traced throughout the entire Old Testament and the entire New Testament. They move like an unbroken thread from Genesis 1, all the way through the rest of the Bible, to their grand climax in Revelation 22.

This fact alone tells us that God has never given up on His eternal purpose. Even in the midst of the fall, He has still been working it out.

An exercise that will be well worth your time is to identify all of the common items that appear in Genesis 1 and 2 and Revelation 21 and 22. You will be surprised at how many there are. Once you've discovered them, trace each one throughout the entire Bible. To do this thoroughly could take years. But it will give you enormous insight into God's ultimate purpose.

For the sake of time and space, I will briefly list ten of the most important items that appear in these four chapters. If you tie them all together,
you will get a fairly clear glimpse of the divine purpose. They are:

1. *A Corporate God.* In Genesis 1:26, the Lord says, "Let *us* make
man in *our* image." This is the Godhead speaking. And not only speaking, but planning. The triune God is taking counsel with Himself, and
He is conceiving an eternal plan. "Let us," He says. This is divine corporateness and divine community—an exchange of divine fellowship. The
Godhead is giving birth to His eternal purpose.

2. *Man.* There's a man in Genesis 1 and 2, and there's a man in Revelation 21 and 22. The Bible is a story of two men. An old man and a
new man. And these two men have been in an enormous battle from the
dawn of the fall until now.

Adam was the new man, but he quickly turned into the old man. All
who are born of Adam are part of the lineage of the old man. Jesus Christ
is the Head of the new man. And that new man has a body.

The old man is the founder of organized religion. Organized religion
is built on human ritual and hierarchy. By contrast, Christianity began as
organic. But as time went on, it adopted the hierarchical structure of the
Roman Empire. All of our denominations have adopted that same organizational structure. This structure can be traced to the old man. It originally
came from the Babylonians and was passed on to other cultures, including
the Romans.

The new man is a spiritual organism, not an institutional organization. He's an organic body. Thus God's eternal purpose is wrapped up
with the creation of a new man.

3. A Corporate Humanity. Genesis 1:26 says, "Let us make man ... and let *them* ..." God said, "Let *us* [plural] make man ... and let *them* [plural] ..." Within the Godhead stands an enormous purpose that is corporate. And at the center of that purpose is a humanity that was created to live and act corporately unto God and not unto themselves. So there is corporateness in God, and there is corporateness in man. God's eternal purpose is intensely corporate.

4. Image-Bearing. Genesis 1:26 says, "Let us make man in *our image*." God wanted man to be His image-bearer on the earth. The Almighty Creator, who is invisible, created a visible image of Himself for angels, animals, and Himself to see. The image of God can be traced all throughout the Bible, from Genesis to Revelation.

Note that the task of bearing God's image was not given to any individual. It was given to a *them*. God wanted a corporate expression of Himself in the earth. He was determined to bring His image into this physical realm. Put another way, God desired to have a corresponding community on earth that reflects the community in the Godhead. And since God is corporate, only a corporate people could do that. In the words of Stanley Grenz, "Only in our Spirit-produced corporateness do we truly reflect to all creation the grand dynamic that lies at the heart of the Triune God."[5]

5. Rulership. Genesis 1:26 goes on to say, "Let us make man in our image ... and let them *rule*." This corporate man—the "them" of Genesis 1—was to have dominion over creation, including the creeping things (Gen. 3:1ff.; Luke 10:9; Rev. 12:9). God wanted to rule the earth through a corporate humanity. And that rulership extended to God's own Enemy. (The serpent creeps on the ground.)

6. A Garden. In Genesis 2:8, there is a garden. The garden was an interface of two realms. It was a meeting place. Visible man and the invisible God walked in the garden together. In the garden, we have two realms touching. It was the place where God's space and man's space intersected.

Herein lies an important spiritual principle: From the beginning, God determined to have a marriage of two realms. He was determined to have something on this earth that would bear His image and exercise His dominion.[6] And He will eventually have it. There will be a wedding of the spirituals with the physicals … the visibles with the invisibles … the seen with the unseen … divinity with humanity … God with man. He had this wedding in Jesus Christ, and He will have it in His church.

The garden is also a lumberyard. It contains the materials that God builds with. There's a special tree in the garden called the Tree of Life. And human beings were called to eat from that Tree and live by the life within it. There's also a flowing river in the garden. And that river produces building materials: gold, pearl (bdellium), and precious stone.

You can trace the garden, the tree, the river, the gold, the pearl, and the precious stone all throughout the Bible—from the Old Testament to the New. All of these items have a great deal to do with God's eternal purpose.

When we come to the end of the Bible, we discover that the house of God is built with gold, pearl, and precious stones. The garden has been transformed into a glorious city. And the Tree and the river reappear in magnificent splendor.

7. A Woman. There is also a woman in Genesis 1. But she is hidden. She doesn't make her appearance until Genesis 2. Where is the woman hidden? She is hidden inside the man. In Genesis 2, God puts Adam into a deep sleep and takes a woman out of him.

Consider the fact that man was made in the image of God. Therefore, just as there was a woman hidden inside of Adam, there has also been a woman hidden inside of God.

The bride of Christ was chosen in Christ before time (Eph. 1:4–5). And when the fullness of time came, the Son of God entered the earth. After His ministry on earth was complete, God the Father put His Son into a deep sleep on a hill called Calvary. Then in His resurrection, He released that woman onto the earth—and her name is *ekklesia* (Rom. 5:14; Eph. 5:23–33). She is the church of the living God—the bride of Christ. And the wonderful news is that you and I are part of that woman!

You can trace this woman from Genesis 1 and 2 all the way through the Bible. In fact, the gospel of Jesus Christ begins with this woman. In John 3, a prophet named John the Baptist declares, "I am the friend of the Bridegroom" (John 3:29). God's eternal purpose, therefore, has something to do with a mystery hidden in God from ages past—and that mystery is a woman (Eph. 3:1–9; 5:32; Col. 1:26–27). This woman reappears in Revelation 21 and 22 in her glorious state.

8. An Earth. In Genesis 1, we have the first mention of the earth and the land. Throughout biblical history, a battle has raged over the earth and the land. That battle has been between God and His Enemy. The central issue of that battle is this: *Who will have the dominion?*

This battle relates to the kingdom of God, which is a major theme of Scripture. The eternal purpose, therefore, has a great deal to do with God's ruling the earth through a corporate humanity.

Unfortunately, many evangelicals have been taught that when Adam and Eve fell, God decided to scrap the earth and redeem a small group of people out of it that He will take to heaven. But God loves the earth, and He wishes to redeem it (Ps. 78:69; Eccl.1:4; Rom. 8:20ff.). He has promised to fill the earth with His glory as the waters cover the sea (Isa. 11:9; Hab. 2:14). Ultimately, God will bring heaven to the earth (Rev. 22), just as it was in the garden of Eden.

In this regard, one of the postfall purposes of the church is to continue the ministry of Jesus outlined in Luke 4:18, which is to preach the good news of the kingdom to the poor, to heal the brokenhearted, to set the captives free, to relieve the oppressed, and to give sight to the blind.

The body of Christ is not only called to be local communities that serve as pilot projects of the new heaven and the new earth; but it's also called to be God's agent of redemptive healing to this fallen world. The church is called to fulfill the Abrahamic promise, which was to be a "blessing to all nations" (Gen. 18:18; 22:18; Gal. 3—4). In all these ways, the Lord's prayer that God's will be done "on earth as it is in heaven" is given visible expression through the church.

9. Sonship. There are three ways a person can become a son. One is by creation. Another is by adoption. Still another is by birth. Adam is called the son of God (Luke 3:38). But Adam was a son of God by creation. He had no father but God.

God, however, wanted Adam to partake of His divine life through the Tree of Life—thus making him a son by birth. Adam failed to do this. But Jesus Christ entered the earth as the second Adam, and all who partake of Him today become authentic sons of God (John 1:12; 6:57). You can trace the theme of sonship all throughout the Old Testament and the New. God's purpose is to make His only begotten Son the firstborn among many brethren, and to bring many sons unto glory (Rom. 8:28–29; Heb. 2:10). In other words, God wants a family.

10. Oneness. Finally, there is oneness in Genesis 1 and 2. Genesis 2 ends with the man and the woman becoming one. You can trace the theme of oneness all throughout the Scriptures. This theme reaches its climax in Revelation 21 and 22, when the bride of Christ becomes the wife of God, and the two become one.

Drawing It All Together

All of the above elements teach us a great deal about God's eternal purpose. From the beginning, God wanted a bride to marry, a house to dwell in, a family to enjoy, and a visible body through which to express Himself. All of these images—the bride, the house, the family, and the body—point to the church of the Lord Jesus Christ, which is from Him, through Him, and, ultimately, to Him (Rom. 11:36).

Not to us, O LORD, not to us but to your name be the glory. (Ps. 115:1)

As Miroslav Volf says, "The church lives from something and toward something that is greater than the church itself."[7] That something is God and His eternal purpose.

The church, then, is not only called to proclaim the gospel, but to embody it by its communitarian life. Unfortunately, the church in the West is dominated by individualistic, anticommunal forces. Its obsession with consumerism, individualism, and materialism has kept it from fulfilling God's ultimate intention.

On this score, Gilbert Bilezikian says, "Christ did not die just to save us from sins, but to bring us together into community. After coming to Christ, our next step is to be involved in community. A church that does not experience community is a parody, a sham."[8]

Simply put, the purpose of the church is to stand for God's eternal purpose. It's called to live in the foretaste of Revelation 21 and 22. Thus from the viewpoint of God's eternal purpose, the church exists to be

- the incarnation and manifestation of the ultimate passion of God
- the organic expression and physical extension of the Trinitarian Community
- the corporate image-bearer of the Lord Jesus Christ on the earth
- the family of God
- the divine building whereby every living stone is being transformed, reshaped, and fitted together to form the Lord's temple
- the colonial outpost of the coming kingdom
- the masterpiece of God
- the spiritual "Bethany" where Jesus of Nazareth is received, obeyed, and adored in the midst of a rejecting world[9]
- the vessel in which the power of Christ's resurrection life is visibly displayed
- the object of God's supreme affection and delight
- the willing vehicle for Christ's manifested presence
- the torchbearer of the testimony of Jesus
- the "one new man"—the new species—the "third race"
- the fiancée of Jesus Christ—His very body, His very bride
- the new humanity marked out in the Son of God before time and brought into existence by His cross

- the Christian's native habitat
- the spiritual environment where face-to-face encounters between the bride and Bridegroom take place
- the living witness to the fullness and headship of God's Son
- the colony from heaven that bears the image of its Ruler

In short, whenever the church gathers together, its guiding and functioning principle is simply to incarnate Christ (1 Cor. 12:12).

Questions That Must Be Faced

- What stood out to you the most in this chapter? Explain.
- If you had been asked about God's eternal purpose and ultimate passion (before reading this chapter), what would you have said? Explain.
- What could be some of the results if Christians turned their faces from meeting their own needs to fulfilling God's ultimate intention?
- Are you willing to discard the man-centered gospel that's commonly preached today and center your life on God's governing purpose? If so, how?

PART TWO
LEADERSHIP AND ACCOUNTABILITY

CHAPTER 8
REIMAGINING LEADERSHIP

The New Testament doctrine of ministry rests therefore not on the clergy-laity distinction but on the twin and complementary pillars of the priesthood of all believers and the gifts of the Spirit. Today, four centuries after the Reformation, the full implications of this Protestant affirmation have yet to be worked out. The clergy-laity dichotomy is a direct carry-over from pre-Reformation Roman Catholicism and a throwback to the Old Testament priesthood. It is one of the principal obstacles to the church effectively being God's agent of the Kingdom today because it creates a false idea that only "holy men," namely, ordained ministers, are really qualified and responsible for leadership and significant ministry. In the New Testament there are functional distinctions between various kinds of ministries but no hierarchical division between clergy and laity. —Howard Snyder

When we go back to the Word of God and read it afresh, we see that the clergy profession is the result of our human culture and history and not of God's will for the church. It is simply impossible to construct a defensible biblical justification for the institution of clergy as we know it. —Christian Smith

Today, the leadership structure that characterizes the contemporary church is hierarchical and positional. In the following pages, we'll examine this structure and reimagine a form of leadership that's completely different. One that is envisioned in Scripture and rooted in the triune God.

The present-day leadership structure is derived from a *positional mind-set*. This mind-set casts authority in terms of slots to fill, job descriptions to carry out, titles to sport, and ranks to pull. It resonates with concern over explicit leadership structures. According to the positional mind-set, terms like *pastor, elder, prophet, bishop*, and *apostle* are titles representing ecclesiastical offices. (An office is a sociological slot that a group defines. It has a reality apart from the character and actions of the person who fills it.)

By contrast, the New Testament notion of leadership is rooted in a *functional mind-set*. It portrays authority in terms of how things work organically. That is, it focuses on the expression of spiritual life.

Leadership in the New Testament places a high premium on the unique gifting, spiritual maturity, and sacrificial service of each member. It lays stress on functions, not offices. It emphasizes tasks rather than titles. Its main concern lies in activities like pastor-*ing*, elder-*ing*, prophesy-*ing*, oversee-*ing*, apostle-*ing*, etc.

To frame it another way, positional thinking is hung up on nouns, while functional thinking stresses verbs.

In the positional leadership framework, the church is patterned after the military and managerial structures of contemporary culture. In the functional leadership framework, the church operates by life—divine life. Mutual ministry comes forth naturally when God's people are equipped and hierarchical structures are absent.

Native to hierarchical/positional-oriented churches is a political machine that works behind the scenes. This machine promotes certain people to positions of ecclesiastical power and authority. Native to functionally oriented churches is the mutual responsibility and collegial interplay of its members. They listen to the Lord together. They affirm each other in their Spirit-endowed gifts. They encourage one another toward Christ.

In sum, the New Testament orientation of leadership is organic and functional. The hierarchical/positional orientation is fundamentally worldly.

Jesus and the Gentile/Hierarchical Idea of Leadership

Our Lord contrasted the hierarchical leadership style of the Gentile world with leadership in the kingdom of God. After James and John implored Jesus to grant them the glorified powerseats beside His throne, the Lord replied, saying,

> You know that the rulers of the Gentiles lord it over them, and their great men exercise authority over them. It is not this way among you, but whoever wishes to become great among you shall be your servant, and whoever wishes to be first among you shall be your slave; just as the Son of Man did not come to be served, but to serve, and to give His life a ransom for many. (Matt. 20:25–28 NASB)

And again,

> The kings of the Gentiles lord it over them; and those who have authority over them are called "Benefactors." But it is not this way with you, but the

one who is the greatest among you must become like the youngest, and the leader like the servant. (Luke 22:25–26 NASB)

Significantly, the Greek word for "exercise authority" in Matthew is *katexousiazo*. *Katexousiazo* is a combination of two Greek words: *kata*, which means over; and *exousiazo*, which means to exercise authority. Jesus also used the Greek word *katakurieuo* in this passage, which means to "lord it over" others.

What Jesus is condemning in these texts is not oppressive *leaders* as such. He's condemning the hierarchical *form* of leadership that dominates the Gentile world.

That bears repeating.

Jesus was not just condemning tyrannical leaders. He was condemning the hierarchical form of leadership itself.

What is the hierarchical form of leadership? It's the leadership style that's built on a chain-of-command social structure. It's rooted in the idea that power and authority flow from the top down. Hierarchical leadership is rooted in a worldly concept of power. This explains why it's endemic to all traditional bureaucracies. It's present in the vicious forms of liege/lord feudalism and master/slave relationships. But it's also present in the highly stylized spheres of military and corporate America.

While often bloodless, the hierarchical leadership style is undesirable for God's people. Why? Because it reduces human interaction into command-style relationships. Such relationships are foreign to New Testament thinking and practice. Yet hierarchical leadership is employed everywhere in secular culture. And the institutional church operates by it.

Summing up our Lord's teaching on this style of leadership, the following contrasts come into sharp focus:

- In the Gentile world, leaders operate on the basis of a political, chain-of-command social structure—a graded hierarchy. In the kingdom of God, leadership flows from childlike meekness and sacrificial service.
- In the Gentile world, authority is based on position and rank. In the kingdom of God, authority is based on godly character. Note Christ's description of a leader: "Let him *be* a servant," and "let him *be* as the younger." In our Lord's eyes, *being* precedes *doing*. And *doing* flows from *being*. Put differently, function follows character. Those who serve do so because they *are* servants.
- In the Gentile world, greatness is measured by prominence, external power, and political influence. In the kingdom of God, greatness is measured by humility and servitude.
- In the Gentile world, leaders exploit their positions to rule over others. In the kingdom of God, leaders deplore special reverence. They rather regard themselves "as the younger."

In brief, the hierarchical leadership structure characterizes the spirit of the Gentiles. The implanting of these structures into the church, therefore, is at odds with New Testament Christianity. Our Lord didn't mince words in declaring His implicit disdain for the Gentile notion of leadership: *"It shall not be so among you!"* (Matt. 20:26 KJV) is His explicit feeling on it.

All in all, there is no room in the teaching of Jesus for the hierarchical leadership model that characterizes the institutional church.

Jesus and the Jewish/Positional Model of Leadership

Our Lord also contrasted leadership in the kingdom with the leadership model that marks the religious world. In the following text, Jesus vividly expresses God's perspective on authority in contrast to the Jewish perspective. Note His words:

> But do not be called Rabbi; for One is your Teacher, and you are all brothers. Do not call anyone on earth your father; for One is your Father, He who is in heaven. Do not be called leaders; for One is your Leader, that is, Christ. But the greatest among you shall be your servant. Whoever exalts himself shall be humbled; and whoever humbles himself shall be exalted. (Matt. 23:8–12 NASB)

Gathering up the content of this text, we may glean the following:

- In the religious climate of the Jews, a class system exists made up of religious, guru-like specialists and nonspecialists. In the kingdom, *all* are brethren in the same family.
- In the Jewish world, religious leaders are accorded with honorific titles. (examples: teacher, father, reverend, pastor, bishop, minister, etc). In the kingdom, there are no distinctions of protocol. Such titles obscure the unique honor of Jesus Christ and blur the New Testament revelation that envisions all Christians as ministers and priests.
- In the Jewish world, leaders are exalted into positions of prominence and outward display. In the kingdom, leaders find their identity in the lowly towel of servitude and in the unassuming basin of humility.
- In the Jewish world, leadership is rooted in status, title, and position. In the kingdom, leadership is rooted in inward life and character.

(In this vein, the current fad of bestowing honorary "doctorates" before the names of countless clergy is one example of how the contemporary church mirrors those values that run contrary to God's kingdom.)

In sum, leadership according to Jesus is a far cry from what it is in the institutional church. Our Lord dealt a deathblow to both Gentile/hierarchical and Jewish/positional leadership models.

These ego-massaging models are incompatible with the primitive simplicity of the organic church and the upside-down kingdom of Jesus Christ. They impede the progress of God's people. They suppress the free functioning of the believing priesthood. They rupture the image of the church as family. They do violence to the leadership that exists in the triune God. And they place severe limitations on the headship of Christ. For these reasons "it shall not be so among" those who bear the name of the Savior.

The Modern Clergy System

Scripture makes clear that Jesus condemned the hierarchical/positional leadership structure. But what about Paul and the other apostles?

Contrary to popular thinking, the New Testament letters never cast church leaders in terms of "offices" and other conventions of human social organization. (We'll deal with the various passages that are commonly used to support church "offices" in chapter 9.)

Whenever the New Testament describes people who are *chiefly* responsible for spiritual oversight, it does so by mentioning the work they do. Functional language dominates. Verbs are prominent.

In this connection, the modern clergy system is a religious artifact that has no biblical basis. This system has allowed the body of Christ to lapse into an audience due to its heavy reliance on a single leader. It has turned church into the place where Christians watch professionals perform. It has transformed the holy assembly into a center for professional pulpiteerism supported by lay-spectators.

Perhaps the most daunting feature of the clergy system is that it keeps the people it claims to serve in spiritual infancy. Because the clergy system usurps the Christian's right to minister in a spiritual way during corporate gatherings, it ends up debilitating God's people. It keeps them weak and insecure.

Without question, many—if not most—of the people who are part of the clergy profession love God's people and desire to serve them. Many of them sincerely want to see their fellow brethren take spiritual responsibility. (Numerous clergy have expressed their frustration with not seeing their congregations take more responsibility. But few of them have traced the problem to their own profession.)

Yet the clergy profession ends up disempowering and pacifying the believing priesthood. This is the case regardless of how uncontrolling the person who fills the clergy position may be.

Here's how it works. Since clergy carries the spiritual workload, the majority of the church becomes passive, lazy, self-seeking ("feed me"), and arrested in their spiritual development.

Just as serious, the clergy system warps many who occupy clerical positions. The reason? God never called anyone to bear the heavy burden of ministering to the needs of the church by himself.[1] Yet regardless of the spiritual tragedies the clergy profession engenders, the masses continue to rely on, defend, and insist upon it. For this reason the so-called laity is just as responsible for the problem of clericalism as is the clergy.

If the truth be told, many Christians prefer the convenience of paying someone to shoulder the responsibility for ministry and shepherding. In their minds, it's better to hire a religious specialist to tend to the needs of God's people than to bother themselves with the self-emptying demands of servanthood and pastoral care.

The words of the ancient prophet capture the Lord's disposition toward this mind-set: "They have set up kings, but not by me: they have made princes, and I knew it not." (Hos. 8:4a KJV). In short, the modern clergy system is far removed from the thought of God. It puts the living, breathing organism of the church into an Old Testament straightjacket.

In light of these sobering facts, one may intelligently ask how it is that the clergy profession remains to be the commonly accepted form of church leadership today. The answer lies deeply entrenched in the history of the Reformation. And it continues to be reinforced by current cultural imperatives.

In short, the clergy profession is little more than a one-size-fits-all blending of administration, psychology, and oratory that's packaged into one position for religious consumption. As such, the sociological role of clergy, as practiced in the West, has few points of contact with anything or anyone in the New Testament.

Again, clergy need not be despots in order to hinder mutual ministry. Most of them are well-intentioned and gifted Christians who sincerely believe that God has called them to their profession. Many are benevolent dictators. Some are spiritual tyrants with a Machiavellian quest for power who imprison and freeze the life of their congregations.

The point is that clergy need not use vicious forms of authority to be harmful to body life. The mere presence of the one-up/one-down hierarchical mode of leadership suppresses mutual ministry. This is true regardless of how nonauthoritarian in temperament the clergyman may be.

The mere presence of clergy has the deadening effect of conditioning the congregation to be passive and perpetually dependent. Christians are taught from childhood that pastors (and priests) are the religious specialists. They are the qualified ones who handle the "spiritual" things of God, while everyone else is called to secular work. Because clergy are viewed as the religious specialists, the rest of the church sees themselves as passive recipients.

As Christian Smith says, "The problem is that, regardless of what our theologies tell us about the purpose of clergy, the actual effect of the clergy profession is to make the body of Christ lame. This happens not because clergy intend it (they usually intend the opposite) but because the objective nature of the profession inevitably turns the laity into passive receivers."[2]

The average believer is probably unaware that his or her notion of leadership has been shaped by centuries of ecclesiastical history (about seventeen hundred years' worth). For this reason, the clergy concept is so embedded in our thinking that any attempt to deviate from it will often meet fierce opposition.

Many modern Christians are just as resistant to the idea of dismantling the clergy as are the clergy themselves. The words of Jeremiah have pertinent application: "The prophets prophesy falsely, and the priests bear rule by their means; and *my people love to have it so*" (Jer. 5:31 KJV). In short, clergy and nonclergy alike are responsible for the ailments of the present-day church.

The truth is that many of us—like Israel of old—still clamor for a king to rule over us. We want a visible mediator to tell us what "God hath said" (Ex. 20:19; 1 Sam. 8:19). The presence of a human mediator in a church is a cherished tradition to which many Christians are fiercely committed. But it doesn't square with Scripture. And in my judgment, it suppresses the free functioning and full maturing of Christ's body.

To repeat the point: The trouble lies not with clergy as people. It lies with the system to which they belong. Christian Smith puts it beautifully:

The clergy profession is fundamentally self-defeating. Its stated purpose is to nurture spiritual maturity in the church—a valuable goal. In actuality, however, it accomplishes the opposite by nurturing a permanent dependence of the laity on the clergy. Clergy become to their congregations like parents whose children never grow up, like therapists whose clients never become healed, like teachers whose students never graduate.

The existence of a full-time, professional minister makes it too easy for church members not to take responsibility for the on-going life of the church. And why should they? That's the job of the pastor (so the thinking goes). But the result is that the laity remain in a state of passive dependence. Imagine, however, a church whose pastor resigned and that could not find a replacement.

Ideally, eventually, the members of that church would have to get off of their pews, come together, and figure out who would teach, who would counsel, who would settle disputes, who would visit the sick, who would lead worship, and so on. With a bit of insight, they would realize that the Bible calls the body as a whole to do these things together, prompting each to consider what gift they have to contribute, what role they could play to build up the body.[3]

Some modern pastors would deny that their office is part of a clerical hierarchy. However, Kevin Giles cuts through the fog of this denial. In describing pastor-led churches, he makes this pointed critique:

> *The stranger paradox is that in such churches there is usually also a strong emphasis on lay ministry, sometimes expressed in terms of the exercise of charismatic gifts, but what we find is that the ministry of the whole body is always seen as in some way very different to that of the pastor who represents God. In these churches, teaching on authority structures in the church and the home is constantly given. It is emphasized that the pastor or pastors have been set over the flock, leadership is a male preserve, and the flock is to obey. This is seldom described as a hierarchical order, but this is what it is in reality.[4]*

In light of the above, it's no wonder that eminent scholar James D. G. Dunn said that the clergy-laity tradition has done more to undermine New Testament authority than most heresies.[5] Dunn also observes:

> *Increasing institutionalism is the clearest mark of early Catholicism— when church becomes increasingly identified with institution, when authority becomes increasingly coterminous with office, when a basic distinction between clergy and laity becomes increasingly self-evident, when grace becomes increasingly narrowed to well-defined ritual acts ... such features were absent from first generation Christianity, though in the second generation the picture was beginning to change.[6]*

On that sober note, let's reimagine a new kind of leadership in the church. One that's based on the organic nature of the body of Christ and grounded in God Himself.

Questions That Must Be Faced

- Do you think the church would be better off if we followed the teachings of Jesus on leadership rather than accepting the hierarchical/positional form of leadership? Explain.
- If the clergy profession is foreign to the church that Jesus and the apostles established, should we continue to support and affirm it? Explain.
- In Colossians 2:8, Paul exhorts the believers in Colosse not to allow any man to spoil them through the philosophies and rudiments of this world. Do you believe this includes the rudiments and philosophies of the business world? Explain.

CHAPTER 9
REIMAGINING OVERSIGHT

The clerical system of church management is exceedingly popular, but the whole thought is foreign to Scripture. In a church all the members are active. He [God] appointed some to take oversight of the work so that it might be carried on efficiently. It was never His thought that the majority of the believers should devote themselves exclusively to secular affairs and leave church matters to a group of spiritual specialists.

—Watchman Nee

There is thoroughly entrenched in our church life an unbiblical two-caste system. In this two-caste system there is a clergy-caste which is trained, called, paid, and expected to do the ministering. And there is the laity-caste which normally functions as the audience which appreciatively pays for the performance of the clergy—or bitterly criticizes the gaping holes in that performance (and there are always gaping holes). No one expects much of the lower or laity caste (except attendance, tithe, and testimony). And everyone expects too much of the upper or clergy caste (including the clergy themselves!). The greatest problem in the whole business is the fact that the Bible's view of ministry totally contradicts this system.

—Robert C. Girard

Every church has leadership. Whether it's explicit or implicit, leadership is always present. In the words of Hal Miller, "Leadership is. It may be good or bad. It may be recognized and assented to or not. But it always is." Depending on who is doing the leading, leadership can be the church's worst nightmare or its greatest asset.

Because of leadership's "Jekyll and Hyde" potential, there's a tremendous need for Christians to take a fresh look at the subject. The New Testament identifies two kinds of leadership: that of *oversight*, and that of *decision-making*. In this chapter, we'll deal with oversight. In the next, we'll discuss decision-making. Consider the following passages:

From Miletus he sent to Ephesus and called for the elders of the church.... Therefore take heed to yourselves and to all the flock, among which the Holy Spirit has made you overseers, to shepherd the church of God which He purchased with His own blood. For I know this, that after my departure savage wolves will come in among you, not sparing the flock. (Acts 20:17, 28–29 NKJV)

The elders who are among you I exhort, I who am a fellow elder and a witness of the sufferings of Christ, and also a partaker of the glory that will be revealed: Shepherd the flock of God which is among you, serving as overseers, not by compulsion but willingly, not for dishonest gain but eagerly; nor as being lords over those entrusted to you, but being examples to the flock; and when the Chief Shepherd appears, you will receive the crown of glory that does not fade away. (1 Peter 5:1–4 NKJV)

For this reason I left you in Crete, that you would set in order what remains and appoint elders in every city as I directed you, namely, if any man is above reproach, the husband of one wife, having children who believe, not accused of dissipation or rebellion. For the overseer must be above reproach as God's steward, not self-willed, not quick-tempered, not addicted to wine, not pugnacious, not fond of sordid gain. (Titus 1:5–7 NASB)

Elders, Shepherds, and Overseers

In the Greek language, elder (*presbuteros*) merely means an old man. A first-century elder, therefore, was a seasoned Christian. A senior. One who had experience and wisdom. Elders were also called "overseers." This is a term that described their function of supervising the affairs of the church. The task of the elders is also depicted by the metaphor of a "shepherd." This is because they were caretakers. Just as literal shepherds care for literal sheep, elders care for their fellow Christians.

While all elders were "apt to teach" and all had the gift of shepherding, not all who shepherded and taught were elders (Titus 2:3–4; 2 Tim. 2:2, 24; Heb. 5:12). Teaching could come from any Christian who had a word of instruction for the church (1 Cor. 14:24–26).

Consequently, those who provided oversight in the church were called elders, overseers, and shepherds. This is simply because they elder-*ed*—they acted as seasoned models to the less mature (1 Peter 5:3). They over*saw*—they watched out for the spiritual well-being of the church (v. 2). And they shepherd-*ed*—they cared for the needs of God's people (v. 2).

That said, equating elders with a sociological slot (an office) can only be done at substantial risk. In order to do so, we have to evacuate "shepherd" of its intended meaning (one who cares for God's people). We also have to evacuate "elder" from its intended meaning (an old man). Not to mention having to evacuate "overseer" from its native meaning (one who watches out for others).

Elders, then, were overseers and shepherds. The term *elder* refers to their *character*. The term *overseer* refers to their *function*. And the term *shepherd* refers to their *gifting*. Their chief responsibility was to instruct and oversee the church during times of personal crisis.

Our Western obsession with offices and titles has led us to superimpose our own ideas of church order onto the New Testament. Yet the very ethos of the New Testament militates against the idea of a single pastor. It also militates against the idea of offici-elders. ("Offici" is shorthand for official.)

Scripture is equally at odds with the "*senior* pastor" concept. This is the common practice of elevating one of the elders to a prominent authoritative position. Nowhere does the New Testament sanction the notion of *primos inter pares*—"first among equals." At least not in any official or formal way.

The disconnect between the "pastor" and the other elders was an accident of church history. But because it meshes perfectly with our acculturated religious mind-set, contemporary believers have little trouble reading this false dichotomy into Scripture.

While elders provided oversight, they didn't monopolize the ministry of the church gatherings. Nor did they make decisions on behalf of the church. Instead, they superintended the church as it experienced the rigors of community life.

Please note that superintending is largely a passive role. The supervision of the elders didn't stifle the life of the church. Nor did it interfere with the ministry of the other believers. While gifted elders had a large share in teaching, they did so on the same footing as all the other members. They didn't monopolize the meetings of the church.

To be more specific, New Testament elders didn't operate like spiritual CEOs who presided over their spiritual enterprises. Instead, the elders were fully aware that the church didn't belong to them. It rather belonged to their beloved Master—the Lord Jesus. He alone had the right to "walk in the midst of the ... lampstands" (Rev. 2:1 NKJV). A first-century elder, therefore, would no doubt cringe if you used phrases like "his church" or "his people."

First-century elders were simply spiritually mature men—exemplary Christians who superintended (not controlled or directed) the affairs of the church.

Elders were not organizational figureheads. They weren't hired pulpiteers, professional clergy, or ecclesiastical chairmen. They were simply older brothers (elders-in-fact) carrying out real functions (elder-*ing*, shepherd-*ing*, oversee-*ing*, etc.).

Their chief task was threefold: to *model* servanthood in the church; to *motivate* the believing community toward works of service; and to *mold* the spiritual development of the younger believers (1 Peter 5:1–3). The elders also dealt with sticky situations in the church (Acts 15:6ff.). But they never made decisions for the church. The New Testament method for decision-making was neither dictatorial nor democratic. It was consensual. And it involved all the brothers and sisters. (See chapter 10.)

As overseers, the elders *supervised* the work of others (instead of *substituting* for it). They were the ones who prayed with their eyes open. They had their spiritual antennae continually raised to check for wolves. As older men, their wisdom was sought after in times of crisis. And when they spoke, their voices possessed the weight of experience.

Perhaps a modern-day example will help to explain how elders functioned in this way. One particular church I was a part of had about thirty people in it. Over the course of four years, three of the more seasoned brothers rose to the surface. Whenever people in the church got into personal trouble, they would naturally go to one of these three men.

The church instinctively trusted these men for their compassion and wisdom. Tellingly, most of their ministry was done outside of church meetings. It happened in private homes, in restaurants over coffee, or on the phone.

These men helped navigate the Lord's people through personal crises. In this particular church, they were never called "elders." And in the church meetings, they were indistinguishable from the other believers. Visitors could never tell who the elders were. The reason? Because the meetings of the church belonged to the whole church, never to the elders. Everyone was free to share, minister, and function on equal footing.

In this way, the role of the elders can be likened to the human liver. The liver works invisibly, filtering out poisons and other toxic substances. It resists infections by producing immune factors and removing bacteria from the bloodstream. The liver organically detoxifies the human body, causing it to function properly. But it does so in a quiet and hidden way. In a similar fashion, the elders detoxify the church behind the scenes so that the body can function without hindrance.

Simply put, elders were spiritual facilitators who supplied guidance, provided nurture, and encouraged faithfulness in the church. Eldership, therefore, is something that one *does*. It's not a slot that one *fills*.

The New Testament bears this out rather clearly. If Paul and the other apostles wanted to paint elders as officers, there were numerous Greek words they could have used to do so. Surprisingly, however, the following Greek terms are missing from the apostles' ecclesiastical vocabulary:[1]

- *arche* (a rank-and-file leader, head, or ruler)
- *time* (an officer or dignitary)
- *telos* (the inherent power of a ruler)
- *archisunagogos* (a synagogue official)
- *hazzan* (a public worship leader)
- *taxis* (a post, position, or rank)
- *hierateia* (a priest's office)
- *archon* (a ruler or chief)

The New Testament never uses any of these words to describe leadership in the church. Like that of Christ, the apostles' favorite word to portray church leaders is *diakonos*—which means a servant or a waiter.

Therefore, the penchant to depict servant-leaders in the church as officers and professional clerics guts the true meaning of the biblical language and cuts the nerve of the believing priesthood.

The Principle of Shared Oversight

The New Testament presents a vision of shared oversight. The apostles always established *plural* oversight within the churches they planted. There were elders (plural) in Jerusalem (Acts 11:30). There were elders in the four churches in South Galatia (Acts 14:23). There were elders (plural) in Ephesus (Acts 20:17). There were elders (plural) in Philippi (Phil. 1:1). There were elders in the churches in Judea (James 5:14). And elders (plural) were to be acknowledged in each city in Crete (Titus 1:5).

In short, the Bible unshakably demonstrates that a plurality of elders oversaw the activity of the early churches.[2] No church in the first century had a single leader.

Consequently, the commonly accepted notion of *sola pastora* (single pastor) is at odds with the New Testament. The Bible knows nothing of a person who stands at the helm of a local church, directs its affairs, preaches to it every Sunday, conducts its baptisms, represents it in the world, officiates its Communion (or Lord's Supper), blesses civic events, marries the living, and buries the dead. No such person exists in the entire New Testament. (If you doubt that, see if you can find this person in your Bible. I have money hidden in my shoes that says you cannot.)

While the New Testament calls Paul an "apostle," Philip an "evangelist," Manaen a "teacher," and Agabus a "prophet," it never identifies anyone as a pastor. In fact, the noun "pastor" is used only once in the entire New Testament. (See Eph. 4:11.) And it's used as a descriptive *metaphor*, never as an ecclesiastical office. It is also plural, not singular.

This flies in the face of common practice. Today the "pastor" is regarded as the figurehead of the church. His name is exclusively splashed on church marquees all across the Western landscape. (One wonders why other ministries don't appear on these marquees when they are given far more attention in the New Testament.)

In our book, *Pagan Christianity*, George Barna and I demonstrate historically that the modern pastoral office is a postbiblical novelty that evokes a tradition of humane (but not so helpful) sacerdotalism. (Sacerdotalism is the belief that priests act as mediators between God and humans.) It's essentially a carryover from the priest of Roman Catholicism. As such, it better reflects the weak and beggarly elements of the Levitical priesthood than anything found in the New Testament.

(Incidentally, those who point to the single leaders of the Old Testament to justify the single pastor system make two mistakes. First, they

overlook the fact that all the single leaders of the Old Testament—
Joseph, Moses, Joshua, David, Solomon, etc.—were types of the Lord
Jesus Christ, not a human officer. Second, they typically ignore the
pattern for oversight that is clearly spelled out throughout the New
Testament.)

First-century elders all stood on equal footing. Perhaps some were
more spiritually mature than the others. And they undoubtedly had different giftings. But there was no hierarchical structure among them.

A careful reading of the book of Acts will show that while God often
used different overseers as temporary spokesmen for specific occasions
(sometimes James, sometimes Peter, etc.), no overseer occupied a permanent position of supremacy above the others.

Consequently, the modern offices of "senior pastor," "chief elder," and
"head pastor" simply did not exist in the early church. The first-century
Christians didn't mark off one man among the college of elders and ele-
vate him to a superior position of authority. The elders were not part of a
chain of command that put them under Christ and over the church. They
weren't part of a hierarchical pyramid. They were simply members of the
body of Christ, not an elite oligarchy.

Again, the single pastor system of our day was utterly foreign to the
New Testament church. Nowhere in the New Testament do we find one
of the elders transformed into the status of a super apostle and accorded
with supreme administrative authority.

Such authority was reserved for only one person—the Lord Jesus
Christ. He alone was the exclusive Head of the church. As such, only
He had the right to command His own sheep. Plural oversight in the
church protected the sole headship of Christ. It also served as a check
against despotism and corruption among the overseers.

The Public Acknowledgment of the Elders

The oversight of the church was not only shared, but it was *indigenous*. This means that the elders were *local* brothers who were spiritually reared within the church. Therefore, the accepted practice of importing a leader (typically a pastor) from another locality to lead a church has no basis in the New Testament. Instead, the elders were resident men whom God raised up from *within* the existing assembly.

Just as important, the elders always emerged *long after* a church was born. It took at least fourteen years after the birth of the Jerusalem church for elders to emerge within it (Acts 11:30). A good while after they planted the four churches in South Galatia, Paul and Barnabas acknowledged elders in each of them (Acts 14:23). Five years after Paul planted the church in Ephesus, he sent for the elders of the church to meet him in Miletus (Acts 20:17). When Paul wrote to the church in Philippi, which was twelve years old, he greeted the overseers who were present (Phil. 1:1).[3]

Point: There's no case anywhere in the New Testament where elders appear in a church immediately after it was planted. As with all spiritual gifts, the church is a spiritual organism that produces elders naturally. They are in her DNA. But it takes time for them to emerge. Consequently, house churches that rush to appoint elders have no scriptural justification for doing so.

In addition, elders never appointed themselves. Scripture consistently shows that traveling apostolic workers acknowledged them after they emerged from within the congregation. The elders didn't install themselves.

(Before the elders emerged, the oversight of the church was in the hands of the apostolic worker who planted it—1 Thess. 2:7–12. Afterward, the oversight shifted to the hands of the elders.)

The elders' authority to oversee was tied to their spiritual maturity. It was not tied to a sacerdotal office that was conferred upon them externally through an ordination service.

After the Holy Spirit *chose* the elders, apostolic workers later *confirmed* their calling publicly (Acts 14:23; 20:28; Titus 1:5). But the function preceded the form.

It's a tragic mistake, therefore, to equate the public endorsement of elders with the establishment of a separate class system like the clergy profession of our day. Acknowledgment of elders by apostolic workers was no more than the public recognition of those who were already "elder-ing" in the church. (See Num. 11:16 for this principle.) It was not "ministerial ordination" as we know it today.[4] The church simply trusted those who it recognized to be "elder-ing."

Unfortunately, the Western penchant for "offices" and "positions" has caused many Christians to bring these ideas to the biblical text and view elders as official. But such thinking confuses the oversight of the early church with modern social conventions. It also strips the leadership terminology found in the Bible of its native meaning.

Again, "elder" means mature man. "Shepherd" means one who nurtures and protects a flock. And "overseer" means one who supervises. Put plainly, the New Testament notion of oversight is *functional,* not *official.* True spiritual authority is rooted in spiritual life and function, not title or position.

In other words, New Testament leadership can best be understood in terms of *verbs* rather than *nouns.* Recall that our Lord Jesus rejected the authoritative pecking orders of His day (Matt. 20:25–28; Luke 22:25–27). In His eyes, spiritual authority was found in a towel and a basin, not in an external post (Matt. 23:8–12).

Character vs. Gifting

The elders mentioned in the New Testament were men of trusted character, not extraordinary gifting (1 Tim. 3:1–7; Titus 1:5–9). They were leading-servants, not slave drivers (Matt. 20:25–26). They were faithful brothers, not high-powered administrators.

The elders were examples to the flock, not lords over it (1 Peter 5:3). They didn't do the work of others; they supervised others as they worked. They functioned as bond-slaves, not as spiritual Caesars (Luke 22:24–27). They were facilitators, not tyrants. Fathers, not despots (1 Tim. 3:4; 5:1).

The elders were persuaders of the truth, not ecclesiastical autocrats whose egos thrived on power (Titus 1:9). They were nurturers, not brow beaters. Spiritual superintendents, not professional pulpiteers (Acts 20:28–35).

The elders were kingdom seekers, not empire builders. They were ordinary Christians, not multitalented, ultraversatile, superhuman, iconized, celebrity-like performers. They were servants, not dictators. They didn't control, manipulate, or terrorize the people of God.[5] (Regrettably, I've met many Christians who were hurt by elders who acted in ways that are reflected in the above sentences. On the other hand, I've met many who fit my description of first-century elders.)

The elders' training was not academic, formal, or theological. Instead, it was cultivated within the context of organic church life. Their qualification came not from professional schools or licenses, but from the Spirit of God (Acts 20:28). They didn't deem themselves qualified to oversee by acquiring a blend of accounting, public speaking, and amateur psychology skills. Their oversight was an organic, natural outgrowth of their life in the church.

The elders were not regarded as religious specialists, but as faithful and *trusted* brethren. They were not career clergy, but self-supporting family men with secular jobs (Acts 20:17, 32–35; 1 Tim. 3:5, 7; Titus 1:6; 1 Peter 5:2–3).

Because of their tireless labor, some elders received double honor from the church. But double honor is just that—extra respect.

On that note, some have tried to argue for a professional clergy from one isolated text in 1 Timothy, which says,

> *The elders who direct the affairs of the church well are worthy of double honor, especially those whose work is preaching and teaching. For the Scripture says, "Do not muzzle the ox while it is treading out the grain," and "The worker deserves his wages." (1 Tim. 5:17–18)*

However, the context of this passage reveals otherwise. First, the specific Greek words that the New Testament uses for "pay" or "wages" (*misthos* and *opsonion*) are not used to refer to what the elders are due. The Greek word for "honor" in this passage is *time,* and it means to "respect" or "value" someone or something.

The same word is used four times in 1 Timothy. In every case, it means respect. God is to receive honor from man (1:17; 6:16), elders are to receive honor from the church (5:17), and masters are to receive honor from slaves (6:1). Another form of the word is used when Paul says that widows are to be honored by the church (5:3). (Note that *time* is never used in first-century literature to refer to "honorarium.")

Second, all believers are called to honor (*time*) one another (Rom. 12:10). It would be absurd to take this to mean that all believers are to receive payment from one another. Again, those elders who serve well are to receive more honor—or greater respect.

Third, the fact that respect is what Paul had in mind is borne out by verse

19. Paul goes on to say that the elders are not to be accused (dishonored) unless there are two or three witnesses to confirm the accusation (1 Tim. 5:19).

Granted, double honor may have included freewill offerings as a token of blessing from time to time (Gal. 6:6; 1 Tim. 5:17–18). But this was not the dominating thought. It is *honor* (respect) that elders deserve, not a salary. Consequently, 1 Timothy 5 is perfectly consistent with Paul's words to the Ephesian elders recorded in Acts 20:

> *I have not coveted anyone's silver or gold or clothing. You yourselves know that these hands of mine have supplied my own needs and the needs of my companions. In everything I did, I showed you that by this kind of hard work we must help the weak, remembering the words the Lord Jesus himself said: "It is more blessed to give than to receive." (Acts 20:33–35)*

Paul told the elders in Ephesus to follow his example. That example was not to take money from God's people, but instead, to work for a living and give to their needs. Note that 1 Timothy 5:17–18 and Acts 20:33–35 were addressed to the same group of people—the elders in Ephesus.[6] Thus there is no contradiction. Paul's argument in 1 Timothy 5:17–18 is simply this: Just as the working ox deserves food and the working employee deserves payment, the elders who serve well should receive double respect.[7]

That said, the elders of the early church were not dependent on the church. Instead, they made sure that they were in a position to give to it. They certainly didn't receive a fixed salary like that of today's professional pastors. Nor were they biblically sanctioned to receive full financial support like itinerant apostles who traveled to plant churches (1 Cor. 9:1–18).

Because Paul was an itinerant apostolic worker, he had a legitimate right to receive full financial support from the Lord's people. But he intentionally waived that right whenever he worked with a new church (1 Cor. 9:14–18; 2 Cor. 11:7–9; 12:13–18; 1 Thess. 2:6–9; 2 Thess. 3:8–9).

Paul waived this right because he didn't want to burden any church financially while he served it. Thus the Pauline principle regarding financial support can be summed up in the phrase "When I was *present* with you … I was chargeable to no man" (2 Cor. 11:9 KJV).[8]

Again, the New Testament church knew nothing of a resident, hired clergy. Because they were simply brothers, the elders didn't stand *over* the flock. Nor did they stand *apart* from it. Instead, they served the church as those who were *among* the flock (1 Peter 5:1–3).

The Dramatic Lack of Attention Given to Leadership in the New Testament

Paul's letters make a lot of noise about exemplary action. And they show no interest in titular or official position. Consider this: Every time Paul wrote to a church in crisis, he always addressed the *church itself* rather than the elders. This is consistent from Paul's first letter to his last.[9]

Let me repeat that. Every time Paul wrote a letter to a church, he addressed the *whole* church. He never addressed the elders. Here's the record:

Paul, an apostle … To the churches in Galatia. (Gal. 1:1–2)

Paul, Silas and Timothy, To the church of the Thessalonians. (1 Thess. 1:1)

Paul, Silas and Timothy, To the church of the Thessalonians in God our Father and the Lord Jesus Christ. (2 Thess. 1:1)

Paul, called to be an apostle of Christ Jesus by the will of God, and our brother Sosthenes, To the church of God in Corinth, to those sanctified in Christ Jesus and called to be holy, together with all those everywhere who call on the name of our Lord Jesus Christ—their Lord and ours. (1 Cor. 1:1–2)

Paul, an apostle of Christ Jesus by the will of God, and Timothy our brother, To the church of God in Corinth, together with all the saints throughout Achaia. (2 Cor. 1:1)

Paul, a servant of Christ Jesus, called to be an apostle and set apart for the gospel of God.... To all in Rome who are loved by God and called to be saints. (Rom. 1:1, 7)

Paul, an apostle of Christ Jesus by the will of God, and Timothy our brother, To the holy and faithful brothers in Christ at Colosse. (Col. 1:1)

Paul, an apostle of Christ Jesus by the will of God, To the saints in Ephesus, the faithful in Christ Jesus. (Eph. 1:1)

Paul and Timothy, servants of Christ Jesus, To all the saints in Christ Jesus at Philippi, together with the overseers and deacons. (Phil. 1:1)

More striking, every church that Paul wrote to in the New Testament was in a crisis. (The exception was the recipients of the Ephesian letter.) Yet Paul never appeals to or singles out the elders in any of them.

Take for instance Corinth, the most troubled church mentioned in the New Testament. Throughout the entire Corinthian correspondence, Paul never appeals to the elders. He never chastises them. He never commends obedience to them. In fact, he doesn't even mention them.

Instead, Paul appeals to the *whole church*. He shows that it's the church's responsibility to deal with its own self-inflicted wounds. Paul charges and implores the "brethren" more than thirty times in 1 Corinthians. And he writes as if no officers exist. This is also true for all his other letters to churches in crisis.

If church officers did exist in Corinth, surely Paul would have addressed them to solve its woes. But he never does. At the end of the letter, Paul tells the Corinthians to subject themselves to the self-giving Stephanas and his household. But he widens this group to others, saying, "And to everyone who does likewise."

Notice that Paul's stress is on function, not position. His instruction is placed upon the shoulders of the whole church. The entire book of Corinthians is a plea to the whole assembly to handle its own problems.

Probably the most acute example of the absence of offici-elders in Corinth is found in 1 Corinthians 5. There Paul summons the whole church to discipline a fallen member by handing him over to Satan (1 Cor. 5:1ff.). Paul's exhortation clearly runs against the grain of current understanding. In today's thinking, only those possessing "ecclesiastical clout" are regarded as qualified for such weighty tasks.

The difference in the way Paul thinks of elders and the way most modern churches think of them could hardly be more striking. Paul doesn't utter a whisper about elders in any of his nine letters to the churches. This includes his ultracorrective treatise to the Galatians. Instead, Paul persistently entreats the "brethren" to action.

In his last letter to a church, Paul finally mentions the *overseers* in his opening greeting. But he does so in a fleeting way. In addition, he greets the overseers only *after* he greets the whole church. His letter opens with: "Paul and Timothy, servants of Christ Jesus, To all the saints in Christ Jesus at Philippi, together *with the overseers and deacons"* (Phil. 1:1). This is a rather strange order if Paul held to the idea of church officers.

Following this greeting, Paul talks to the church about its present problems. And he never again mentions the overseers.

This trend is highlighted in the book of Hebrews. Throughout the entire epistle, the writer addresses the entire church. Only at the very end of the letter does he offhandedly ask the believers to greet their overseers (Heb. 13:24).

In sum, the deafening lack of attention that Paul gives to elders demonstrates that he rejected the idea that certain people in the church possessed formal rights over others. It also underscores the fact that Paul didn't believe in church officers.

Peter's letters make similar noise. Like Paul, Peter writes his letters to the churches—never to their leaders. He also gives minimal airtime to elders. When he does, he warns them against adopting the spirit of the Gentiles. In fact, he makes the specific point that the elders are *among* the flock, not lords *over* it (1 Peter 5:1–2).

The elders, says Peter, are not to "lord it over [*katakurieuo*] the people" (1 Peter 5:3 NLT). Interestingly, Peter uses the same word that Jesus used in His discussion on authority in Matthew. The Lord's exact words were "You know that the rulers in this world lord it over [*katakurieuo*] their people.... But among you it will be different" (Matt. 20:25–26 NLT).

This same emphasis is found in the book of Acts. There Luke tells the story of how Paul exhorted the Ephesian elders to "be on guard for yourselves and for all the flock, *among* which the Holy Spirit has made you overseers" (Acts 20:28 NASB). Notice that the elders are "among," not "over," the flock.

James, John, and Jude write in the same strain. They address their letters to churches and not to overseers. In fact, they all have very little to say about oversight. And they have nothing to say about official eldership.

It's quite clear, then. The New Testament consistently rejects the notion of ecclesiastical officers in the church. It also greatly downplays the role of elders.

Eldership vs. Brotherhood

It would serve us well to ask why the New Testament gives so little airplay to elders. The oft-ignored reason may be surprising to institutional ears: The bulk of responsibility for pastoral care, teaching, and ministry in the *ekklesia* rests squarely upon the shoulders of *all* the brothers and sisters.

In fact, the richness of Paul's vision of the body of Christ stems from his continual emphasis that *every member* is gifted, has ministry, and is responsible in the body (Rom. 12:6; 1 Cor. 12:1ff.; Eph. 4:7; 1 Peter 4:10). As a consequence, ministerial responsibility is never to be closeted among a few.

This explains why the word *adelphoi*, translated "brethren," appears 346 times in the New Testament. It appears 134 times in Paul's epistles alone. In most places, this word is Paul's shorthand way of referring to *all* the believers in the church—both women and men. By contrast, the word "elders" appears only five times in Paul's letters. "Overseers" appears only four times. And "pastors" appears only once.

The stress of the New Testament, then, is upon *corporate* responsibility.

It's the *believing community* that is called to carry out pastoral functions. To be more specific, all the Christians in a local assembly are called to

- be devoted to one another (Rom. 12:10)
- honor one another (Rom. 12:10)
- live in harmony with one another (Rom. 12:16; 1 Peter 3:8)
- love one another (Rom. 13:8; 1 Thess. 4:9; 1 Peter 1:22; 1 John 3:11)
- edify one another (Rom. 14:19; 1 Thess. 5:11b)
- accept one another (Rom. 15:7)
- instruct one another (Rom. 15:14)
- greet one another (Rom. 16:16)
- agree with one another (1 Cor. 1:10)
- discipline fallen members (1 Cor. 5:3–5; 6:1–6)
- organize the church's affairs (1 Cor. 11:33–34; 14:39–40; 16:2–3)
- care for one another (1 Cor. 12:25)
- prophesy one by one (1 Cor. 14:31)
- abound in the work of the Lord (1 Cor. 15:58)
- serve one another (Gal. 5:13)
- bear one another's burdens (Gal. 6:2)
- bear with one another (Eph. 4:2)
- be kind and compassionate to one another (Eph. 4:32)
- speak to one another with psalms, hymns, and spiritual songs (Eph. 5:19)
- submit to one another (Eph. 5:21)
- forgive one another (Col. 3:13)
- teach one another (Col. 3:16)
- admonish one another (Col. 3:16)

- encourage one another (1 Thess. 5:11)
- warn the unruly (1 Thess. 5:14)
- comfort the feeble (1 Thess. 5:14)
- support the weak (1 Thess. 5:14)
- exhort one another (Heb. 3:13; 10:25)
- incite one another to love and good works (Heb. 10:24)
- pray for one another (James 5:16)
- confess sins to one another (James 5:16)
- offer hospitality to one another (1 Peter 4:9)
- be humble toward one another (1 Peter 5:5)
- fellowship with one another (1 John 1:7)

With dramatic clarity, all of these "one-another" exhortations incarnate the fact that every member of the church is to share the responsibility for pastoral care. Leadership is a corporate affair, not a solo one. It's to be shouldered by the entire body.

Consequently, the idea that elders direct the affairs of the church, make decisions in all corporate matters, handle all of its problems, and supply all of its teaching is alien to New Testament thinking. Such an idea is pure fantasy and bereft of biblical support. It's no wonder that in elder-led churches spiritual maturity atrophies and members grow passive and indolent.

Stated simply, the New Testament knows nothing of an elder-ruled, elder-governed, or elder-directed church. And it knows even less about a pastor-led church. The first-century church was in the hands of the brotherhood and the sisterhood. Plain and simple.

Elders are organic to the church. They exist within her DNA. Like fingernails and eyebrows on an infant, they develop organically as the child grows up. Any church that's properly planted and is living by the life of Christ will naturally produce elders. By the same token, elders should emerge out of brotherhood. For when they do, they will become overseers rather than overlords.

In the final analysis, the leadership of the church really boils down to one basic issue—the headship of Christ. It rests upon the thorny question of who will be Head: Jesus Christ or human beings?

Questions That Must Be Faced

- Why do you believe we've made something normative that has no scriptural support (the modern pastor and official elders) and neglected that which Scripture teaches in abundance (plural elders who are part of a functioning Christian community)?
- What model of leadership do you believe best reflects leadership in the triune God: the single pastor, official elders, or the community of believers under the Spirit's guidance? What is your church's model?
- Can you discern the wisdom of God in designing the church to organically produce a group of elders to oversee it rather than a single pastor (or an imported minister) to run it? Explain.

CHAPTER 10
REIMAGINING DECISION-MAKING

The Trinity understood in human terms as a communion of Persons lays the foundations for a society of brothers and sisters, of equals, in which dialogue and consensus are the basic constituents of living together in both the world and the church. —Leonardo Boff

Guidance on matters affecting the community's life was principally granted to members when they met together to discern what God required of them. They received this guidance from the Spirit through their exercise of gifts of knowledge, revelation, wisdom, and so on. In all this Paul never tires of insisting that every member of the community has the responsibility to impart the particular insights they have been given. Thus, the most characteristic setting in which the community received guidance was when Christians assembled to share and evaluate the gifts given to them. Here, in a variety of complementary ways, guidance was conveyed through each to all and through all to each. —Robert Banks

In our last chapter, we discovered that the New Testament promotes no other form of leadership than a shared form. The Lord has chosen to lead His church through a many-membered community. Elders emerge over time. They model pastoral care for the rest of the church, and they provide oversight. In addition, elders are always plural in a church.

Yet the mere presence of a plurality of elders doesn't ensure that a church will be healthy. If the elders don't oversee according to the life and grace of Christ, they can do more damage than a single leader. (Unfortunately, I've witnessed my share of heavy-handed elders who muscled God's people into a decision. While these men never perceived themselves to be spiritual oppressors, the rest of the church did.)

It is for this reason that the question of decision-making in the church becomes crucial. Unlike the modern clergy system, first-century elders were never regarded as the prominent figures in the church.

As we've previously noted, there's a deafening lack of attention given to elders throughout the New Testament. This omission is significant. It vigorously challenges the Protestant notion of the preeminence of the pastor and equally challenges the popular "house church" notion of the preeminence of elders. Both ideas are at odds with New Testament principles.

In chapter 8, we learned that the biblical model of leadership militates against the poisons of forced submission, top-heavy authority structures, and hierarchical relationships (Matt. 23:11; Mark 10:42–45; Luke 22:26–27). The New Testament model of leadership serves as a safeguard to the real and living headship of Christ. It's also a check against authoritarianism. The budding of Aaron's rod beautifully illustrates that the basis of spiritual authority rests upon resurrection life (Num. 17:1–11). It's never based on position.

The overseers of the early church oversaw by example—not by coercion or manipulation. The respect they received from the other members was in direct proportion to their sacrificial service (1 Cor. 16:10–11,15–18; Phil. 2:29–30; 1 Thess. 5:12–13; 1 Tim. 5:17). Their authority was rooted in their spiritual maturity rather than in a sacerdotal position. In the words of Peter, they didn't oversee by "being lords over God's heritage, but [by] being *examples* to the flock" (1 Peter 5:3 KJV).

To be an example means setting forth a pattern for others to follow. Because elders were examples, (1) they were active in ministry (for they set the example), and (2) they encouraged the church to be just as active (others followed their example).

Therefore, if an elder desired others to win the lost, it was incumbent upon him to model soul-winning. Why? Because he was an example. In this regard, the notion that pastors don't win souls because "shepherds do not breed sheep, but sheep breed sheep" is a classic example of twisting the Scripture.

If we push the shepherd-sheep metaphor beyond its intended meaning, we'll readily see its foolishness. Shepherds are incapable of breeding sheep. They also steal their wool and eat them for dinner!

Simply put, oversight in the New Testament was not a slavish obligation, nor a grim necessity. Instead, it was a valuable family resource marked by humility, relatedness, and servanthood.

A Borrowed Leadership Paradigm

Institutional Christianity has baptized secular leadership patterns and passed them off as being biblically valid. The result: Our modern notion of church leadership is culturally captive to the spirit of this age.

Seeing that the great weight of biblical teaching on leadership has been lost to the prevailing notions of our culture, the scriptural ground needs to be reclaimed.

As we saw in chapter 5, the chief metaphor for the church is the family.

This explains why the biblical image of leadership is that of a mother and a father (1 Thess. 2:6–12). Notwithstanding, even the parental image of leadership can become distorted and turned into cold prose if not viewed against the backdrop of the priesthood of *all* believers and our relationship with each other as brothers and sisters (Matt. 23:8).

Plainly stated, leadership in the early church was nonhierarchical, nonaristocratic, nonauthoritarian, noninstitutional, and nonclerical. God's idea of leadership is *functional, relational, organic,* and *communal*—just as it is in the Godhead.

To have the leadership of the church function according to the same principles as that of a corporate executive in a business or an aristocrat in an imperial caste system was never our Lord's thought. It is for this reason that the New Testament authors never chose to use hierarchical and imperial metaphors to describe spiritual leadership.

The New Testament authors deliberately depict leadership with images of slaves and children rather than lords and masters (Luke 22:25–26). While such thinking comes in direct conflict with today's popular practice of "spiritual authority," it meshes perfectly with the biblical teaching of the kingdom of God—the realm in which the weak are strong, the poor are rich, the humble are exalted, and the last are first (Luke 6:20–26; Matt. 23:12; 20:16).

Since the elders of the early church knew that the church didn't belong to them, they didn't have their own agendas to push. Nor did they roadblock or muscle others into mindless submission by an appeal to their "authority." (While many elders do not operate this way, some unfortunately do.)

The elders of the early church didn't operate as an oligarchy (absolute rule by a few) nor as a dictatorship (monarchical rule by one person).

Again, they were simply older men whom the church organically and naturally looked to in times of crisis.

By the same token, the early church didn't operate like our contemporary democracy. Many mistakenly think that our American democratic system is rooted in biblical theology. But there isn't a single example in the entire New Testament where church decisions were made by a show of hands. Granted, every Christian is equal in spiritual life, but each has a different gift (Rom. 12:3–8). The church is not a pure democracy.

The Divine Rule of Consensus

So what was the New Testament pattern for decision-making in the early church? It was simply by consensus. "Then it seemed good to the apostles and the elders, *with the whole church*," and, "it seemed good *to us*, having become of *one mind*" was the divine model for making corporate decisions (Acts 15:22, 25 NASB). In other words, the decision-making of the early church was not in the hands of the elders. It was in the hands of *all* the brothers and sisters.

Because the church is a body, all the members should agree before it moves forward in obeying the Head (Rom. 12:4–5; 1 Cor. 12:12–27; Eph. 4:11–16). In fact, a lack of unity and cooperation among the members reveals a failure to embrace the Head (Christ).

Majority rule, dictatorial rule, and a *Robert's Rules of Order* mentality do violence to the body image of the church. And they dilute the unvarnished testimony that Jesus Christ is the Head of one unified body. For this reason, Paul's epistles to the churches are saturated with exhortations to be of one mind (Rom. 15:5–6; 1 Cor. 1:10; 2 Cor. 13:11; Eph. 4:3; Phil. 2:2; 4:2). Recall the Lord's teaching in the following text:

Again, I tell you that if two of you on earth agree about anything you ask for, it will be done for you by my Father in heaven. (Matt. 18:19)

Significantly, the word *agree* in this passage is translated from the Greek word *sumphoneo*. *Sumphoneo* means to sound together—to be in one accord. Our word *symphony* is derived from this term. So the meaning is clear. When the church is in sympathetic harmony, God will act.

In this connection, consensus mirrors the decision-making activity within the triune God, whose nature we were created to reflect. God acts when Father, Son, and Spirit agree. Decision-making in the Godhead is communal and marked by mutual submission. In other words, it's consensual.

Even in the Old Testament economy, the Bible associates consensus with spiritual fullness (1 Chron. 12:38–40; 13:1–4; 2 Chron. 30:4–5). Conversely, it associates divided judgment with spiritual ruin (1 Kings 16:21–22).

Again, the elders of the early church bore the bulk of spiritual oversight and pastoral care for the assembly (Heb. 13:7, 17, 24). But they didn't make decisions on behalf of the church. Nor were they solely responsible for the church's direction.

Therefore, an elder had no biblical or spiritual right to bark out commands to a passive congregation. Instead, the elders (once they emerged) worked together with the whole church toward reaching a *unanimous* decision and a *single* mind (Acts 15:22, 28). But it was the church, as a whole, that made the decision as "one new man."

But what about Hebrews 13:17? In that text, some translations have, "Obey them that are over you." The Greek word for "obey" in this passage is not *hupakuo*, the garden-variety word for obedience used elsewhere in

Scripture. It's *peitho* (middle-passive form), which means to yield to persuasion. The author of Hebrews was simply saying, "Allow yourselves to be persuaded by those who are more mature in Christ than you are."

So within the decision-making process of the early church, the role of the elders was to help the church reach a consensus on a matter. By virtue of their relative spiritual maturity, they were sometimes able to persuade the church into a unified understanding of the Lord's mind. But they had no right to force the church to adopt their view. The elders were people who simply demonstrated qualities that built family solidarity (1 Tim. 3:4–5; Titus 1:6).

The Meaning of Consensus

A church reaches a consensus when all of its members have come to a unanimous agreement in support of a particular decision.

Granted, the church may agree with a decision with varying degrees of enthusiasm (some consenting "with a heavy heart"). Yet a consensus is reached when all have come to the place where they have set aside their objections and can support the decision in good faith.

When a church operates by consensus, decisions are delayed until agreement is reached. This process requires that all the members equally participate in and accept responsibility for reaching the mind of the Lord on a given matter. (Incidentally, the mind of Christ doesn't belong to an individual. It's a corporate discovery—1 Cor. 2:9–16.)

When the church reaches a consensus, murmuring and complaining are eliminated. Why? Because every member has had an equal share in the decision. The church owns the decision. It was made *by* and *for* the church under the Holy Spirit's guidance.

Decision-making by consensus stands at odds with modern pragmatism. Pragmatism is the American attitude that says, "If it works, it's good; if it produces results, it's true." Those who look through the prism of modern pragmatism regard consensus to be idealistic and impractical. Yet it's the only sure safeguard to ensure that a group of people have obtained the mind of Christ.

Some may retort that this method would never work in our day. But this simply isn't true. I've been part of a number of churches where it was practiced.

To be sure, consensus is *humanly* impossible. But so is salvation (Matt. 19:26). It is the indwelling Spirit who makes decision-making by consensus a practical reality and a fruitful testimony to the indivisible life of Christ.

The Challenge Before Us

The disconnect between the institutional church's practice of decision-making and the New Testament reality is indeed profound. And it should give us pause to question why we have strayed so far.

In many institutional churches, the pastor (and sometimes the "board") makes decisions independently of the church. The same is true in some house churches where elders have the rule. In those particular churches, the elders decide without any regard for the concerns or judgments of the congregation. Members are without a voice in the church's affairs. What is more, they are encouraged to "go elsewhere" if they don't "line up."

In those churches that decide on the basis of majority rule, those who "lose the vote" are left to question the judgment of the populace. (Sometimes they are left to question the very ethics of the procedure.) The fact that Scripture is filled with examples where the majority was wrong is conveniently over-looked.[1] So often, when the 52 percent see a great victory, the 48 percent are still grumbling and seeking to undermine the majority decision.

There's no doubt that consensus is costly. It imposes responsibility upon all the members of a church to seek the Lord for themselves. It demands that each believer patiently wrestle and struggle with one another to secure the Lord's mind. It often means trading quick decisions for gaining confidence through delay. But what building together it affords! What working out of patience. What expression of mutual love and respect. What exercise of Christian community. What restraint imposed upon the flesh. What bearing of the cross. What dying to our own agendas.

Is such a cost not worth the value of securing the Lord's mind for His body? Is it not worth giving Him the opportunity to work in us more deeply as a people? Does not confidence in getting the mind of the Lord on a matter relating to *His* church outweigh the convenience of making premature decisions—decisions that can damage the lives of our brethren and miss the Lord's will? We so often forget that, in God's eyes, the means is just as important as the end. Once again, Christian Smith puts it beautifully:

> *Consensus is built on the experience of Christian community. It requires strong relationships able to tolerate struggling through issues together. It requires mutual love and respect to hear each other when there is disagreement. Consensus also requires a commitment to know and understand other people more than a desire to convince or railroad them. Consensus, as a way to make decisions in the church, is not easier, just better. To paraphrase Winston Churchill, consensus is the worst form of decision-making in the church, except for all the others. Consensus is not strong*

on efficiency, if by that we mean ease and speed. It can take a long time to work through issues, which can become quite frustrating. Consensus is strong on unity, communication, openness to the Spirit's leading, and responsible participation in the body. In achieving those values, consensus is efficient. Deciding by consensus, then, simply requires belief that unity, love, communication, and participation are more important in the Christian scheme than quick, easy decisions. It requires the understanding that, ultimately, the process is as important as the outcome. How we treat each other as we make decisions together is as important as what we actually decide.[2]

In approaching the matter of consensus, some have sacrificed God's truth upon the altar of convenience. But human convenience and expediency is a dangerously thin criterion for judging actions in the spiritual realm.

The core question that must be asked, therefore, is not, "Is this convenient and expedient?" but, "Is this scriptural, and is it in harmony with the organic nature of the church?" You can rest assured that if the Lord has bid us to follow something, it will be possible and practical by His grace.

In summary, the following is what leadership in the early church did: It encouraged every member to exercise his or her gifts; it helped to form spiritual solidarity among believers; it fostered a sense of community, cohesion, and unity within the church.

The ability to wield power or impose one's will on others does not characterize biblical leadership. Leadership is characterized by the ability to weld the church together to reach undivided judgments on critical affairs. Any person who does this at a given time is leading at that moment.

All in all, the New Testament knows nothing of an authoritative mode of leadership. Nor does it know a "leaderless" egalitarianism. It rejects both hierarchical structures as well as rugged individualism. Instead, the New Testament envisions leadership as coming from the entire church. The brothers and sisters supply direction and decision-making by consensus. Seasoned brothers supply oversight.

In this way, the early churches were guided democracies. Decision-making was communal. It stood between hierarchical structures on the one hand and egalitarian individualism on the other. Elders were called to exercise pastoral oversight in the context of mutual subjection rather than in a hierarchical structure of subordination (Eph. 5:21; 1 Tim. 5:19–20).

Questions That Must Be Faced

- Is it possible that many of the problems that plague the institutional church today are directly rooted in our arrogant assumption that we've found a better way to lead God's house in the twenty-first century than what we find taught and modeled in the New Testament? Explain.
- Do you think that the biblical example of decision-making by consensus better ensures that the Lord's mind has been reached compared to that of allowing a leader to dictate decisions to God's people? Explain.
- Do you believe that discerning the mind of the Lord on a church matter through consensus outweighs the convenience of making hasty decisions by a few people in power? Explain.

CHAPTER 11
REIMAGINING SPIRITUAL COVERING

While the "clergy/laity" distinction is embedded and assumed in religious circles, it cannot be found in the New Testament. Because the New Testament knows nothing of "clergy," the fact that a separate caste of the "ordained" permeates our vocabulary and practice illustrates rather forcefully that we do not yet take the New Testament very seriously. The "clergy" practice is a heresy that must be renounced. It strikes at the heart of the priesthood of all believers that Jesus purchased on the cross. It contradicts the shape that Jesus' kingdom was to take when He said, "You are all brethren." Since it is a tradition of man, it nullifies the Word of God. The clergy system stands as a monumental obstacle to genuine reformation and renewal.

—Jon Zens

Much Christian leadership is exercised by people who do not know how to develop healthy, intimate relationships and have opted for power and control instead. Many Christian empire builders have been people unable to give and receive love.

—Henri Nouwen

So who is your covering? This is the terse query raised by many modern Christians whenever they encounter those who meet outside the institutional church. But what is at the heart of this inquiry? And what biblical basis undergirds it?

It's my contention that a great deal of confusion and subnormal Christian behavior is connected with a teaching known as "spiritual covering." (It's sometimes called "protective covering.") This teaching holds that Christians are protected from doctrinal error and moral failure when they submit themselves to the authority of another believer or religious organization.

The painful experience of many has led me to conclude that the "covering" teaching is a matter that greatly troubles Zion today. And it desperately begs for critical reflection.

In the next three chapters, I will attempt to cut through the fog that surrounds the difficult issues attached to the "covering" teaching. Particularly the thorny subjects of authority and submission.

Is "Covering" Covered in the Bible?

Since I've been gathering outside the institutional church, I've observed many who have suffered opposition from leaders in the organized church. These brave souls have generated acute questions about ecclesiastical authority. In fact, they have been asked the same questions that religious leaders asked our Lord centuries ago: "By what authority are You doing these things? And who gave You this authority?" (Matt. 21:23 NKJV). Or to put it in modern parlance, "Who is your covering?"

If we strip it down to its bare roots, the idea of "covering" rests upon a top-heavy, hierarchical understanding of authority. This understanding is borrowed from the structures that belong to this world system. It in no way reflects the kingdom of God. Consequently, there is a natural affinity between the hierarchical/positional orientation of leadership and the modern "covering" teaching.

Interestingly, the word *covering* only appears once in the entire New Testament. It is used in connection with a woman's head covering (1 Cor. 11:15). While the Old Testament uses the word sparingly, it typically uses it to refer to a piece of natural clothing. It never uses it in a spiritual way.

So the first thing we can say about spiritual "covering" is that there is scant biblical evidence to support it. Yet despite this fact, countless Christians glibly parrot the "who-is-your-covering?" question. Some even push it as a litmus test to measure the authenticity of a church or ministry.

This leads me to ask a question of my own: If the Bible is silent with respect to "covering," what do people mean when they ask, "Who is your covering?" Most people (if pressed) would rephrase the question as "Who are you accountable to?"

But this raises another sticky point. The Bible *never* consigns accountability to human beings. It always consigns it exclusively to God (Matt. 12:36; 18:23; Luke 16:2; Rom. 3:19; 14:12; 1 Cor. 4:5; Heb. 4:13; 13:17; 1 Peter 4:5).

Consequently, the biblically sound answer to the "who-are-you-accountable-to?" question is simply "I'm accountable to the same person you are—God." Strangely, however, this answer is usually a prescription for misunderstanding and a recipe for false accusation.

So while the timbre and key of "accountability" sounds slightly different from that of "covering," the song is essentially the same. And it's one that doesn't harmonize with the unmistakable singing of Scripture.

Unearthing the Real Question Behind Covering

Let's widen the question a bit. What do people *really* mean when they push the "covering" question? I submit that what they're really asking is "Who controls you?" Common (mis)teaching about "covering" really boils down to questions about who controls whom. And the modern institutional church is structured around such control.

Of course, people rarely recognize that this is what's at the bottom of the issue. For it's typically well clothed with religious garments. In the minds of many Christians, "covering" is merely a protective mechanism.

But if we dissect the "covering" teaching, we'll soon discover that it's rooted in a one-up/one-down, chain-of-command style of leadership. Within this leadership style, those in higher ecclesiastical positions have a tenacious hold on those under them. And it's believed (rather oddly) that, through such top-down control, believers are "protected" from error.

The concept goes something like this. Everyone must answer to someone else who is in a higher ecclesiastical position. In the garden-variety, postwar evangelical church, this translates into the "laymen" answering to the pastor. In turn, the pastor must answer to someone with more authority.

The pastor typically traces his accountability to a denominational headquarters, to another church (often called the "mother church"), or to an influential Christian worker. (The worker is perceived to have a higher rank in the ecclesiastical pyramid.)

So the layman is "covered" by the pastor, who is "covered" by the denomination, the mother church, or the Christian worker. Because each person is accountable to a higher ecclesiastical authority, each one is protected (or "covered") by that authority. So the thinking goes.

This "covering-accountability" template is applied to all spiritual relationships in the church. And each relationship is artificially cut to fit the template. No relationship can be had outside of it—especially those of the "laymen."

But this line of reasoning generates the following questions: *Who covers the mother church? Who covers the denominational headquarters? Who covers the Christian worker?*

Some have offered the pat answer that God covers these "higher" authorities. But such a canned answer begs the question: Why can't God be the covering for the laymen—or even the pastor?

Hmmm ...

The truth is that the guy on top ends up being accountable to no one, while accountability is pushed to the hilt for everyone below him. Of course, the real problem with the "God-denomination-worker-pastor-laity" model goes far beyond the incoherent, pretzel logic to which it leads. The chief problem is that it violates the organic nature of the church. For behind the pious rhetoric of "providing accountability" and "having a covering" looms a system that's bereft of biblical support and driven by a spirit of control. In a word, the underlying issues that lurk behind the "covering" teaching have to do with power and control.

Covering is Smothering

It is my opinion that the doctrine of "spiritual covering" fundamentally supplants the headship of the Lord Jesus Christ. Therefore, the attempt to critically examine the "covering" teaching and all that's bound up with it is far more than an arcane, theological exercise. It touches the very purpose of God—a purpose that is wholly occupied with the absolute sovereignty and supremacy of Jesus Christ in His church.

In the 1970s, God raised up many organic churches in virtually every part of America. Yet misteaching about spiritual authority caused the demise of virtually all of them. They experienced the smothering that follows "covering." Those who waded into the swirling waters of spiritual covering capsized under the crosscurrents of human power and control.

May it not be so in our day.

While we are subject to the same foibles as those who have gone before us, we don't have to succumb to their mistakes. If we have to make mistakes, let's make new ones.

As in the 1970s, the Lord is now reawakening His people to His all-consuming purpose of restoring His house. In light of this new awakening, may we scrap the old leaking wineskins that have hindered the flow of God's new wine.

Would to God that there would be scores of Christian groups who are gathering unto His Son alone. Groups that express His body in all of its fullness. Groups that are not hidebound by authoritarian leadership models or denominational structures.

May you, dear reader, be added to their tribe.

Questions That Must Be Faced

- How familiar are you with "covering" terminology? Have you ever used it as a standard by which to judge people and churches?
- Does the word *control* or *smothering* describe your "covering" experience? Explain.
- If "covering" is a foreign concept to you, do any of the descriptions of it in this chapter resonate with experiences that you or your friends have had in the past? Explain.

CHAPTER 12
REIMAGINING AUTHORITY AND SUBMISSION

No one sews a patch of unshrunk cloth on an old garment, for the patch will pull away from the garment, making the tear worse. Neither do men pour new wine into old wineskins. If they do, the skins will burst, the wine will run out and the wineskins will be ruined. No, they pour new wine into new wineskins, and both are preserved.

—Jesus Christ in Matthew 9:16–17

Within the fellowship of the Trinity there is no lusting after power and position. No trinitarian Person considers himself better than the other two, but in loving deference esteems the other two more highly.

—Roderick T. Leupp

In Christianity today, a great deal of talk about authority and submission is circulating. Granted, the Bible has something to say about authority and submission. However, it spills far more ink in teaching us about love and service than it does about authority and submission. They are but footnotes in the unfolding drama that the Bible portrays.

My experience has been that when the fundamental aspects of love and servanthood are mastered in a church, the issues of authority and submission amazingly take care of themselves. (In this connection, those who put undue emphasis on these subjects are typically more interested in making *themselves* an authority figure than they are in serving their fellow brethren.)

So while the Bible doesn't make a lot of noise about authority and submission, the subjects are present. And they are germane to bearing ministry, receiving ministry, and pleasing Christ—the Head of all authority.

To my mind, using unbiblical jargon like "covering" only obscures the issue of authority and submission. It makes our conversation cluttered and our thoughts murky. If we stay with a New Testament vocabulary, we'll be better able to cut through the matted layers of human tradition that have obscured the subject.

Let me be candid. Most of what passes today for "spiritual authority" is a study in absurdity. The discipleship-shepherding movement of the 1970s is a classic example of the unspeakable tragedies that occur when bogus and foolish applications of authority are made. The aforementioned movement was riddled with spiritual mixture. And it degraded into extreme forms of control and manipulation.

Here is a summary of the discipleship-shepherding teaching. Every Christian must find a shepherd to disciple and "cover" him or her. The shepherd is "God's delegated authority." Therefore, his advice must always be followed. To disobey one's shepherd is to disobey God Himself. Thus, all Christians must trust in their shepherd's judgment above their own. If a person fails to submit to his or her shepherd, he or she has moved outside of divine "covering" and will experience loss—either spiritual or physical.

The major error of the discipleship-shepherding teaching rests upon the false assumption that submission is the equivalent of unconditional obedience. Equally flawed is the idea that God vests certain people with unquestioned authority over others.

To be sure, the leaders of the discipleship-shepherding movement were gifted men with noble motives. They didn't envision the direction that the movement would take. (Some of them have since apologized for their role in spawning it.) Even so, countless lives were devastated as a result. In many segments of the discipleship-shepherding movement, spiritual abuse was rationalized under the oft-repeated platitude that God works good despite the actors in the cast. God, it was taught, will hold individual "shepherds" responsible for wrong decisions. The "sheep" bear no responsibility so long as they mindlessly obey their shepherds—regardless of what they command the sheep to do.

Under this rationale, the movement constructed new yokes of control that were whittled and shaped to fit the laity caste. These new yokes suffocated the believing priesthood. And they exhibited the same domination of souls that characterize the cults. So-called shepherds were transformed into God-surrogates for other Christians, seizing control over the most intimate details of their lives. All of this was done in the name of "biblical accountability."

In the aftermath, the movement left a trail of broken and disillusioned Christians who continue to mistrust any semblance of leadership today. (Some suffered crueler fates.) As a result, those who were clergy-whipped in the movement developed an aversion to words like *authority, submission,* and *accountability.* Even today, they still struggle to discard the distorted images of God that were etched in their minds by their "shepherding" experience.

The subjects of authority and submission, therefore, represent a sensitive and highly charged history for many. So much so, that when leadership terminology is merely uttered, alert lights go off and the red flag of victimization is raised.

More than thirty years later, spiritual authority continues to be an emotionally laden and flammable subject. Despite the highly divergent take on the issue that's contained in this book, we are still treading on the edges of a hazardous minefield.

Keep in mind that erroneous teachings never spring from the mere employment of biblical words. They rather stem from running roughshod over what they meant to their original hearers. Words like *authority* and *subjection* have been debased for so long that they need to be "redeemed" from the bogus connotations that have been attached to them.

Therefore, the safeguard to false teaching is not found in discarding these biblical terms. It's rather found in rising above the fray and recasting them according to their original renderings. To put it another way, we must learn not only to speak *where* the Bible speaks. But we must also learn to speak *as* the Bible speaks.

The New Testament Notion of Subjection

The Greek word most often translated "submit" in the New Testament is *hupotasso. Hupotasso* is better translated "subjection." In its New Testament usage, subjection is a voluntary attitude of giving into, cooperating with, and yielding to the admonition or advice of another.[1]

Biblical subjection has nothing to do with control or hierarchical power. It's simply an attitude of childlike openness in yielding to others.

Biblical subjection exists, and it's precious. But it must begin with what God wants and what the New Testament assumes. Namely, that we are individually and corporately subject to Jesus Christ; we are subject to one another in the believing community to which we belong; and we are subject to those proven and trustworthy Christian workers who sacrificially serve our believing community.

I stress "proven and trustworthy" because false prophets and pseudo-apostles abound. It's the responsibility of the local brethren to examine those who claim to be Christian workers (1 Thess. 1:5; 2 Thess. 3:10; Rev. 2:2). For this reason, the Bible exhorts us to subject ourselves to spiritual leaders because of their noble character and sacrificial service (1 Cor. 16:10–11,15–18; Phil. 2:29–30; 1 Thess. 5:12–13; 1 Tim. 5:17; Heb. 13:17). Perhaps the most luminous text to consider in this discussion is in Ephesians:

Submit to one another out of reverence for Christ. (Eph. 5:21)

Again, the Bible never teaches "protective covering." Instead, it teaches *mutual subjection*. Mutual subjection rests upon the New Testament notion that all believers are gifted. As such, they can all express Jesus Christ. Therefore, we are to be in subjection to *one another* in Christ.

Mutual subjection is equally rooted in the biblical revelation of the body of Christ. God's authority has been vested in the *entire* body rather than to a particular section of it (Matt. 18:15–20; 16:16–19; Eph. 1:19–23). In God's ecclesiology, the *ekklesia* is a theocratic, participatory society where divine authority is dispersed to all who possess the Spirit. In this way, the church reflects the triune God where the relationship of the three divine persons is communal and nonhierarchical.

Make no mistake about it: God has not deputized His authority to any individual or segment of the church. Instead, His authority resides in the entire community. As the members of a believing community discharge their ministries, spiritual authority is dispensed through their Spirit-endowed gifts.

At bottom, mutual subjection demands that we realize that we are members of something larger than ourselves—a body. It also demands that we acknowledge that we are inadequate in ourselves to fulfill God's highest purpose. In other words, mutual subjection is rooted in the humble yet realistic affirmation that we need the input of our fellow brethren. It admits that we cannot be good Christians by ourselves. In this way, mutual subjection is indispensable to the texture of a normal Christian life.

God's Idea of Authority

The flip side of subjection is authority. Authority is God-given privilege to carry out a particular task. The New Testament word that's closest to our word "authority" is *exousia*. *Exousia* is derived from the word *exestin*, which means a possible and rightful action that can be carried out without hindrance.

Authority (*exousia*) has to do with the communication of power. Scripture teaches that God is the sole source of all authority (Rom. 13:1). And this authority has been vested in His Son (Matt. 28:18; John 3:30–36; 17:2).

In other words, Jesus Christ alone possesses authority. The Lord plainly said, "*All* authority in heaven and on earth has been given to me" (Matt. 28:18). At the same time, Christ has delegated His authority to men and women in this world for specific purposes.

For instance, in the natural order, the Lord has instituted various and sundry spheres in which His authority is to be exercised. He has established certain "official authorities" that are designed to keep order under the sun. Governmental officials like kings, magistrates, and judges are given such authority (John 19:10–11; Rom. 13:1ff.; 1 Tim. 2:2; 1 Peter 2:13–14).

Official authority is vested in a static office. The authority works regardless of the actions of the persons who populate the office. Official authority is fixed and positional. As long as a person holds office, he or she has authority.

When official authority is given to someone, the recipient becomes an "authority" in his or her own right. It is for this reason that Christians are charged to be subject to governmental leaders—regardless of their character (Rom. 13:1ff.; 1 Peter 2:13–19).

Our Lord Jesus as well as Paul exhibited the spirit of subjection when they stood in the presence of official authority (Matt. 26:63–64; Acts 23:2–5). In like manner, Christians are always to be subject to such authority. Lawlessness and the despising of authority are marks of the sinful nature (2 Peter 2:10; Jude 8). Yet subjection and obedience are two very different things. And it's a profound error to confuse them.

Subjection vs. Obedience

How does subjection differ from obedience? Subjection is an attitude; obedience is an action. Subjection is absolute; obedience is relative. Subjection is unconditional; obedience is conditional. Subjection is internal; obedience is external.

God summons His people to have a spirit of humble subjection toward those whom He has placed in authority in the natural order. Yet we must not obey them if they command us to do something that violates His will.

For the authority of God is higher than any earthly authority.

In other words, one can disobey while submitting. That is, a person can disobey an earthly authority while maintaining a spirit of humble subjection to the authority's office. One can disobey while having an attitude of respect as opposed to a spirit of rebellion, reviling, and subversion (1 Tim. 2:1–2; 2 Peter 2:10; Jude 8).

The disobedience of the Hebrew midwives (Ex. 1:17), Rahab (Josh. 2:1ff.), the three Hebrew young men (Dan. 3:17–18), Daniel (Dan. 6:8–10), and the apostles (Acts 4:18–20; 5:27–29) all exemplify the principle of being subject to official authority while disobeying it when it conflicts with God's will. It's also possible to correct a person in an authoritative office while still having a submissive attitude toward him or her (Matt. 14:3-5; Acts 16:35–39).

While God has established official authority to operate in the natural order, He hasn't instituted this kind of authority in the church. Granted, God gives believers authority (*exousia*) to exercise certain rights. Among them is the authority (*exousia*) to become the children of God (John 1:12); to own property (Acts 5:4); to decide to marry or live celibate (1 Cor. 7:37); to decide what to eat or drink (1 Cor. 8:9); to heal sickness and drive out devils (Matt. 10:1; Mark 3:15; 6:7; Luke 9:1; 10:19); to edify the church (2 Cor. 10:8; 13:10); to receive special blessings associated with certain ministries (1 Cor. 9:4–18; 2 Thess. 3:8–9); to govern nations and to eat of the Tree of Life in the future kingdom (Rev. 2:26; 22:14).

Yet astonishingly, the Bible never teaches that God has given believers authority (*exousia*) over other believers. Recall our Lord's words in Matthew 20:25–26 and Luke 22:25–26 where He condemned *exousia*-type authority among His followers. This fact alone should give us pause for serious reflection.

Therefore, it's a leap in logic and an overextrapolation of reason to suggest that church leaders wield the same kind of authority as dignitaries. Again, the New Testament never links *exousia* with church leaders. Nor does it ever suggest that some Christians have *exousia* over other Christians.

To be sure, the Old Testament portrays prophets, priests, kings, and judges as official authorities. This is because these "offices" stood as shadows of the authoritative ministries of Jesus Christ Himself. Christ is the real Prophet, the real Priest, the real King, and the real Judge. But never do we find any church leader described or depicted as an official authority in the New Testament. This includes local overseers as well as apostolic workers.

To be blunt, the notion that Christians have authority over other Christians is an example of forced exegesis. As such, it's biblically indefensible. When church leaders wield the same type of authority that governmental officials do, they become usurpers.

Admittedly, authority does function in the church. But the authority that works in the *ekklesia* is drastically different from the authority that works in the natural order. This only makes sense because the church is not a human organization, but a spiritual organism. The authority that operates in the church is not *official* authority. It's *organic* authority.

Official Authority vs. Organic Authority

What is organic authority? It's authority that's rooted in spiritual life. Organic authority is *communicated* authority. That is, when a person communicates God's life through word or deed he or she has the support and backing of the Lord Himself.

By virtue of the fact that they have the life of the Spirit, all Christians are capable of communicating organic authority. This is why the New Testament enjoins us to subject ourselves one to another out of reverence for Christ (Eph. 5:21). But those who are more seasoned in spiritual life tend to express God's will more consistently than the carnal and the immature (Heb. 5:14).

Organic authority finds its source in Christ's *immediate* direction rather than in a static office. Organic authority is not intrinsic to a person or a position. It doesn't reside in humans or in an office they may hold (as is the case with official authority).

Instead, organic authority operates outside of the individual. This is because it belongs to Christ. Only when Christ directs a person to word or action does that person exercise authority. Put another way, a person has the right to be heard and obeyed only when he or she reflects the Lord's mind. Organic authority, therefore, is communicative.

The communicative nature of organic authority can be understood within the framework of the body metaphor that Paul draws for the church. When the Head (who is the source of all authority) signals the hand to move, the hand possesses the authority of the Head. The hand, however, has no authority in itself. It derives authority only when it acts in accordance with the communication of the Head. Insofar as the hand represents the will of the Head, to that degree the hand is an authority.

Note that the movement of the physical head in relation to the physical body is organic. It's based on the fact that a human being is a living organism. The same principle holds true for the spiritual Head and the spiritual body. Christians only exercise spiritual authority when they are representing Christ in their words and deeds.

Organic authority, therefore, is flexible and fluid. It's not static. Organic authority is transmitted, not innovative. Therefore, it's not an irrevocable possession.[2] Organic authority is also evaluated and affirmed by the body.

Because organic authority is not officiated but derived, believers don't assume, inherit, confer, or substitute for God's authority. They merely represent it. This is a blunt distinction. Failure to understand it has led to untold confusion and abuse among God's people.

When discussing spiritual authority, the emphasis ought always to be on *function* and *service* rather than on a mystical notion of "spirituality." Claiming authority on the basis of one's spirituality is practically the same as making oneself an official authority. For the *claim* to "spirituality" (in contrast with actual spirituality) can easily constitute a veiled office.

If one is truly spiritual, his or her spirituality will be manifested in how he or she lives and serves. Spirituality can only be discerned by the latter and not by the touted claims of the person who assumes it. In this way, keeping the focus on service and function helps protect organic churches from devolving into personality cults.

A Helpful Comparison

Let's isolate some of the differences between official authority and organic authority.

1. Official authorities must be obeyed as long as what they declare does not violate the will of a higher authority (Acts 5:29; 1 Tim. 3:1). By contrast, those exercising organic authority never demand obedience to themselves. They rather seek to *persuade* others to obey God's will. Paul's letters are wonderful examples of this principle. They resonate with

appeals and pleas rather than commands. They're littered with the language of persuasion. (More on this later.)

2. Official authorities bear full responsibility when they lead those under them into wrong practices. In Numbers 18, we learn that the burden of iniquity fell upon the shoulders of the priests—the official authorities in Israel.

By contrast, organic authority never nullifies the responsibility of others. In the church, believers bear full responsibility for their actions—even when they choose to obey the counsel of others.

It is for this reason that Scripture gives multiple injunctions to test the fruit of others. It equally teaches that deception brings divine judgment (Matt. 7:15–27; 16:11–12; 24:4–5; 1 Cor. 14:29; Gal. 1:6–9; 2:4; Phil. 3:2–19; 1 Thess. 5:21; 1 Tim. 2:14; 1 John 3:4–10; 4:1–6). The New Testament never teaches that if a Christian obeys another person he is no longer responsible for his actions.

3. Official authorities may be less mature, less spiritual, and less righteous than those they have authority over. Organic authority, however, is directly linked to spiritual life. It cannot be separated from it.

We often tell our children "obey your elders" because those who are older (in natural life) tend to be more mature in their counsel. Thus they deserve our respect and subjection (1 Peter 5:5a). The same principle applies in the spiritual realm.

Those who have grown further in spiritual life bear a greater measure of organic authority. (Note that a person cannot exercise spiritual authority unless he or she is under God's authority.) A sure sign of greater spiritual maturity is a spirit of servanthood and childlike meekness. Consider the following texts that exhort us to esteem those who display both characteristics:

Now I urge you, brethren (you know the household of Stephanas, that they were the first fruits of Achaia, and that they have devoted themselves for ministry to the saints), that you also be in subjection to such men and to everyone who helps in the work and labors. I rejoice over the coming of Stephanas and Fortunatus and Achaicus, because they have supplied what was lacking on your part. For they have refreshed my spirit and yours. Therefore acknowledge such men. (1 Cor. 16:15–18 NASB)

Receive him [Epaphroditus] then in the Lord with all joy, and hold men like him in high regard; because he came close to death for the work of Christ, risking his life. (Phil. 2:29–30a NASB)

And we ask you, brethren, to know those labouring among you, and leading you in the Lord, and admonishing you, and to esteem them very abundantly in love, because of their work. (1 Thess. 5:12–13 YLT)

Let the elders who take the lead [among the saints] well be esteemed worthy of double honour, specially those labouring in word and teaching. (1 Tim. 5:17 DARBY)

Remember those who led you, who spoke the word of God to you; and considering the result of their conduct, imitate their faith. (Heb. 13:7 NASB)

Be obedient to [Greek: persuaded by] those leading you, and be subject, for these do watch for your souls, as about to give account, that with joy they may do this, and not sighing, for this [is] unprofitable to you. (Heb. 13:17 YLT)

You younger men, likewise, be subject to your elders. (1 Peter 5:5 NASB)

Clearly, the New Testament exhorts Christians to give weight to those who tirelessly labor in spiritual service. Such esteem is both spontaneous and instinctive. It should never be absolutized or formalized.

The honor that a believer receives from the church is always earned by humble service. It's never demanded or asserted. Those who are truly spiritual don't claim to have spiritual authority over others. Nor do they boast about their spiritual labor and maturity. In fact, people who make such claims reveal their *immaturity*. The person who declares that he is "God's anointed man of strength and power for the hour"—or similar self-accolades—simply proves one thing: *He has no authority.*

Contrarily, those who receive esteem in the church have *proven* themselves to be trustworthy servants. Not in mere words, but in experience (2 Cor. 8:22; 1 Thess. 1:5; 2 Thess. 3:10). Earned recognition and trust from the body is the only valid benchmark for one's spiritual authority.

4. Official authorities possess their authority for as long as they hold office. And their authority works regardless of whether they make unwise or unrighteous decisions. For example, as long as King Saul sat on Israel's throne, he retained his authority. This was true even after the Spirit of God departed from him (1 Sam. 16:14; 24:4–6).

On the other hand, organic authority operates only when Christ is being expressed. So if a believer exhorts the church to do something that doesn't reflect the will of the Head (even if it may not violate a prescribed mandate of God), there's no authority to back his exhortation. Again, only Jesus Christ has authority. And only that which flows from His life carries authority.

5. Official authorities virtually always function in a hierarchy. Organic authority is never related to hierarchy (Matt. 20:25–28; Luke 22:25–27). In fact, organic authority is always distorted and abused when allied with hierarchy. For this reason, hierarchical imagery is absent from the New Testament Epistles.

In short, organic authority doesn't flow from the top down. Nor does it function in a chain-of-command, hierarchical mode. Equally so, organic authority doesn't work from the bottom up. That is, it doesn't flow from the church to the person. For even if a church decides to give someone authority for a specific task, it lacks authority if it doesn't reflect the mind of Christ.

Organic authority works from the inside out. When the indwelling Christ leads a believer or a church to speak or act, the authority of the Head backs him or her. Jesus Christ, as represented by the indwelling Spirit, is the exclusive wellspring, mainstay, and source of all authority. And there is no covering over His Head.

The upshot is that leadership problems in the institutional church stem from an obscenely simplistic application of official authority structures to Christian relationships. This faulty application is rooted in a one-size-fits-all mentality of authority. Indeed, it's a profound mistake to transplant the official authority template into the church of the living God.

Organic Authority Is Always Framed in Love

Whenever a Christian is exercising organic authority in the church, we do well to recognize it. To rebel against such authority is to rebel against Christ. Why? Because the only authority that exists is Christ. And when He is speaking through the church, genuine authority is at work.

Scripture plainly says that "God is love" (1 John 4:8, 16). For that reason, when God's authority is being expressed, love is present. To put it another way, the exercise of divine authority is always framed in love. Let me try to unravel that sentence.

Love is willing to admonish others when they falter. It rejects freelancing, do-it-yourself, lone-ranger spirituality. Instead, it values the interdependence of the body.

Love realizes that because we are members one of another and have the same ancestry, our actions have a profound effect on our fellow brethren. Love deplores individualistic, privatized Christianity. Instead, it affirms its need for the other members of the church.

Love is sometimes sweet, kind, and nice. But when it faces the horrors of unrepentant sin, it can be combative and unbending. Love is patient, respectful, and gentle. It's never strident, demeaning, or dictatorial. Love repudiates pompous and inflated claims to authority. Instead, it's stamped with humility and meekness.

Love isn't flabby or sentimental, but keenly perceptive and discerning. It never manipulates or imposes its own will. It never threatens, forces, demands, or coerces.

Love propels us to accept responsibility in being our "brother's keeper." But it forbids us from becoming intrusive meddlers into his life. Love never usurps the place of God nor judges the motives of others' hearts. Nor does it think the worst of them.

Love recognizes that we are called to *represent* the Holy Spirit's will to one another, not to *substitute* for His person or *replace* His work.

Consequently, organic authority isn't a license to probe into the intimate affairs of our fellow brethren to "make sure" they're walking aright. The Bible never gives us liberty to quiz our spiritual siblings about their financial investments, how they make love to their spouses, or other areas of privacy.

This kind of unnecessary probing—exercised under the guise of "accountability"—is the stuff that authoritarian cults are made of. Such thinking will ultimately turn any believing community into a psychological pressure cooker. (Of course, if a believer *willingly* desires to confide in another person about such personal matters, that's a different story. But that's a choice, not a duty.)

We should never lose sight of the fact that the Bible puts a high premium on individual Christian liberty, freedom, and privacy (Rom. 14:1–12; Gal. 5:1; Col. 2:16; James 4:11–12). So respect for these virtues should be high among believers. Unless there's good reason to suspect that a brother or sister is living in gross sin, it's profoundly unchristian to poke and pry into their personal and domestic affairs.

The New Testament warns us against being "busybodies" in other people's matters, "speaking things which [we] ought not" (1 Tim. 5:13 KJV; 1 Peter 4:15). By the same token, if a Christian is in serious straits spiritually—struggling with grave sin—love demands that he or she both seek and welcome help from others.

In sum, because divine authority is always couched in love, it engenders a culture of spiritual safety and security. Subjection to God's authority isn't control. It's aid. It's never static or frozen into a formal system. It's not official, legal, or mechanical. Instead, it's relational and organic.

Danger looms whenever God's authority is transformed into a human institution—no matter what name it flies under. As Christians, we have a spiritual instinct to subject ourselves to spiritual authority. And the church always benefits when we do so.

Whenever we welcome others to speak into our lives, we wedge the door open for the Lord to encourage, motivate, and protect us. It's for this reason that Proverbs repeatedly stresses that "in the *multitude* of counselors there is safety" (Prov. 11:14 NKJV; 15:22; 24:6). Love, then, is the divine umbrella that affords spiritual protection. Yet thankfully, it's not as narrow as the hearts of some who live under its reach. In the final analysis, only love has "covering" power. For "love covers over a multitude of sins" (1 Peter 4:8; Prov. 10:12; 17:9).

The Cost of Mutual Subjection

Mutual subjection is radically different from unilateral subordination to authoritarian structures. At the same time, it should never be confused with the highly individualistic, morally relative, tolerant anarchism that marks postmodern thinking.

Mutual subjection is costly. Let's face it. Our egos don't like being subject to anyone. As fallen creatures, we want to do what is right in *our own* eyes—without the interference of others (Prov. 12:15).

So the inclination to reject organic authority is deeply rooted in our Adamic nature (Rom. 3:10–18). Receiving correction, admonition, and reproof from other mortals constitutes a big cross to bear (Prov. 15:10; 17:10; 27:5–6; 28:23). It is for this reason that mutual subjection serves as an antidote to our rebellious flesh as well as to our lawless culture.

Exercising spiritual authority is equally painful. Unless one is a control freak, the task of reproving others is both difficult and risky. Scripture tells us that a brother who is offended is harder to be won than a walled city (Prov. 18:19). Hence, the awkwardness of correcting others, coupled with the fear of confrontation, makes obeying the Lord in areas of expressing His authority hard on our flesh. (This awkwardness merely highlights the importance of cultivating loving, accepting relationships within the assembly.)

It's far easier just to let things go. It's far simpler just to pray for our erring brethren and leave it at that. It's far harder to confront them lovingly with patience, humility, and compassion. (Again the exception to this is the self-righteous control freak. Such a person seems to relish correcting others.)

All of this simply underscores the arresting fact that love is to govern our relationships with others. For if we love the brethren, we will subject ourselves to their counsel and admonition.

Likewise, love will compel us to approach our failing brethren in a spirit of meekness whenever they need our help (Gal 6:1; James 5:19–20). And we will refrain from imputing evil motives to their hearts (Matt. 7:1–4; 1 Cor. 13:5). At bottom, the way of love is always the way of self-denial.

Mutual Subjection Is Rooted in the Triune God

Let's return our discussion of mutual subjection to the archetype of the church: the Godhead. Because mutual subjection is based in love, it's rooted in the very nature of the triune God. God, by nature, is Community. The one God is made up of a Community of three persons who eternally share Their lives with one another.

Within the Godhead, the Father pours Himself into the Son. In turn, the Son gives Himself unreservedly to the Father. And the Spirit, as the Holy Mediator, pours Their love from each to each. Within this divine dance of love, there exists no hierarchy. There exists no control. There exists no authoritarianism. There exists no conflict of interests. Instead, there's mutual love, mutual fellowship, and mutual subjection.

The mutual sharing that perpetually flows within the Godhead is the cornerstone of love. In fact, it's the very reason that John could say, "God is love" (1 John 4:8). For if God were not Community, there could have been no one for Him to love before creation. The act of loving requires the presence of two or more persons.

The church is the community of the King. As such, it's called to mirror the reciprocal love relationship that eternally flows within the triune God. Thus within the fellowship of the church, there is mutual subjection governed by mutual love. There is no hierarchy, no control, and no authoritarianism. Why? Because the church is called to live by divine life—the same life that exists within the Godhead (John 6:57; 17:20–26; 2 Peter 1:4).

Within the family environment of the church, mutual subjection creates unity. It builds love, provides stability, and fosters growth. It gives rich meaning to Christian living. The Christian life was never meant to be lived outside of a face-to-face community. The *ekklesia*—the community of the King—is our natural habitat.

In this regard, mutual subjection is an antiseptic against hard-line Nicolaitanism (clericalism). It emphasizes power *for* and power *among* rather than power *over*. It encourages the empowerment of all rather than the power of a few.

While our culture encourages self-reliance, individualism, and independence, these things are incompatible with the ecology of organic Christianity. Because God is Community, His children are designed for community. Our new nature calls out for it.

We Christians are not isolated beings. Like the triune God who we were created after, our species is communal (Eph. 4:24; Col. 3:10). We thrive on meaningful relationships with others of the same kind. The modern "covering" doctrine obscures this unearthing insight. But the principle of mutual subjection brings it into sharp relief.

Stated simply, the Trinitarian nature of God serves as both the source and the model for all human community. And it is within the love relationship of the Godhead that the principle of mutual subjection finds its true value. As Miroslav Volf says, "The more a church is characterized by symmetrical and decentralized distribution of power and freely affirmed interaction, the more it will correspond to the trinitarian communion."[3]

Mutual subjection, therefore, isn't a human concept. It instead stems from the communal and reciprocal nature of the eternal God. And it is that very nature that the *ekklesia* is called to bear. In this way, mutual subjection enables us to behold the face of Christ in the very fabric and texture of organic church life.

To borrow language from John Howard Yoder, the authority and submission that Scripture envisions "gives more authority to the church than does Rome, trusts more to the Holy Spirit than does Pentecostalism, has more respect for the individual than Humanism, makes moral standards more binding than Puritanism, and is more open to the given situation than 'The New Morality.'"[4]

In sum, mutual subjection creates a culture that appreciates spiritual leadership without absolutizing it. It responds to spiritual authority without turning it into an instrument of control. For when "mentoring relationships," "accountability partnerships," and "spiritual direction" are governed by mutual subjection, they become spiritually healthy and mutually enriching. They also bear no resemblance to the modern practice of hierarchical "covering."

Perhaps a closing metaphor will help sum up all that I've said in this chapter. We can compare mutual subjection to good music. When it functions in the context of intelligent humility and deep faithfulness to the headship of Christ, it makes a beautiful melody that resonates with the sweet harmony of the New Testament song. But when it is replaced by hierarchical systems that characterize the spirit of the Gentiles, its sound is distorted. Still worse, when it's rejected in favor of the postmodern sins of wholesale individualism and independence, its timbre and key cease altogether, and the dead chill of silence stands in its wake.

Questions That Must Be Faced

- Where do you think your current thinking on "covering" and "accountability" originates? Explain.
- Do you have any stories of damage by people who uttered "no covering" platitudes and thoughtlessly waved their hands at buzz words like "accountability"? Explain.
- Are we not obligated by Scripture to cease from applying the concept of official authority in the church and instead return to the New Testament concept of mutual subjection to organic authority? Explain.
- This chapter points out that the New Testament does not support the idea that some Christians have authority over other Christians. How do you feel about this? Explain.

CHAPTER 13
REIMAGINING DENOMINATIONAL COVERING

What life have you if you have not life together? There is no life that is not in community, and no community not lived in praise of God. —T. S. Eliot

You are still worldly. For since there is jealousy and quarreling among you, are you not worldly? Are you not acting like mere men? For when one says, "I follow Paul," and another, "I follow Apollos," are you not mere men? What, after all, is Apollos? And what is Paul? Only servants, through whom you came to believe—as the Lord has assigned to each his task. —Paul of Tarsus in 1 Corinthians 3:3–5

Many Christians believe that denominations protect us from error. But this is an illusion.

"Denominational covering" is built on the superstitious idea that if I belong to a Christian denomination, I'm somehow magically "covered" and "protected" from error. But this idea is a charade. Countless Christians who have belonged to a denomination have gone off the beam theologically and morally.

Consequently, the notion that people are "covered" by tracing their accountability to a top-down organization is pure fiction.

The only protection from error is in submitting ourselves to the Spirit of truth and the Word of God in the context of the body of Christ (1 John 2:20, 27). God's idea of accountability works from community to person. Not from *parson* to person. Spiritual protection comes from relatedness to the Holy Spirit and spiritual connectedness with other Christians. Therein lies the genius of Christian community. By contrast, the complicated, legalized, over-under system of denominational accountability is a man-made substitute for mutual subjection.

The Tyranny of the Status Quo

If you doubt that the denominational system is built on top-down control, try questioning it. If you do, it's quite likely that you will hear the rhetoric engines kick in.

The frightening truth is that, all too often, those who raise questions about ecclesiastical authority send tremors through the ecclesiastical system. And they are often vilified as a result.

If you are a dissenter who leaves the institutional church because you believe it to be unscriptural, you might be branded a "heretic," a "boat-rocker," a "troublemaker," a "loose cannon," or an "unsubmissive rebel." Such invocation of religious rhetoric is designed to stifle thought. It's calculated to derail honest dissent with the partisan status quo.

Sometimes the religious machinery will concoct the most vicious and hurtful rumors on those who dissent. I have a good friend who used to be a pastor. He was part of the local pastors association in his hometown. After having a crisis of conscience regarding the biblical legitimacy of the modern pastoral office and the denominational system, he gave up being a pastor and left the institutional church for good.

Not long after, his fellow pastor friends in town began to spread vile rumors about him and his family. To their minds, a man couldn't leave the pastorate without being embroiled in some sort of scandal that forced him to leave. So they made one up out of thin air.

None of the rumors were true. But my friend tasted firsthand the tremendous power of the religious system. More importantly, he learned to suffer with his Lord "outside the camp, bearing His reproach" (Heb. 13:13 NASB). Such is the price that many have paid for leaving the religious system.[1]

Interestingly, advocates of the denominational system argue that denominations are a safeguard from the cults. But here's the irony: The concept of "denominational covering" is very much like the skewed, master/slave notion of leadership that marks most modern cults. Let me explain.

In the denominations, members unreservedly follow a single leader, a board of "lay-leaders," or an organization. By contrast, the biblical principle of mutual subjection emphasizes submission to *one another* as opposed to unquestioned obedience to a human leader or hierarchical organization.

To put an even finer point on it, the "covering" teaching is often used as a bludgeon to dismiss those Christians who don't meet under a denominational flag. "Covering" has too often become a weapon in the hands of partisan religious groups to secure the theological terrain. And that weapon has often been fueled by sectarian bigotry.

Autonomous yet Related

Every church born within the first seventeen years of Pentecost was spawned from the Jerusalem church. But these new churches had nei-

ther a formal nor a subservient relationship to the church in Jerusalem.
In this regard, the New Testament *always* envisions autonomous (independent), but fraternally related, churches. The early churches made
their decisions apart from external control. It is for this reason that Paul
admonishes the assemblies he worked with to take charge of their own
internal problems.

In God's thought, every church is one in life with all other churches.
But every church is independent, self-governing, and responsible to
God alone for its decision-making. Hence, the concept of a governing
"mother church," or denominational headquarters, is based on a wooden
interpretation of Scripture.

Scriptural principle affirms that each church is independent in its
decision-making and oversight. (Consider our Lord's words to the seven
churches of Asia. He dealt with each assembly according to its unique
problems—Rev. 1, 2, 3.)

This principle is also underscored in Paul's letters. Paul consistently
treats each church as an autonomous, self-governing organism. To Paul's
mind, each church is directly responsible and accountable to God (Eph.
5:24; Col. 1:9–10).

It's a gross mistake, therefore, to spin local churches together with
the thread of religious federationism. Every church stands under the
same Head. They are all one in life. Consequently, churches should
cooperate with, learn from, and help one another just as they did in
the first century (Acts 11:28–30; Rom. 15:25–29; 16:1; 1 Cor. 16:19;
2 Cor. 8:1–14; 13:13; 1 Thess. 2:14; Phil. 4:22). At the same time,
each church should embrace the tradition that the apostles established
for "every church" (1 Cor. 4:16–17; 7:17; 11:16; 14:33; 16:1; 1 Thess.
2:14).

According to divine principle, each church should develop its own oversight, ministry, and unique testimony. On the other hand, there should be spiritual relatedness and mutual helpfulness among the churches.

In short, there's no evidence in Scripture that a church has the right to regulate, control, or intrude upon the affairs, teachings, or practices of another assembly. The denominational system betrays this principle.

The Church Council of Acts 15

As a counterargument, some have sought to tease out of Acts 15 a biblical precedent for a governing "mother church." But a careful analysis of this text shows that this is an unwarranted application. On the surface, it could appear that Paul and Barnabas went to the Jerusalem church because it had unilateral authority over every other church. However, this notion falls apart when the chapter is read in context.

Here's the story. Some from the Jerusalem church introduced a false teaching to the church in Antioch. Paul and Barnabas were prompted to pay Jerusalem a visit to settle the matter. Why? *Because the teaching had originated from Jerusalem* (Acts 15:1–2, 24).

If the false teaching had come out of the Antioch church, Paul and Barnabas would have dealt with it locally. But because the doctrine came from the Jerusalem church, the two men went to Jerusalem to determine who introduced the false teaching. They also wanted to make sure that the Jerusalem elders and the twelve apostles didn't affirm it.

Upon their arrival, those in the Jerusalem church who taught the doctrine were identified (15:4–5). This led to a temporary church council, and the church repudiated the doctrine publicly (vv. 6ff.).

The decision reached by the council, which included the approval of the twelve apostles, the elders, and the whole church, was circulated among the Gentile churches. This was done in the event that other churches would someday face the same troubling issue. The church's decision carried God's authority because the Holy Spirit inspired it (15:28) and the church affirmed it (vv. 23, 28, 31).

To read anything else into this story reflects a failure to take seriously the historical specifics behind the account. It's an example of reading one's own biases into the text rather than reading meaning and direction out of it. Consequently, the idea of an authoritative "mother church" lacks scriptural merit.

To be sure, the Jerusalem church was loved, appreciated, and helped by other churches (Rom. 15:26–27; 2 Cor. 9:11–13). But there's nothing in the New Testament that would lead us to believe that it possessed supreme authority, or that all other churches were subservient to it. Rather, each church was autonomous and directly responsible to God. None were subordinate to any other.

Denominationalism Is Self-Defeating

Another problem with the denominational system is that it frequently crushes that which it claims to protect. It effectively *breaks* up that which it alleges to *build* up. Like the misguided sectarian zeal that drove ancient Roman Catholicism, Protestant denominationalism has too often descended into a human institution that cracks the whip of despotism before its dissenters. It adeptly defends the party line. And it damns others for alleged doctrinal trespasses.

It is for this reason that Paul thunders against the Corinthian Christians when they denominated themselves into separate camps (1 Cor.

1:11–13; 3:3–4). That God's family today be pressed into the partisan straitjacket of denominationalism is biblically unjustifiable. But today, it's part of the Christian subculture, and few people wince at it.

(Incidentally, many so-called nondenominational, interdenominational, and postdenominational churches are just as hierarchical as mainline denominations. The same is true for many modern Christian "movements." These also belong to the denominational *system*.)

More striking, the denominational system actually helps perpetuate heresy—the very thing it claims to curb. Think about it. If the autonomous nature of every church were preserved, the spreading of error would be strongly localized. But when a denominational headquarters is infected with a false teaching, every church connected with it embraces the same falsehood. Thus the heresy becomes widespread.

When every church is autonomous, it's difficult for an ambitious false teacher to emerge and seize control over a cluster of churches. It's also virtually impossible for a "pope-like figure" to emerge. Not so in a denomination. All related churches stand or fall together.

It can also be argued quite soundly that to form a denomination is to commit heresy. Denominations are formed when some Christians split off from the larger body of Christ to follow their favorite doctrines or practices and create a movement with them.

The sin of heresy [Greek: *hairesis*] is the act of choosing to follow one's own tenets. So a person can be a heretic with the truth if he uses it to fracture the body of Christ. A person can be technically "orthodox" and yet be a "heretic" by using an orthodox belief to divide Christians from one another.

While the typical institutional church makes its boast about being "covered" by a denomination, it actually affords less face-to-face accountability than organic churches. In the average evangelical church, for example, the pastor is said to "cover" the congregation. But in most churches of this ilk, the bulk of the congregation barely knows the pastor (let alone one another). It's not uncommon for "churchgoers" to say less than three sentences to each other during a typical Sunday-morning service. By contrast, in an organic church, all the brethren know one another intimately. This includes the extralocal workers who help the church (1 Thess. 5:12a).

All in all, "denominational covering" is artificial. It turns the church of Jesus Christ into a hierarchical society. And it maps poorly to scriptural example.

In a word, the denominational system has fragmented the one body of Christ by religious partisanship. It has alienated the family of God into separate tribes. It has disintegrated the fabric of our spiritual brotherhood and sisterhood into an endless morass of religious parties. It has fractured the fellowship of God's people. It has slashed the body of Christ into pieces. It has carved the church into splintered fragments. It has spawned thousands of warring clans out of the one family of Christ. (Shockingly, there are more than thirty-three thousand Christian denominations on the planet today.)[2] In a word, the contemporary denominational morass has polluted the Christian landscape.

Advocates of denominationalism believe that this system is helpful. To them, the different denominations represent the different parts of the body of Christ. But the denominational system is foreign to New Testament principle. It's incompatible with Christian oneness. It's based on human divisions that are biblically unjustifiable (1 Cor. 1, 2, 3). It stems from a fractured vision of the body of Christ. And it runs contrary to the unified diversity of the triune God.

A Word About Christian Orthodoxy

Clearly, the mere employment of institutional church structures like the pastor system of Protestantism, the bishop system of Anglicanism, the priestly system of Roman Catholicism, and the denominational system of Christendom can never safeguard the Lord's people from doctrinal error. Barring the raft of independent churches that have gone off the rails of Christian orthodoxy, many clergy-led denominations have followed in the same path.[3]

Historic Christian teaching on the essential doctrines of the faith plays a crucial role in keeping a church on scriptural track. Throughout the centuries, Christians have preserved the core beliefs of our faith: Jesus Christ is God and man, He was born of a virgin, He was crucified for our sins, He rose again in bodily form, etc.

These core beliefs do not belong to any one ecclesiastical tradition or denomination. Instead, they are the heritage of all genuine believers. And they reflect the voice of the church throughout history.

These "essentials of the faith" embody what C. S. Lewis called *Mere Christianity*—"the belief that has been common to nearly all Christians at all times."[4] Thus the call to recover the ecology of the New Testament church doesn't translate into a summons to reinvent the religious wheel on every theological issue. Nor does it include a rejection of all that has been passed down to us by our spiritual forefathers. At the same time, everything that is postapostolic is subject to scrutiny and should be critiqued by the apostolic tradition itself.

The call to restore organic Christianity sides with every voice of the past that has remained true to apostolic revelation—no matter what segment of the historic church to which they may have belonged. The primitive church was rooted in the soil of Christian truth. And staying within that soil requires that we stand on the shoulders of those who have gone before us. As C. H. Spurgeon affirmed, "I intend to grasp tightly with one hand the truths I have already learned, and to keep the other hand wide open to take in the things I do not yet know."

By What Authority?

When the Lord Jesus was on earth, the religious leaders of His day pressed the vexing question: "By what authority are You doing these things and who gave You this authority?" (Matt. 21:23 NKJV).

Ironically, not a few in today's religious establishment are raising the same questions to those simple communities that are gathering around Jesus Christ alone—without clerical control or denominational partisanship. "Who is your covering?" is essentially the same question as "By what authority do you do these things?"

At bottom, the modern notion of ecclesiastical "covering" is a thinly veiled euphemism for control. For this reason it doesn't map well with God's idea of mutual subjection. And it represents a wholesale departure from the New Testament concept of authority.

While some Christians carry on rather loudly about it, the notion of "covering" would be repudiated by all first-century Christians. To be sure, ideological divisions, doctrinal heresies, anarchic independence, and individualistic subjectivism are severe problems that plague the body of Christ today. But denominational/clerical "covering" is bad medicine for purging these ills.

The "covering" teaching is really a symptom of the same problem masquerading as a solution. As such, it compounds the problems of rugged individualism and independence by blurring the distinction between official and organic authority. It also creates a false sense of security among believers. At the same time, it introduces further divisions in the body of Christ.

Just as serious, the "covering" teaching inoculates the believing priesthood from carrying out its God-ordained responsibility to function in spiritual matters. Intentional or not, the "covering" doctrine strikes fear into the hearts of multitudes of Christians. It asserts that if believers take responsibility in spiritual things without the approval of an "ordained" clergyman or denomination, they will be raw meat for the Enemy.

(On this score, many clergy chew up a great deal of Christian airtime touting how necessary they are to our spiritual well-being. They assert that they are essential for providing direction and stability in the church. It's the old "without-a-vision-the-people-perish" sermon. But it's routinely the clergyman's isolated vision that we are hopelessly perishing without.)

In this way, the covering teaching contains an implicit threat that the "uncovered" are to blame for all the horrible things that will happen to them. As such, few things so paralyze the ministry of the body than does the doctrine of "covering."

To put it succinctly, if we try to finesse the ills of the church by employing a technique of "covering," we'll end up with an illness that's worse than the maladies it's intended to cure. Stated simply, the "covering" teaching brings with it very specific tones, textures, and resonances that have little to do with Jesus, Paul, or any other apostle. While it avows to scratch a peculiarly modern itch, it's alien to God's chosen method for displaying His authority.

It is my judgment that the spiritual antidote for the ills of heresy, independence, and individualism is not "covering." It's mutual subjection to the Spirit of God, mutual subjection to the Word of God as understood in Christian community, and mutual subjection to one another out of reverence for Christ. Nothing short of this can protect the body of Christ. And nothing less can heal its open wounds.

Questions That Must Be Faced

- If the early church didn't create denominations, and Paul rebuked the Corinthians for denominating themselves, why do we unthinkingly accept them today? Explain.
- What spiritual risks might we run by acting condemnatory and smug toward those churches and ministries that have chosen not to wed themselves to a denomination or a religious institution? Explain.
- If we took our cue for relationships in the church from the Community of the Godhead instead of the denominational system or the clergy system, what might happen? Explain.

CHAPTER 14
REIMAGINING THE APOSTOLIC TRADITION

There can be no doubt that every one of the great churches of the Reformation has developed its own masterful tradition, and that tradition today exercises massive influence not only over its way of interpreting the Bible and formulating its doctrine, but over the whole shape and direction of its life. Those who shut their eyes to this fact are precisely those who are most enslaved to the dominant power of tradition just because it has become an unconscious canon and norm of their thinking. It is high time we asked again whether the Word of God really does have free course among us and whether it is not after all bound and fettered by the traditions of men. The tragedy, apparently, is that the very structures of our churches represent the fossilization of traditions that have grown up by practice and procedure, and they have become so hardened in self-justification that even the Word of God can hardly crack them open.

—Thomas F. Torrance

Tradition is the living faith of the dead, and traditionalism is the dead faith of the living.
—Jaroslav Pelican

Virtually every segment of the body of Christ operates on the basis of some historical tradition handed down to them by their spiritual forefathers. For some denominations, these traditions comprise the very fabric that holds their members together. They define the church's purpose through statements of faith, confessions, creeds, and canons.

In response to this tendency, many neodenominations hold anything that smacks of the word "tradition" to be anathema. And they have distanced themselves from any practice remotely routine or binding. (Interestingly, most churches that claim to be free from the influence of tradition have merely created their own.)

The irony of these two tendencies lies here. Much attention has been given to the calcified, ecclesiastical traditions of men. But very little has been given to the divine tradition passed on by the apostles of Jesus Christ.

Consider the following passages that allude to this tradition:

Therefore I urge you to imitate me.… my way of life in Christ Jesus, which agrees with what I teach everywhere in every church. (1 Cor. 4:16–17)

I praise you because you remember me in everything and hold firmly to the traditions, just as I delivered them to you. (1 Cor.11:2 NASB)

But if one is inclined to be contentious, we have no other practice, nor have the churches of God. (1 Cor. 11:16 NASB)

So then, brethren, stand firm and hold to the traditions which you were taught, whether by word of mouth or by letter from us. (2 Thess. 2:15 NASB)

Now we command you, brethren, in the name of our Lord Jesus Christ, that you keep away from every brother who leads an unruly life and not according to the tradition which you received from us. (2 Thess. 3:6 NASB)

What the Apostolic Tradition Is Not

The tradition of the apostles is not a codified set of prescribed rules that the apostles created. Neither is it a detailed manual for church practice. (The truth is, no such manual exists.)

As stated in chapter 1, some hold to the concept of "biblical blueprintism." According to this paradigm, the New Testament is a detailed manual for church practice. We simply need to study the practices of the early church, imitate them, and presto, we'll have a "New Testament church."

But this viewpoint is flawed on two counts. First, it turns the New Testament into a modern replica of ancient Judaic Law. Second, those who hold to the biblical blueprint model disagree with one another as to which practices ought to be followed to create a "New Testament church."

Some, for example, focus on speaking in tongues, signs, wonders, and healings. They assert that if a church practices these things, that makes it an authentic "New Testament church." Others focus on taking the Lord's Supper as a meal. Others focus on having a plurality of elders. Others focus on baptizing new converts in the name of Jesus. Others focus on meeting in houses. The list is endless.

Point: Technical correctness and outward conformity to a prescribed form of church order has never been God's desire. Such cold formalism will only yield death. It will also smother the organic life of the body of Christ. As John W. Kennedy once said, "The church of Jesus Christ is a living body, not a corpse. The imposition of a pattern has never yet made a church. It can never be too strongly or too often emphasized that the imposition of a pattern, or simply the gathering of people together, does not bring the church into being. A church cannot be organized, it has to be born."[1]

For this reason, the New Testament doesn't supply us with a detailed blueprint for church practice. It's a gross mistake, therefore, to try to tease out of the apostolic letters an inflexible code of church order that's as unalterable as the law of the Medes and Persians. Such a written code belongs to the other side of the cross.

This, of course, doesn't mean that the New Testament is silent when it comes to church practice. It certainly isn't. But the New Testament isn't a manual for church practice. It's rather a record of how the living, breathing organism called the *ekklesia* expresses herself on the earth.

Understanding that the church is organic safeguards us from turning the New Testament into a method or a technique. It also enables us to see that the church is bound up with something far higher than a *pro forma* adherence to a prescribed pattern.

Be assured: The Spirit of God will never lead us into a dead orthodoxy based on the imitation of external forms. Instead, the Spirit always works according to the DNA that exists within the triune God—for the church possesses that very DNA.

To put it another way, God is a living person. As such, He has certain habits and tendencies that are innate to His divine nature. The apostolic tradition is simply the physical expression of those habits and tendencies.

Recovering the Place of Tradition

The New Testament word for tradition is the Greek word *paradosis*. It means "that which is handed down."

What, then, is the apostolic tradition? First, it contains the stories and teachings of Jesus. These are contained in the Gospels. Second, it includes the commands and practices of the apostles that were passed on to all the churches (1 Cor. 11:23ff.; 15:1–3; 2 Peter 3:1–2).

The apostolic tradition, therefore, represents the normative beliefs and practices of the church of Jesus Christ. Beliefs and practices that were *prescribed* for each and every church (1 Cor. 4:16–17; 11:16; 14:33–38).[2]

Put another way, the apostolic tradition is the embodiment of those organic practices that the apostles modeled in every church during the first century. It is these practices that constitute the new wineskin that God has fashioned to preserve His new wine. In referring to the apostolic tradition, F. F. Bruce says, "Paul indeed seems to have attached some importance to preserving a certain measure of uniform practice throughout his churches."[3]

Simply put, If our church practices are derived from spiritual life, they will be in harmony with the apostolic tradition. Consequently, what is written in the New Testament shouldn't be viewed as irrelevant history. It's a benchmark to test whether or not our church practices have a sound foundation.

Some may argue that if we are rightly following the Holy Spirit's guidance there's no need to give our attention to New Testament teachings and practices. But this argument ignores the fact that we are fallible creatures who easily confuse the Spirit's guidance with our own. Not to mention that it's relatively easy to confuse human tradition with God's will. Thus in order for us to discover the source of our leading, our church practice must have a biblical basis.

To ignore apostolic traditions is to put us in the dangerous position of unknowingly substituting our own misguided feelings and unfounded thoughts for the Holy Spirit's leading. The New Testament is our standard for faith and practice. Both for individual conduct as well as for corporate life.

Voltaire once said, "God made man in his image, and man returned the favor." In like manner, God created the church in His own image, and man returned the favor. When we ignore the record of the early church and fail to recognize that it's a description of her spiritual DNA at work, we end up creating a church in the image of fallen humanity.

All that to say, if we ignore what Scripture teaches by *precept* and *example* about the church, we're in danger of making the perilous mistake of creating a church after our own image. And that's exactly what we have on the earth today.

Where Modern Evangelicalism Has Gone Wrong

While the church is an organism, it does have a form. Look at your physical body. It's a living entity. Yet it has a specific form—a particular expression. And within that expression there's a certain harmony and order.

Whenever the body of Christ gathers together, a form will eventually emerge. The form may be liberating or oppressive. It may be scriptural or unscriptural. It may be helpful or harmful. But it always exists.

In the words of Howard Snyder, "All life must have form. Life without form is sick and dies; it perishes because it cannot sustain itself. That is the way it is with all life, whether human, spiritual, or botanical, for God in His creation is consistent."[4]

Fact: There is both order and life—form and function—in the church of Jesus Christ. And if the church is operating according to its organic nature—its DNA, if you please—it will produce a certain form.

Many modern evangelicals have embraced the benighted idea that only those things that are "explicitly commanded" in Scripture are binding. Everything else can be safely ignored. Ironically, most who espouse this idea deny it in their practice.

Equally problematic is the notion that only the "commands" of the New Testament are to be heeded, while its "practices" are irrelevant and antiquated. This idea has deluded many Christians into embracing a raft of humanly devised practices that violate the DNA of the church. For example, salaried clergy, single pastors, hierarchical leadership structures, denominations, and pulpit-pew-styled services in basilica-like spaces (regarded as the equivalent of "church") are all at odds with the organic nature of the body of Christ.[5]

Point: Normative apostolic *commands* are binding on the contemporary church. But normative apostolic *practices* are as well. By normative, I mean those practices that contain a spiritual subtext and are the outworking of the organic nature of the body of Christ.

Such practices are not purely narrative. They carry prescriptive force. This means that they reflect the unchanging nature of God Himself. And they naturally emerge whenever God's people live by divine life together—irrespective of culture or time.

In that connection, the book of Acts and the Epistles are awash with references to the apostolic tradition. In 1 Corinthians 4:17, Paul declares how he *taught* his *ways* "everywhere in every church." To Paul's mind, doctrine and duty—belief and behavior, life and practice—are inseparable.

In short, that which is included in the apostolic tradition is normative for all churches yesterday and today. The exhortations of Paul to "hold firmly to the traditions just as I delivered them to you" and to practice what "you have learned and received and heard and seen in me" are the considerations that should guide our church life.

The Correlation Between Theology and Practice

Observing the apostolic tradition doesn't mean reenacting the events of the first-century church. If so, we would have to hold our meetings in an upper chamber with many lights (Acts 20:8), cast lots to appoint leaders (Acts 1:26), and climb upon rooftops at the hour of prayer (Acts 10:9). Not to mention having to speak and dress like all first-century believers did, in sandals and togas.

Instead, observing apostolic traditions means being faithful to what was *theologically* and *spiritually* significant in the experience of the early church. The apostolic tradition, therefore, represents the balance between *reenacting* the practices of the first-century church and *ignoring* them.

The truth is that there are numerous practices of the early church that are normative for us today. These practices are not culturally conditioned. Instead, they are native to the organic nature of the triune God and deeply rooted in biblical theology. They are the church's DNA in operation. As such, they are the divine means for expressing the divine purpose.

To put it in a sentence: Apostolic tradition incarnates the apostolic teaching that the church is a spiritual organism whose taproot can be traced back to the Godhead. Consider the following examples:

- Open-participatory church meetings are solidly based on the well-established doctrine of the priesthood of all believers and the every-member functioning of the body of Christ. They are also the organic outflow of the mutual, self-giving exchange of fellowship within the triune God. By contrast, equating church with a service in which a professional clergy is active and the rest of the body is passive violates both scriptural principle and the organic nature of the Godhead. (See chapter 2.)

- Observing the Lord's Supper as the communal meal of the church is built upon the centrality of Jesus Christ and the covenantal relationship of the believing community. It's also a tangible expression of the mutual partaking of divine life within the Godhead, which is often depicted by eating and drinking. By contrast, taking the Supper as a ritual that's guided by a clergyman and removed from a meal is a departure from the apostolic tradition and does violence to the mutual participation that's present in the triune God. (See chapter 3.)

- House church meetings rest squarely on the fact that the church is a face-to-face community—a close-knit, extended family that engages in mutual sharing and mutual edification. As such, they provide the best atmosphere for fleshing out the familial love that flows between the Father and the Son through the Spirit. By contrast, it's virtually impossible to embody these elements in a building where the architecture fosters passivity among the congregation. (See chapters 4 and 5.) In addition, the idea of a sacred building contradicts Jesus' teaching that worship is to be desacralized (John 4:21–24).

- The practical expression of the church's unity is rooted in the New Testament teaching that there is only one body. It's also based on the unified diversity and oneness that the Father, Son, and Spirit share in the Godhead. The denominational system violates this principle and distorts the indivisible oneness that exists within the body of Christ and the triune God. (See chapter 6.)

- Plural oversight and decision-making by consensus are firmly grounded in the biblical teaching that Jesus Christ is Head of His church. It's also rooted in the mutual decision-making within the triune God. By contrast, a single pastor system (or rule by elders) supplants the headship of Christ and contradicts the organic principle of decision-making found within the Godhead. (See chapters 8, 9, and 10.)

Granted, there are other first-century practices beyond the ones just mentioned. Church planting by itinerant apostolic workers; gospel witness; missional living; social outreach; the baptizing of new converts; and the training of apostolic workers are just some examples.[6]

That said, the tradition of the apostles is vitally connected to the organic nature of the church, which is rooted in the triune God. And that nature is grounded in the unshakable teaching of the New Testament.

For that reason, when the Holy Spirit has His sovereign way in birthing a church, it will spontaneously gather in a biblical fashion. The church will be led of the Spirit to fulfill the apostolic tradition. As Paul said, those who follow the Spirit (those who are "spiritual") will adhere to the apostolic tradition regarding church practice (1 Cor. 14:37).

Regrettably, the tradition of the apostles has been largely ignored today. It's been viewed as irrelevant in the eyes of many contemporary Christians. In other words, the *apostolic* tradition has been buried under a mountain of *human* tradition.

The Importance of the Apostolic Tradition

Paul responded with unusual sharpness toward those who departed from the apostolic tradition, saying,

Did the word of God originate with you? Or are you the only people it has reached? If anybody thinks he is a prophet or spiritually gifted, let him acknowledge that what I am writing to you is the Lord's command. If he ignores this, he himself will be ignored. (1 Cor. 14:36–38)

Surprisingly, a gathering of Christians may abandon the apostolic tradition in lieu of their own self-constructed forms and still receive God's blessing. This has caused many people to conclude that the New Testament record isn't important. But this conclusion is profoundly flawed. We must not be deceived into thinking that God's *blessing* equals His *approval*. Just because God uses something doesn't mean that He sanctions it.

The history of Israel teaches us that God can still bless a people who disregard His ways for their own. Throughout Israel's wilderness journeys, God met His people's needs. This happened despite the fact that He was continually at odds with them.

When the children of Israel clamored for a king in their rebellion against the divine will, the Lord condescended to their carnal desire (1 Sam. 8:1ff.). And He continued to bless them despite their disobedience.

Yet tragic consequences followed their self-motivated decision (1 Sam. 8:11–18). The nation lost its freedom under a raft of evil monarchs. And it suffered a series of divine judgments. There's a sad parallel between the condition of Israel and many "churches" that have opted for an earth-tied, man-managed religious system.

So it bears repeating: God's blessing doesn't equal His approval.

Because of His infinite mercy, the Lord will bless any group of people if He can find some ground to do so. But whenever they choose their own ways in place of His, they limit His blessing.

How quickly we forget that the church belongs to God and not to us. It's part of our fallen nature to follow our own ideas regarding church practice. To enshrine our own traditions. To canonize our own personal preferences. To institutionalize what fits our own ideas of success rather than to follow what Jesus and the apostles have handed down to us.

Whose House Are We Building?

An unmistakable theme of the Bible is that God leaves nothing crucial for man to decide concerning His house. It's God's house that He's building in His way.

Consequently, the Lord's chief concern is not the size of the building. It's what the building is composed of (1 Cor. 3:9–15). In the Lord's eyes, *how* we build and *what* we build with are more important than the size of the building.

"Unless *the LORD* builds the house," declares the psalmist, "its builders labor in vain" (Ps. 127:1). God alone is the Master "architect and builder" (Heb. 11:10). Especially when it comes to His own dwelling place.

In God's work, the governing principle is always, "LORD … all that we have accomplished you have done for us" (Isa. 26:12). Those who hold to the idea of a "culturally relevant" church have a penchant for forgetting that the church belongs to God, and not to human beings. The church is not a toy that's been given to mere mortals to experiment with. Neither is it the property of a special class of "ministers" to shape the way they wish. It's an organic, living entity that has a specific expression. And it belongs to our Lord.

The tragic story of King David's presumptuous act of placing the ark of God upon a wooden cart is the summary witness that God's work must be done His way (2 Sam. 6:1–7). The humanly devised scheme of placing the holy ark upon a cart appeals to modern pragmatic ears. Yet the idea was borrowed from the heathen Philistines, and it contradicted the Lord's plain instruction (Ex. 25:12–16; Num. 4:5–15).[7]

Perhaps a simple illustration will help to underscore the force of what I've tried to communicate in this chapter. Suppose that you hired a carpenter to build a den as an addition to your home. You sketched out a diagram specifying how you wanted the den to be built. You then carefully explained it to the carpenter.

After returning from a weeklong vacation, you are shocked to find that your new den barely resembles the image that you sketched out for him. You ask the carpenter why he failed to adhere to your plan. He responds by saying, "I thought my ideas were better than yours."

Have we not done the same with the *Lord's* house?

Regrettably, scores of Christians have had no qualms with rearranging the spiritual furniture in God's house without consulting the Owner. Tragically, David is still placing the holy ark upon a Philistine cart. And Uzzah's human hand continues to try to steady it.

May we not be so unwise.

Questions That Must Be Faced

- Do you believe we have the right to change New Testament principles and ignore the tradition of the apostles in preference for our own? Explain.
- What current problems in the church could be the result of replacing plural oversight with hierarchical forms of government; replacing

open-participatory meetings with program-based, man-officiated services that foster passivity and suppress functioning; and replacing the
organic expression of the body with a business organization run by
hired professionals? Explain.

• If your church practices conflict with New Testament revelation, will
  you continue to support them? Explain.

CHAPTER 15
WHERE DO WE GO FROM HERE?

What is called "Christianity"—and what has come to be called "the church"—has become a tradition, an institution, and a system quite as fixed, rooted, and established as ever Judaism was, and it will be no less costly to change it fundamentally than was the case with Judaism. Superficial adjustments may be made—and are being made—but a very heavy price is attached to the change which is necessary to really solve the great problem. It may very well be, as in the time of the Lord, that the essential light will not be given to very many because God knows that they would never pay the price. It may only be a "remnant"—as of old—who will be led into God's answer because they will meet the demands at all costs.

—T. Austin-Sparks

All church structure (including the structure of authority) must come forth spontaneously from life. The river (life) makes its own riverbed (structure). We cannot make the riverbed (structure) and then invite the river (life) to come through our construction. Rather, the river moves and as it does it makes its own riverbed to flow through. So the life of the Spirit in the assembly will form its own structure. However, the basic structure of the church is set forth in the Scriptures and should be studied and restudied so as to check the structure being formed. The Spirit does not bring structures that are in opposition to the Word. —Rudy Ray

In this book, I've argued that the church of Jesus Christ has *departed,* rather than *developed,* from her original foundations. Many Christians—including church leaders, scholars, and theologians—would agree with me. However, not all agree on what should be done to remedy the situation.

Some have championed the idea of renewing the institutional church from the inside out. But those who have sought to revamp the established church have met serious resistance and frustration.

My experience suggests that unless the extrabiblical clergy system is dismantled in a particular church, efforts to recover the organic nature of church life will be handcuffed. The following disheartening results will most likely occur: The pastor will feel threatened; the staff will resist the disruption of the status quo; the congregation will be thrown into a panic; individual believers will be utterly confused; and the people calling for change will find themselves the target of personal attack. That said, let's take a brief look at some recent movements that have sought to renew the institutional church.

Before you read on, let me make a few introductory remarks. First, I thank God for all of the following movements. The Lord has used them all, without a doubt. Second, I'm taking the liberty to critique them because I strongly feel that if we accept them as the answer to reforming the church, the Lord will get shortchanged in the end. Add to that, I'm not critiquing them from afar. I have experienced all of these movements at one time in my life.

Third, I acknowledge that I could be completely wrong in my assessments, and I am open to standing corrected. Fourth, when I'm finished, I will offer another alternative. One that some, I'm sure, will be all too happy to critique themselves. I welcome this. But I only ask that those who make such critiques *first* experience for themselves what they are setting out to critique.

Shopping at a Supermall

The superstore megachurch trend is just one example of a failed attempt at renewing the church. Event-driven, shopping-mall churches have created specialized boutiques for every sociological slice in America today. From single parents, twelve-step recoverers, homebuilders, premarital couples, parents of adolescents, Generation Xers to working mothers, businessmen, actors, artists, and dancers.

Advertised by extraordinarily gifted marketeers and driven by a formidable "growth-industry" mentality, megachurches attract thousands every Sunday morning into their enormous amphitheaters. They use the latest church growth strategies, organizational methods, and marketing techniques.

They provide flawless multimedia worship. They supply pep-rally-like religious services. They offer high-tech visual effects. They possess tightly scripted gospel orations mingled with a heavy dose of comic relief. And they usually focus on the prominent charisma of the senior pastor.

They have seamless, choreographed drama presentations. They attract frequent visits from featured celebrities whose clothes are always color coordinated. They contain a zillion splinter interest groups designed to meet every consumer need.

To top it off, megachurches offer these mass-market religious resources to the public in exchange for minimal commitment, low visibility, and little cost. Stated simply, the megachurch movement is built on a corporate business paradigm that utilizes a market-driven approach to building the kingdom of God. It's no wonder that churches of this ilk are successful at swelling their ranks.

Unfortunately, those who are attracted to these large, flashy, organized Wal-Marts of the religious world can hardly find a place in their hearts for a simple, unextravagant meeting centered around the person of Christ alone. To their minds, choosing between a lavish supermall church and an "organic church" is like choosing between the flamboyant supercenter mall and the corner grocery store.

The weakness endemic to the superstore church is that it so emphasizes the "church scattered" dimension of the body of Christ that the "church gathered" dimension suffers great loss. By focusing all attention on being "sensitive" to the comfort zones of "seeking" unbelievers, many megachurches have failed to adequately disciple their new converts into radical abandonment to Jesus Christ.

They have also failed to nurture close-knit communal relationships in the body. What is more, the business machinery that drives these mammoth institutions obscures the organic nature of the *ekklesia*.

While it labors under the banner of "cultural relevancy," the supermall church bears too striking a resemblance to the shallow business structures of this age. It is for this reason that they don't have any profound or lasting impact on the culture.

Put plainly, the modern techniques used by the supermall church are as worldly as the system from which they're supposed to deliver people. In this way, the gospel has become trivialized, commercialized, and emptied of its power. It's been diluted as just another "product" in our consumer-obsessed culture.

Perhaps it's for this reason that the original innovators of the seeker-sensitive megachurch movement have recently stated that their model has largely been a failed enterprise.[1]

In a word, the megamall church of modern pop-Christian culture bears little similarity to the simple, Spirit-dependent, Christ-centered, spiritually dynamic, mutually participatory communities of the first century—the very churches that turned the world upside down (Acts 17:6).

Pulled Under a Wave

The "third-wave movement" and its cousin, the "restoration movement," have been two highly influential players in the renewal game.

Populated mostly by charismatics and Pentecostals, these movements stress the restoration of apostolic and prophetic power. For brevity's sake, I'll call these related movements *third-wave-restoration*.

Please understand: I have no quarrel with the pressing need for a genuine move of the Holy Spirit in and through the church today. But in my opinion, most third-wave-restoration churches have put the cart before the horse. Namely, they have sought to possess the power of the Spirit *before* they have gone under the flesh-severing knife of the cross. (By the way, I'm speaking of the principle of the cross, which is death to self.)

Scripturally speaking, the cross is the exclusive ground for the Holy Spirit's power. Calvary preceded Pentecost. Our Lord's Jordan baptism preceded the arrival of the heavenly dove. The sacrificial altar preceded the heavenly fire. And the smitten rock preceded the flowing waters at Horeb. In like manner, the Holy Spirit only finds His resting place upon the altar of a crucified life.

Recall the Lord's command to Israel not to pour the sacred oil upon any flesh (Ex. 30:32). This command is an apt figure illustrating how the cross cancels out the old creation. This is crucial because the Spirit cannot do His deepest work through uncrucified flesh.

The dangers of beginning with the Spirit rather than with the cross are numerous. For one thing, it can easily lead a person into an unwholesome quest for power without character. Mystical experience without godliness. Unrestrained soulish excitement without sound discernment. And demonic counterfeits without divine reality.

Not a few Christians who seek renewal routinely pack their bags and flock to the various "Christian Meccas" of revivalism sponsored by third-wave-restoration churches. Such people desperately wish to be touched by God. So much so that they have become consumers of every new wind of doctrine, fad, or experience that blows through the body of Christ (Eph. 4:14).

(A new wind seems to blow through certain Christian movements about every five years. Christians in these movements eventually get burned out with it and then look for another one to pick up. For some, this is a never-ending cycle.)

As a result, many in the third-wave have developed an unhealthy dependence upon phenomenological experience. It's a dependence like that of an addict. They are driven to travel far and wide to acquire the next spiritual fix. Such dependence obscures the role of Scripture in the life of a believer. It equally fosters an unhealthy (and sometimes pathological) spiritual instability.

This is not to suggest that the third-wave-restoration movement has been without value to the body of Christ. The movement has contributed a number of helpful spiritual accents. Most significantly, it has fostered a genuine hunger for and openness to God's moving. It has produced a sound blending of evangelical and charismatic theology. And it has created a vast collection of wonderfully anointed praise and worship music.

But its basic flaws lie in its overemphasis on supernatural experience; its tendency to put power *gifts* on the throne rather than Christ the *Giver;* and its zealous support of the modern clergy system. Quite frankly, the pastor is *king* in the typical third-wave-restoration church. And congregants who have been renewed with the new wine of the Spirit find very little freedom to fully function in their gifts during a typical third-wave service.

While third-wave-restoration churches may boast about possessing the "new wine," they have all too often confined it to an old, leaking wineskin. A wineskin that inhibits mutual ministry, relatedness, community, and freedom. The old wineskin that's employed merely reinforces the "sit-and-soak" mentality that plagues the body of Christ today.

"Christian guruism" is also epidemic in third-wave-restoration churches. High-powered "prophets" and "apostles" are copious in the movement. They are revered as spiritual icons, basking in the limelight of fan-club followings.

A typical renewal crusade is similar to a rock concert where the featured celebrity gives an encore performance and takes his bow in the Christian limelight. It's not uncommon for third-wavers to arrive hours early to secure a prime seat to hear the latest circuit prophet who has come to town.

In effect, the third-wave-restoration movement has so emphasized the so-called fivefold ministry that it has rivaled and obscured the priesthood of all believers. It has stressed the *extra-local* ministry at the expense of the *local* church. And it is the latter that God has established to be the normal environment for spiritual nourishment.

It's no wonder that those who desire the fullness of God, but don't know organic church life, are compelled to try anything that promises them a greater surge of renewal juice.

Regrettably, many in the third-wave-restoration movement have rushed headlong toward spiritual ambiguity. They have wholeheartedly embraced a peculiar phenomenon that has little to no biblical warrant. At the same time, they have shrugged their shoulders at an experience of church life that has abundant biblical merit.

Ironically, the very experience that multitudes in this movement are seeking to achieve can only be found in organic church life. When individuals taste body life, they will be forever cured of the unbridled urge to travel "to and fro" to attend the latest "hot spot" of renewal. Instead, they will discover true and lasting refreshment and stability within the local assembly that's captivated by a revelation of Jesus Christ and God's eternal purpose in Him. Those who wish to "chase God," therefore, will find Him in the *ekklesia* in His fullness. For she is His highest passion.

To spin the metaphor, in seeking to ride the latest spiritual wave, many third-wave-restorationists have been caught in the undertow of a clergy-dominated ecclesiastical structure. As a result, some have been bitten by the sharks of counterfeit spiritual experience. And they are now drowning in the murky waters of religious mysticism and charismatic clericalism.

Sadly, CPR cannot be successfully administered within the institutional matrix of the third-wave-restoration movement. The only hope for recovery lies in pulling the institutional plug to drain the rising water.

Imprisoned in a Cell

Another attempt at renewal in recent years has been the emergence of the "cell church." Cell churches are based on a two-winged approach to worship. They provide a weekly "cell group" meeting (set in a home) and a Sunday "celebration" meeting (set in a building).

The smaller cell meetings are called by different names (small groups, kinship groups, home meetings, life groups, rap groups, etc.). These small home meetings are designed for fellowship, ministry, prayer, and evangelism. The larger meetings are designed for pastoral preaching, corporate worship, and taking a collection.

There is much to be commended about the cell-church model. Particularly, its emphasis on close-knit connectedness, one-anothering, authentic evangelism, and body ministry. But its greatest weakness lies in its leadership structure.

By and large, the cell church model has left the unscriptural clergy system (the pastor and staff) completely untouched. Native to cell churches is a top-heavy, hierarchical leadership structure that ultimately controls the community. (I have a friend who describes this model as the "longer leash.")

The congregation is given a measure of church life weekly at someone's home. Yet through a highly organized hierarchy, the pastoral staff controls the gatherings and steers them according to their own vision and leadings. (Each cell group has a leader over it. And it's not uncommon for the "ministry time" in a cell meeting to be restricted to a discussion of the pastor's latest sermon.)

Not long ago, I was conversing with a cell church leader. He's a friend, and I love and respect him dearly. Interestingly, when he described what his particular cell group was doing, it was evident that he was the one in charge. He went on to explain how *he* gives the members direction, how *he* offers them personal counseling, and how *he* prays during the week to set the agenda for each cell meeting. Clearly, he was the one running the group.

While the cell church model looks impressive on paper, it doesn't quite match the free-flowing, organic expression of the church that's under the direct headship of the Lord Jesus—an expression where decision-making and ministry are shared and the modern pastoral role is glaringly absent.

The cell church deserves our applause for its emphasis on evangelism and its denunciation of "program-based" churches that find themselves mired in bureaucratic structures. But it warrants our disapproval for its blithe espousal of a rigid, multilayered, hierarchical leadership structure.

In many cases, each cell group is an extension of the pastor's vision. And it buries the believing priesthood under layers of human hierarchy. Accordingly, the cell church model often violates the very principle it claims to uphold: that the church is an organism made up of individual "spiritual cells." In stark contrast, many cell groups are nothing more than a facsimile of the same body part—the single pastor—and the leaders who serve under him. In these situations, the cell group is merely another program of the church. It's not the church itself.

Stated simply, the mere addition of home meetings (cells) to a clergy-dominated structure fails to go far enough in restoring the church's native expression. Again, the church isn't an institutional organization. She doesn't operate by chain of command. She's a living entity. For that reason, she discovers her native expression when she is properly planted, equipped, then left on her own. As long as she is controlled by graded hierarchies and chain-of-command leadership structures, she will never discover her organic expression.

Emerging into the Status Quo

In recent years, the emerging church "conversation" has taken the Christian world by storm. The emerging church conversation is a Christian movement whose participants seek to engage postmodern people—especially the unchurched. To accomplish this, "emerging Christians" (sometimes called "emergents") deconstruct and reconstruct Christian beliefs, standards, and methods to accommodate postmodern culture.[2]

The emerging church conversation is a mixed bag. It's by no means a monolith. However, certain streams of the emerging conversation are emphasizing the need to reexamine ecclesiology from top to bottom.[3]

Within these streams, there's a lot of high talk about community, being missional, liberating the laity, God's triune nature, scrapping the old way of doing church, and embracing a new paradigm shift for the body of Christ.

I have many friends who are pioneering in the emerging church. And I applaud much of what they are saying, especially in the area of upholding a "generous orthodoxy" that emphasizes accepting all Christians whom God has received.[4] Equally so, the encouragement to embrace the positive contributions that Christians of all stripes have made in the past is a noble one.

My main criticism of the emerging conversation rests here: When it comes to the practical expression of the church, many emergents have only slightly tweaked it. The old, leaking wineskin invented some five hundred years ago has been largely left unaltered.

Sacral buildings, sermon-based church services, the clergy system, the modern office of the pastor, have all been left unchallenged and unchanged, even among those who carry on the loudest about deconstructing the face of the modern church. By and large, many in the emerging church world still believe that every church needs a "minister" just as every company needs a boss.

Let me give you an example of what I mean. Less than twelve months ago, two highly visible emerging church leaders wrote articles on how the practices of the established church are "Constantinian," and this is one of the major reasons why many postmodern Christians find church to be irrelevant.

When I read these articles, I was thrilled. I then quickly called several friends who lived in the areas in which the authors of these articles were leaders. The report I received back was disheartening. They both said, "Frank, we visited and their services are no different than any other church. They begin with music from the worship team. Announcements are given. Then special singing. Then the pastor preaches a sermon to a passive audience. The only thing we noticed that was different was that there was artwork on the walls of the building and the language was deliberately postmodern. Other than that, it was the same song and dance that you would find in any other Protestant assembly today."

I have found this to be true in my own experience as well.

It seems to me that many of us are willing to tip over any sacred cow *except* the modern pastoral office and the Sunday-morning Protestant ritual. Regardless of how unbiblical these two religious traditions are, they seem to be off limits even to the most radical thinkers.[5]

At this point, I would like to propose a challenge. Can we please be daring enough and creative enough to change this five-hundred-year-old ritual—which incidentally doesn't have a shred of biblical warrant to justify it? Can we accept the challenge to equip God's people to function under the headship of Christ without human control? And if we don't know how to do this, can we please be humble enough to bring in someone who can and see what happens?

Adopting the Right Attitude

What I've said so far isn't meant to place judgment on any of God's dear people. I have respected friends in all of the aforementioned movements, and they are servants of God whom He is using.

Make no mistake about it: God has used and is using the institutional church. Because of His mercy, the Lord will work through any structure as long as He can find hearts in it that are truly open to Him. So there's no question that God is using megachurches, third-wave-restoration churches, cell churches, and emerging churches alike. (In my opinion, He's using them more than so-called house churches that are elitist and sectarian.)

But this isn't the question at hand. The good is often the enemy of the best. And the Lord holds us responsible for following His Word insofar as we understand it. So comparing ourselves with others is shaky ground for seeking His approval (2 Cor. 10:12). Anything less than what God has disclosed in Scripture concerning church practice falls short of His full purpose. I don't say this judgmentally, but soberly. The words of T. Austin-Sparks capture the tone of my spirit:

> *While the sects and denominations, missions, and institutions are a departure from the Holy Spirit's original way and intention, God has undoubtedly blessed and used these in a very real way and has sovereignly done great work through faithful men and women. We thank God that it is so, and pray that every means possible of use may have His blessing upon it. This is not said in any patronizing or superior spirit: God forbid. Any reserve is only because we feel that there has been much delay, limitation, and weakness due to the departure from the first and full position of the first years of the church's life, and because of a heart-burden for a return thereto. We cannot accept the present "disorder" as all that the Lord would or could have.[6]*

The Symptom Masquerading as the Cause

I strongly believe that genuine church renewal requires that we distinguish between the *symptom* and the *root* of the problem. Elton Trueblood has rightly said, "The basic trouble [with the modern church] is that the proposed cure has such a striking similarity to the disease."

Conferences for burned-out clergy, cross-denominational unity gatherings, support groups for pastors who suffer from "sheep bite," and workshops presenting the latest church growth strategy are vivid examples of Trueblood's penetrating observation. All of these supposed "cures" merely coddle the system that's responsible for the church's maladies. They simply treat the symptom while ignoring the real culprit. The result? The same drama continues to play out on a different stage.

It's the clergy system and the institutional structure that inhibits the rediscovery of face-to-face community, supplants the functional headship of Christ, and stifles the full ministry of every believer. Consequently, all attempts at renewal will always be shortsighted until the clergy system and institutional structure is dismantled in a local fellowship. At best, such attempts will bring limited change. At worst, they will invite open hostility.

It's my conviction that the attempt to work for a recovery of organic church life where Jesus Christ is Head from within an institutional church is a futile exercise. Such an attempt can be likened to the dismantling of a tower from the ground. If those disassembling the tower come close to compromising the structure, the tower will fall down on them. The only way to dismantle a tower is to proceed from the top down.

For this reason, renewal movements that merely transplant biblical principles into institutional soil will never succeed in realizing the full purpose of God. As I have often said, organic churches that are planted in institutional soil do not take root. In the words of Arthur Wallis,

> *A church is not fully renewed if the structures are left untouched. To have within a traditional church a live group composed of those who have received the Spirit and are beginning to move in spiritual gifts; to introduce a freer and livelier spirit into the worship with renewal songs; to permit the clapping and the lifting up of the hands and even to dance; to split the weeknight meeting into home groups for the purpose of discipling; to replace "one-man leadership" with a team of elders—all these measures, good though they are, will only prove to be a patching operation. Individuals will undoubtedly be blessed. There will be an initial quickening of the church. But if it ends there, the long-term results will be detrimental. There will be a quiet struggle going on between the new measures and the old structures, and you may be sure the old structures will win in the end. The new patch will never blend in with the old garment. It will always look incongruous.*[7]

For the past fifty years, a plethora of books have been published that have sought to reform and renew the modern church. To my mind, few of these books have produced any real change. The reason? The vast majority of them have offered cosmetic changes to a structure that lacks biblical and spiritual integrity.

Seeking to repair a house that has cracks in its foundation will never prove productive. I believe it's time that we honestly examined the structural integrity of the modern church system. I strongly believe that the clergy *system*, which includes the modern pastoral *office*, is what needs to be abandoned. It's the system that's one of the main culprits, not the people, the motives, or the intentions. Experience has taught me that an institutional church will never fully embody the dream of God until it recognizes that the framework within which it operates is inadequate and self-defeating. Despite the good intentions of the persons who populate it, the interior design of the organized church sets us up for defeat.

True renewal, therefore, must be radical. That means it must go to the root. Recovering the organic expression of the church and the practical headship of Jesus Christ necessitates that we forsake our ecclesiastical patches and Band-Aids.

In this connection, I thank God for those Christians who have left their clerical professions and laid down their high-powered hierarchical positions to learn what it means to be a simple brother in an organic expression of the church. Sound radical? Perhaps. But it's certainly not impossible. I personally know numerous men who have left the clergy system out of conscience. Some of them are church planters today, and God is using them mightily. (By the way, all of them first learned to be non-leaders in organic church life before they went out to plant such churches themselves.)[8]

A few of these men helped the churches they pastored make the transition from an institutional church to an organic church. But such a move is profoundly drastic. It goes well beyond the typical tweaking that many leaders feel comfortable with these days.[9]

As would be expected, those who have left their salaried, clergy positions have paid a tremendous price. For this reason, such a thought strikes a sensitive chord in the heart of the average religious professional, and many have violently resisted it. They have reacted in a way not dissimilar to the silversmiths of Ephesus who withstood Paul's message because it endangered their craft (Acts 19:24–27).[10] Consequently, unless pastors are ready to examine this issue openly before God, any discussion of the matter will remain a highly flammable topic that can easily turn torrid.

Despising Not the Day of Small Things

Recall that after Israel's seventy-year captivity in Babylon, God called His people out of Babylon to return to Jerusalem to rebuild His house. While Israel was in captivity in a foreign land, she still assembled to worship God in the various synagogues that she built on her own. Israel still belonged to God. But God's will for her was to leave Babylon and return to Jerusalem to build the temple that He Himself ordained.

Sadly, only a tiny remnant responded to the Lord and returned to the land (Ezra 9:7–8; Hag. 1:14). Most were unwilling to pay the price of leaving their comfortable lifestyles, their new jobs, their new homes, and the convenient new synagogue worship that they had constructed.

I believe the call of God to Israel to leave Babylon foreshadows the present cry of the Spirit to His people today. In view of the fact that only a small, seemingly insignificant remnant returned to Jerusalem to rebuild God's house, the prophet Zechariah issued this challenging rebuke: "Who hath despised the day of small things?" (Zech. 4:10 kjv).

Why did the prophet issue such a word? Because despite the seeming smallness of the endeavor, God was in it. Despite the fact that most of Israel regarded the rebuilt temple "as nothing" in comparison to the surpassing splendor of the former temple, God was in it (Hag. 2:3). Despite the fact that the elders of Israel wept in despair when they saw the tiny remnant lay down the unimpressive foundation, God was in it (Ezra 3:12).

From Gideon's army of three hundred to Elijah's seven thousand who had "not bowed the knee to Baal"—from the Levitical priests who first entered the Promised Land to the hidden Annas and Simeons of our Lord's day who "looked for the consolation of Israel"—God's most precious work has been accomplished through the small, the weak, and the unnoticed (1 Cor. 1:26–29; 1 Kings 19:11–13).

Success in the eyes of the world is tied to natural measurements. Large numbers, large budgets, large buildings, etc. are all signs of success to the worldly minded. Yet the greatest things in God's eyes are extremely small in the eyes of man.

Let me be clear. The call of God to recover the primitive simplicity of organic church life requires that we begin on an entirely new ground. A ground different from the religious systems and traditions that we fallen mortals have constructed. And that ground is the Lord Jesus Christ.

A Paradigm Shift

To borrow a term from scientific philosopher Thomas Kuhn, we need a "paradigm shift" regarding the church before we can properly rebuild it. That is, we need a new worldview regarding the meaning of the body of Christ. A new model for understanding the *ekklesia*. A new framework for thinking about the church.

Of course, the "new paradigm" that I'm speaking of is not new at all. It's the paradigm that undergirds the entire New Testament.

Our day is not much different from that of Nehemiah's. In Nehemiah's time, Israel had just rediscovered the Law of God after being without it for many years. But once it was discovered, it had to be reexplained and reinterpreted. Consider the words of Nehemiah:

They read from the Book of the Law of God, making it clear and giving the meaning so that the people could understand what was being read. (Neh. 8:8).

In the same way, twenty-first-century Christians must relearn the language of Scripture with respect to the church. The original meaning of countless biblical terms like "church," "minister," "pastor," "house of God," "ministry," "bride of Christ," "family of God," and "fellowship" have largely been lost.

These words have been invested with institutional power. A power that was foreign to those who originally penned them. Therefore, a pressing need today is the rediscovery of biblical language and ideas. We need to rethink our entire concept of church and discover it afresh through the lens of Jesus and the apostles.

Because of common misteaching, we have many deeply buried assumptions that are in need of excavation and examination. Many of us have been mistaught that "church" means a building, a denomination, or a worship service. And that a "minister" is a special class of Christian.

Since our contemporary notion of the church has been so entrenched in human thinking, it requires a conscious effort to view it in the way that all first-century Christians did. It demands that we rigorously plow through the thick and tangled weeds of religious tradition until we unearth the virgin soil of organic Christianity.

As we rethink the church in its scriptural context, we'll be better equipped to distinguish between the biblical notion of church and those institutions that pose as churches. Let's briefly isolate some of those differences now:

The Institutional Paradigm

- is sustained by a clergy system

- seeks to energize the laity

- limits many functions to the ordained

- renders the bulk of its congregants passive in their pews

- associates church with a building, a denomination, or a religious service

- is rooted in unifying those who share a special set of customs or doctrines

- thrusts "ordinary" Christians out of the "Holy of Holies" and chains them to a pew

- places its priority on programs and rituals that keep its congregants at arm's length, insulating them from one another

- depends on forced tithing and huge budgets

The Organic Paradigm

- knows nothing of a clergy system

- doesn't recognize a separate class called laity

- makes all members functioning priests

- allows and encourages all Christians to engage in whatever ministry God has called them to

- affirms that people do not *go to* church; affirms that they (together) *are* the church

- is rooted in unreserved fellowship with *all* Christians based on Christ alone

- liberates all believers to serve as ministers in the context of a nonclerical, decentralized form of church leadership

- places its priority on face-to-face, shared-life relationships, mutual submission, openness, freedom, mutual service, and spiritual reality—the very elements that were built into the fabric of the New Testament church

- depends on the Spirit of God to bring about generous, grace-based giving among members

- spends most of its resources on building expenditures and pastor-staff salaries

- operates on the basis that the pastor/priest is the functional head (while Christ is the nominal Head)

- extols and protects the clergy-dominated, program-centered system that serves as the driving machine of the organized church

- recognizes and affirms hierarchical leadership

- builds *programs* to fuel the church; treats people as cogs in the machine

- encourages believers to participate institutionally and hierarchically

- separates church (ecclesiology) from personal salvation (soteriology); views the former as a mere appendage to the latter

- spends most of its resources on "the poor among you" and travelling workers who preach the gospel and plant new churches

- operates on the basis that Christ is the functional Head through the invisible guidance of the Holy Spirit through the believing community

- rejects the clergy system because it quenches the sovereign exercise of the Holy Spirit; yet lovingly embraces every Christian within that system

- rejects hierarchical leadership; recognizes and affirms the organic leadership of the whole body

- builds *people* together in Christ to provide the momentum for the church

- invites believers to participate relationally and spiritually

- forges no link between personal salvation and the church; sees the two as inextricably intertwined (Scripture has it that when people were saved, they simultaneously became part of the church and immediately met together)

To make the point better by someone else somewhere else, the organic paradigm represents "the winning back to God of things ordinary and the desacralisation of things made sacred by human hands." Because the traditional paradigm has been so entrenched in the minds of so many Christians, the mere notion of "coloring outside the lines" is quite terrifying. The unfortunate result is that those who haven't had a paradigm shift regarding the church will either ignore or oppose those churches that have.

In the eyes of those who see the world through institutional glasses, unless a church meets in the "right" place (a building), has the "proper" leadership (an ordained minister), and bears the "correct" name (one that indicates a "covering"), it's not an authentic church. Instead, it's dubbed with innovative terms like "parachurch."

Hence, among those who haven't yet grown weary of running on the program-driven treadmill of institutional "churchianity," that which is abnormal is considered normal and that which is normal is regarded as abnormal. This is the unhappy result of not basing our faith and practice upon Scripture.

In brief, nothing short of a paradigm shift regarding the church, coupled with an impartation of fresh light from the Holy Spirit, will produce enduring change. Readjustments to the old wineskin, no matter how radical, will only go so far.

Consequently, in my personal judgment, the church doesn't need *renewal*. It needs a complete overhaul. That is, the only way to *fully* renew the institutional church is to wholly disassemble it and build something far different. The brittle wineskin of church practice and the tattered garment of ecclesiastical forms need to be exchanged, not just modified. Some may disagree. But this is my conviction based on my experience, and I'm not ashamed to state it.

In short, what is needed is a *new* wineskin and a *new* garment (Luke 5:36–38).

The words of Frederick Buechner are fitting:

I also believe that what goes on in them [support groups] is far closer to what Christ meant his Church to be, and what it originally was, than much of what goes on in most churches I know. These groups have no buildings or official leadership or money. They have no rummage sales, no altar guilds, no every-member canvases. They have no preachers, no choirs, no liturgy, no real estate. They have no creeds. They have no program. They make you wonder if the best thing that could happen to many a church might not be to have its building burned down and to lose all its money. Then all the people would have left is God and each other.[11]

May we be delivered from carelessly imposing *our* pattern of church organization upon the New Testament authors. And may we have the courage to discard our institutional baggage. Or at least be willing to open our bags and inspect the contents.

Counting the Cost

So what alternative do I recommend? Very simply, a return to organic church life. The very thing that I have sought to reimagine throughout this book.

I believe that we are living in an hour when God is seeking to raise up multitudes in the spirit of the sons of Issachar "who understood the times and knew what Israel [God's people] should do" (1 Chron. 12:32).

The peril of ancient Israel rested in its willingness to follow the multitudes that surrounded it. By contrast, shouldn't we connect our obedience to what God has revealed to us in His Word? In Exodus 23:2, the Lord warned Israel about the peril of following after the multitudes. I think that warning holds good for us today.

As the Scripture says, "*Today,* if you hear his voice, do not harden your hearts" (Heb. 3:15).

Let me be clear. There's a price to pay in responding to the Lord's will for His church. You'll have to reckon with being misunderstood by those who have embraced spectator Christianity. You'll bear the marks of the cross and die a thousand deaths in the process of being built together with other believers in a close-knit community.

You'll have to endure the messiness that's part and parcel of relational Christianity—forever abandoning the artificial neatness afforded by the organized church. You'll no longer share the comforts of being a passive spectator. Instead, you'll learn the self-emptying lessons of becoming a responsible, serving member of a functioning body.

In addition, you'll have to go against the harsh grain of what one writer calls "the seven last words of the church" (*we never did it that way before*). You'll incur the disfavor of the religious majority for refusing to be influenced by the tyranny of the status quo. And you'll incite the severest assaults of the Adversary in his attempt to snuff out that which represents a living testimony of Jesus.

Add to that, living in organic church life is incredibly difficult. The experience is fraught with problems. Read the New Testament letters again with an eye to discovering the many hazards the early Christians encountered when living in close-knit community. When we live in the same kind of community life today, the same problems emerge. Our flesh gets exposed. Our spirituality gets tested. And we quickly find out just how deep the fall goes.

As one person said, "Everybody's normal until you get to know them." This is all too true for those who take the plunge of living in organic church life. The problems are endless. It's much easier to become a "pew potato" two hours on Sunday morning in an institutional church. Anyone can be a perfect Christian then. Organic church life, however, is a wedding of glory and gore. But this is the genius of God. It's His prescribed way to transform us into His image. For "iron sharpens iron" (Prov. 27:17).

Yet regardless of the suffering that follows those who take the road less traveled, the glorious benefits of living in body life far outweigh the costs. The Lord builds on broken lives; His house is constituted out of conflict (1 Chron. 26:27). This being the case, "Let us, then, go to him outside the camp, bearing the disgrace he bore" (Heb. 13:13). For it is there that we may meet the Savior's heartbeat.

Closing Words

If you have understood and accepted the message of this book, then you have drawn two significant conclusions:

1. The institutional church as we know it today does not reflect the church that God originally intended.
2. The church that Scripture envisions is organic in its nature and expression, and the Lord desires to recover it today.

That said, a major decision awaits some of you. To frame it in a question: What is the next step? Some of you are already part of an organic church, so perhaps this book will have helped you better understand your spiritual and biblical roots. Others of you may be content with your present church experience, even though it may not be organic. Still others of you desire to be part of an organic expression of the church.

If you are part of the latter group, a new set of questions faces you. Namely,

- What is the mission of God in relation to the church, and how can I best fulfill it?
- How can I find an organic church where I live?
- How are organic churches planted, and can I start one myself?
- If I'm a leader in an institutional church, is it possible to have organic church life in my present situation? If so, how?
- What are the problems that organic churches face, and how are they best handled?

If you are asking these questions, there's good news.

First, my coworkers have created a Web site that gives practical help to those who are asking these questions. Through the site, you can connect with Christians who are also reimagining church. In addition, you can request the help of those who plant organic churches to assist you in having one planted in your area. The site also includes resources for pastors who are struggling with the issues raised in this book. Just go to **www.HouseChurchResource.org**.

Second, the questions regarding the mission of God as well as planting and sustaining organic church life are not easy to answer. For this reason, I'm writing two other volumes to address them in detail.

The first is titled *From Eternity to Here: Rediscovering the Ageless Purpose of God.* This book will seek to present the sweeping grandeur of God's eternal campaign for a bride, a house, a family, and a body. And it will focus on our place in the eternal drama of God's timeless plan.

The second volume will discuss in great depth the biblical principles for planting and sustaining organic churches. It will also offer practical guidance on how you can apply these principles today. Visit **www.ptmin.org** and you will be notified when these new books are available.

APPENDIX
OBJECTIONS AND RESPONSES ABOUT LEADERSHIP

To be honest is to confront the truth. However unpleasant and inconvenient the truth may be, I believe we must expose and face it.
—Dr. Martin Luther King Jr.

I am not here attacking Christianity, but only the institutional mantle that cloaks it.
—Pierre Berton

For centuries, certain texts in the New Testament have been mishandled to support hierarchical/positional leadership structures in the church. This mishandling has caused no small damage to the body of Christ.

The notion of hierarchical/positional authority is partly the result of mistranslations and misinterpretations of certain biblical passages. These mistranslations and misinterpretations have been influenced by cultural biases that have cluttered the original meaning of the biblical language. Such biases have transformed simple words into heavily loaded ecclesiastical titles. As a result, they have eroded the original landscape of the church.

Thus a fresh reading of the New Testament in its original language is necessary for properly understanding certain texts. For instance, a look at the original Greek yields the following insights:

- Bishops are simply guardians (*episkopoi*), not high-church officials.
- Pastors are caretakers (*poimen*), not professional pulpiteers.
- Ministers are busboys (*diakonos*), not clergymen.
- Elders are wise old men (*presbuteros*), not ecclesiastical officers.

Thankfully, a growing number of New Testament scholars are pointing out that the "leadership" terminology of the New Testament possesses descriptive accents denoting special functions rather than formal positions.

What follows is a list of common objections to the idea that church leadership is nonofficial, nontitular, and nonhierarchical. Each objection is followed by a response.

Objections from Acts and Paul's Epistles

1. Don't Acts 1:20; Romans 11:13; 12:4; and 1 Timothy 3:1, 10, 12 speak of church officials?

The word *office* in these passages is a mistranslation. It has no equivalent in the original Greek. Nowhere in the Greek New Testament do we find the equivalent of *office* used in connection with any ministry, function, or leader in the church. The Greek word for *office* is only used to refer to the Lord Jesus Christ in His high priestly office (Heb. 5—7). It's also used to refer to the Levitical priesthood (Luke 1:8).

The King James Version mistranslates Romans 11:13b to be "I magnify mine office." But the Greek word translated "office" means service, not office. So a better translation of Romans 11:13b is "I magnify my service [*diakonia*]."

Similarly, Romans 12:4b is better translated "All the members do not have the same function [*praxis*]." The Greek word *praxis* means a doing, a practice, or a function rather than an office or position. The NIV and the NASB reflect this better translation.

Finally, 1 Timothy 3:1 says the following in the KJV: "If a man desire the office of a bishop …" But a more accurate translation puts it this way: "If anyone aspires to oversight …"[1]

2. *1 Timothy, 2 Timothy, and Titus are called the Pastoral Epistles. So that means that Timothy and Titus were pastors, right?*

No, it does not. Paul's letters to Timothy and Titus were first dubbed the "Pastoral Epistles" as recently as the eighteenth century.[2] But this is a misguided label.

Timothy and Titus were not local pastors. They were apostolic coworkers who were mostly on the move. They only occasionally spent a long period of time in a single place. (For instance, Paul sent Titus to Crete and Timothy to Ephesus to strengthen the churches there and sort out local problems.)

Because Timothy and Titus were itinerant church planters, Paul never called them pastors or elders. These men were not resident ministers. They were part of Paul's apostolic circle—a circle that was noted for its constant traveling (Rom. 16:21; 1 Cor. 16:10; 2 Cor. 8:23; 1 Thess. 1:1; 2:6; 3:2; 2 Tim. 2:15; 4:10). Therefore, calling these three letters the "Pastoral Epistles" reflects a modern bias, not an objective processing of the truth.

3. Don't Paul's lists of qualifications in the Pastoral Epistles, namely 1 Timo-
thy 3:1–7 and Titus 1:7–9, prove that elders are church officers?

All that's written in 1 Timothy, 2 Timothy, and Titus must be understood from the standpoint that Paul was writing to his apostolic coworkers,
not to churches. This explains some of the differences between these
epistles and the rest of Paul's letters. In Timothy and Titus, for example,
the body metaphor is absent. The "brethren" are only occasionally mentioned. And there is little emphasis on mutual ministry.

By the same token, we don't find anything resembling nascent Catholicism in these epistles. The Spirit of God as well as His gifts are mentioned.
And leaders are understood to gain recognition by their example rather
than by any held position.

What we have in these texts, then, are the essential *qualities* of a true
overseer, not a list of *qualifications* for an office that can be ticked off with
a pencil.

The summation of these qualities is: spiritual character and faithfulness—godliness and responsibility. Paul's lists, therefore, merely served as
guides to Timothy and Titus in helping them identify and affirm overseers in the churches with which they worked (1 Tim. 5:22; Titus 1:5).

In addition, the flavor of these texts in the Greek is one of function
rather than officialdom. Paul himself doesn't call an overseer an office-
bearer, but a "noble task" (1 Tim. 3:1b). Moreover, functional language is
employed when Paul commends honor to those elders who "guide well"
and who "labor" in teaching (1 Tim. 5:17 NKJV).

Consequently, to conflate the overseers in these texts with modern
ecclesiastical officials—like the modern pastor—is pure fantasy. It's a
function of our tendency to bring our organizational conventions to the
New Testament and read them back into it. It's the result of a learned

cultural framework that we bring to the text and nothing more. In short, the language of function rather than office dominates the "Pastoral Epistles" just as it does Paul's other letters.[3]

4. *First Corinthians 12:28 says, "And in the church God has appointed first of all apostles, second prophets, third teachers...." Doesn't this text envision a hierarchy of church officials?*

Again, this question is indicative of our penchant for reading Scripture with the tainted spectacles of human hierarchy. It's a peculiarly Western foible to insist that every relationship be conceived in terms of a one-up/one-down hierarchical mode. Thus whenever we see an ordered list in the New Testament (like 1 Corinthians 12:28), we can't seem to keep ourselves from connecting the dots of hierarchy.

While we twenty-first-century Westerners like to think in terms of organizational flow charts, the Bible never does. So it's an unwarranted assumption to think that every ordered list in Scripture is some sort of a veiled command hierarchy. Simply put, to see hierarchy in Paul's catalog of gifts in 1 Corinthians 12:28 represents a culturally biased misreading of Paul. The question of authority structures is not being asked anywhere in this text. Therefore, we do not exegete hierarchy from it; we impose it upon it.

A more natural reading of this passage understands the ordering to reflect a logical priority rather than a hierarchical one. In other words, the order reflects *greater gifting* with respect to church building. This interpretation meshes nicely with the immediate context in which it appears (1 Cor. 12, 13, 14).

To unfold that, Paul is saying that within the scope of church building, the apostle's ministry is the most fundamental. That's because apostles give birth to the church and sustain it during its prenatal development. Apostles break the ground and plant the seed of the *ekklesia*.

Since apostles lay the foundation of the church, they're also ranked first (chronologically) in the work of church building (Rom. 15:19–20; 1 Cor. 3:10; Eph. 2:20). Significantly, while apostles are placed *first* in the church-building scheme, they rank *last* in the eyes of the world (Matt. 20:16; 1 Cor. 4:9).

Prophets appear second in Paul's list. This indicates that they immediately follow the apostles in their value to church building. Much confusion (and abuse) surrounds the function of the prophet today. Briefly, prophets supply the church with spiritual vision and encouragement through prophetic utterances. Like apostles, prophets unfold the mystery of God's purpose for the present and the future (Acts 15:32; Eph. 3:4–5). They also root out the weeds so the church can grow unhindered.

Teachers are mentioned third. They follow the prophets in their value to church building. Teachers put the church on solid biblical ground. They supply instruction concerning God's ways. They also shepherd God's people through hard times.

To continue the metaphor, teachers water the seed and fertilize the soil so the church can flourish and blossom. If we examine the ministry of the teacher with an eye for chronology, teachers build the superstructure of the church *after* the apostles have established the ground floor.

This interpretation of 1 Corinthians 12:28 follows the path of Paul's thought far better than that of a hierarchical command structure where apostles "pull rank" on prophets, and prophets do the same with teachers. It also brings to the fore an important spiritual principle: The absence of hierarchical authority doesn't mean egalitarian gifting.

While the New Testament affirms that all are gifted and all have ministry, it equally demonstrates that God disperses His gifts in a diverse way (1 Cor. 12:4–6). Every gift is valuable to the body of Christ. But some gifts are greater than others within their respected spheres (Matt. 25:14ff.; 1 Cor. 12:22–24, 31; 14:5).

This doesn't mean that those with greater gifts are greater in authority (or intrinsic worth) in some formal sense. But God has called each of us to a different work. And some have greater gifts for different tasks (Matt. 25:14ff.; Rom. 12:6; Eph. 4:7).

Within the sphere of our gifts, each member is indispensable to the general upbuilding of the church—even those members whose gifts are not outwardly impressive (1 Cor. 12:22–25). Therefore, every Christian in the Lord's house is responsible for using and increasing his or her gifts. And we are all warned against hiding them in the napkin of fear (Matt. 25:25).

In short, the idea that 1 Corinthians 12:28 denotes some sort of church hierarchy lacks argumentative force. The text has in mind greater gifting with a subtext of the chronological order of church building (some plant, then some water, etc.—1 Cor. 3:6). It doesn't indicate a pecking order of an ecclesiastical hierarchy or an authoritative ladder for Christians to climb.

5. Don't Acts 20:28; 1 Thessalonians 5:12; 1 Timothy 5:17; and Hebrews 13:7, 17, 24 say that elders have "the rule over" the church?

The words "rule" and "over" in these texts are a poor fit with the rest of the New Testament. And there's no analog for them in the Greek text. This is yet another case where certain translations have confused the modern reader by employing culturally conditioned religious terminology.

The word "rule" in Hebrews 13:7, 17, 24 is translated from the Greek word *hegeomai*. It simply means to guide or go before. In his translation of Hebrews, New Testament scholar F. F. Bruce translates *hegeomai* into "guides."[4] This word carries the thought of "those who guide you" rather than "those who rule over you."

Similarly, in 1 Thessalonians 5:12, the word "over" is translated from the Greek word *proistemi*. It carries the idea of standing in front of, superintending, guarding, and providing care for. Robert Banks and F. F. Bruce explain that this term doesn't carry the technical force of an official designation, for it's used in the participle rather than the noun form. It's also positioned as the second in the midst of two other nonofficial participles.[5] Bruce translates 1 Thessalonians 5:12–13 as follows: "Now we ask you brothers to know those who work hard among you and care for you in the Lord and instruct you, and esteem them very highly in love because of their work."[6]

The same word (*proistemi*) appears in 1 Timothy 5:17. It, too, is incorrectly translated "rule" in the KJV and NASB. In addition, in Acts 20:28, the Greek text says that the elders are *"en"* (among) the flock rather than "over" them (as the KJV puts it).

In a similar vein, Paul's statement that overseers must "rule [*proistemi*] their own houses well" in 1 Timothy 3:4–5 doesn't point to their ability to wield power. It rather points to their capacity to supervise, manage, and nurture others. Incidentally, managing the household didn't envision managing the nuclear family. It involved much more than that. It involved managing married and unmarried relatives as well as servants.

In all these passages, the basic thought is that of watching rather than bossing. Superintending rather than dominating. Facilitating rather than dictating. Guiding rather than ruling.

The Greek text conveys an image of one who stands within the flock, guarding and caring for it (as a leading-servant would). It's reminiscent of a shepherd who looks out for the sheep—not one who drives them from behind or rules them from above.

Again, the thrust of apostolic teaching consistently demonstrates that God's idea of church leadership is at odds with those conventional leadership roles that are based on top-heavy rule.

6. *Doesn't Romans 12:8 (KJV) teach that God gifts some believers to rule in the church? There Paul says, "He that ruleth, [should do so] with diligence."*

The KJV uses the word "ruleth" in this text. But the Greek word that appears here is *proistemi*. Again, this word envisions one who superintends and gives aid to others. It doesn't refer to one who governs or controls them. So the text is better translated, "He that guards and gives care should do so with diligence." Paul's thought here is clearly one of earnest oversight rather than dictatorial rulership.

7. *Don't Acts 14:23 and Titus 1:5 teach that elders are ordained, implying that they are church officers?*

The mention of apostolic recognition (endorsement) is at least as friendly to the functional mind-set as it is to the positional interpretation. In Titus 1:5, the word translated "ordain" in the Greek is *kathistemi*. One meaning of this word is "to declare, to show to be."

In Acts 14:23, the word is *cheirotoneo*. It means "to stretch forth the hand" or "to choose." Both terms can be understood to mean the acknowledgment of those whom others have already endorsed.

Second, there's not a shred of textual evidence to support the idea that biblical recognition bestows or confers authority. Paul never vested certain ones with authority over the remaining members of the community. The Holy Spirit makes overseers, not overlords (Acts 20:28).

Elders exist in the church *before* they are outwardly recognized. Apostolic endorsement merely makes public that which the Spirit has already accomplished. The laying on of hands is a token of fellowship, oneness, and affirmation. It's not one of special grace or transferred authority. It's a profound error, therefore, to confuse biblical recognition with ecclesiastical ordination. The laying on of hands doesn't qualify religious specialists to do what lesser mortals cannot.[7]

Instead, biblical recognition is merely the outward confirmation of those who have already been charged by the Spirit to a specific task. It serves as a visible testimony that publicly endorses those who "have the goods."

In many contemporary house churches, public recognition constitutes a Trojan horse of sorts. Some men just can't handle the recognition. It inflates their egos. The title gives them a power trip. Worse still, it transforms some people into control freaks.

We must remember that in the first century it was the itinerant workers who publicly acknowledged overseers (Acts 14:23; Titus 1:5). Therefore, it falls upon extralocal workers today (with the input of the church) to discern the timing and method of how overseers are to be acknowledged.[8] The recognition of overseers—when they emerge—should not be pressed into any rigid mold. Some church planters directly recognize overseers. Others do so tacitly.

The bottom line is that when we attach the recognition of elders to special ceremonies, licenses, seminary degrees, etc., we are speaking where the Bible doesn't speak.

We do well to keep in mind that in the New Testament the principle of recognizing elders exists. But the method is open. And it always has the sense of *recognizing* a dynamic function rather than *placing* into a static office.

In addition, we are on safe scriptural ground if elders are recognized by extralocal workers who know the church well. This safeguards the church from being controlled and manipulated by local, self-appointed leadership.

8. *Doesn't Paul use the word "apostle" as an official title when speaking of himself?*

Contrary to popular thinking, most of Paul's correspondence contains a subtext that affirms that he is *not* an offici-apostle. Granted, Paul regularly makes known his special function in the salutation of his letters (e.g. "Paul, an apostle of Jesus Christ"). But he never once identifies himself as "the apostle Paul."

This is a meaningful distinction. The former is a description of a special function based on divine commission. The latter is an official title. As previously stated, nowhere in the New Testament do we find any ministry or function in the body used as a title before the names of God's servants. Christians who are "title happy" need to seriously reflect on this.

9. *Doesn't Ephesians 4:11 envision a clergy? It says, "And He gave some as apostles, and some as prophets, and some as evangelists, and some as pastors and teachers" (NASB).*

Not at all. Ephesians 4 has in view those gifts that equip the church for its diversity of service (vv. 12–16). The gifts listed in this text are actually gifted *persons* who empower the church (vv. 8, 11). They are not the gifts that the Holy Spirit distributes to each *individual* as He wills (1 Cor. 12:11).

Put another way, Ephesians 4 is not discussing gifts given to men and women. It's discussing gifted men and women who are given to the church. Apostles, prophets, evangelists, and pastors/teachers are people given by the ascended Lord to His church for its formation, coordination, and upbuilding. (See my article "Rethinking the Fivefold Ministry" for details, www.ptmin.org/fivefold.htm.)

Their chief task is to nurture the believing community into responsible roles. Their success is rooted in their ability to empower and mobilize God's people for the work of the ministry. In this way, the Ephesians 4 gifts equip the body to fulfill God's eternal purpose.

These ascension gifts are not offices. Nor are they formal positions. The Greek has no definite article connected with these terms. They are merely brethren with peculiar "enabling" gifts designed to cultivate the ministries of their fellow brethren.

In short, Ephesians 4:11 doesn't envision a hired clergy, a professional ministry, or a special priestcraft. Neither are they a special class of Christians. Like Paul's catalog of gifts in 1 Corinthians 12:28, Ephesians 4 has in view special functions rather than formal positions.

10. *Doesn't the mention of "governments" or "administration" in 1 Corinthians 12:28 show that the early church possessed church officials?*

The Greek word translated "governments" in the KJV and "administration" in the NIV is *kubernesis*. According to New Testament scholar Gordon Fee,

> *the noun occurs three times in the LXX [the Greek Old Testament], where it carries the verbal idea of giving "guidance" to someone. Since the word "administration" in contemporary English conjures up the idea of*

*"administrative skills," which is a far cry from what Paul had in mind,
the better translation here might be "acts of guidance," although it is
likely that it refers to giving wise counsel to the community as a whole,
not simply to other individuals.*[9]

In this light, to invest an official form of church polity into this word
is unwarranted and untenable. The only "government" that the *ekklesia* knows is the undiluted government of Jesus Christ (Isa. 9:6). While
overseers supply supervision and guidance to a local church, they don't
"govern" or "rule" it. Thus the terms "governments" and "administration"
are poor translations.

*11. Doesn't the Bible say that Timothy was "ordained the first bishop
of the church of Ephesus"? And doesn't it also say that Titus was
"ordained the first bishop of the church of the Cretians"?*

Some editions of the KJV have these notes annexed to the end of the so-
called Pastoral Epistles. But they don't appear in the Greek text. The
translators of the KJV inserted them in the seventeenth century.

As we have already stated, both Timothy and Titus were not bishops.
Nor were they pastors. They were Paul's apostolic coworkers—church
planters, if you will (Rom. 16:21; 1 Cor. 16:10; 2 Cor. 8:23; 1 Thess. 1:1;
2:6; 3:2; 2 Tim. 2:15; 4:10).

Significantly, the monarchical episcopate (the bishop system) did not
take root until long after the New Testament was completed. Hence, the
historical evidence that Timothy and Titus were "first bishops" is just as
scanty as the idea that Peter was the "first bishop" of Rome. All of these
suppositions conflict with the New Testament narrative as well as with
church history. They are human inventions that have no biblical basis.

12. *Acts 15:22 mentions "chief men among the brethren" (KJV). Doesn't this imply the existence of hierarchical authority in the early church?*

The KJV translates this text using the terms "chief men"—which gives it a hierarchical flavor. However, the Greek word for "chief" is *hegeomai*. And it simply means "leading" or "guiding." (See the NASB and NIV.)

This text underscores the fact that Judas (not Iscariot) and Silas were among the respected brothers in the Jerusalem church. They were *responsible* men—probably elders as well as prophets (Acts 15:32). For this reason the church of Jerusalem selected them as temporary messengers to Antioch (compare with Prov. 10:26; 25:19). Therefore, to extract hierarchy from this verse cannot be justified.

13. *Doesn't Paul's metaphor of the body of Christ demonstrate that authority works in a hierarchical mode? That is, when the Head signals to the hand, it must first signal to the arm. So the hand must submit to the arm in order for it to obey the Head.*

Anyone who is conversant with human anatomy knows that the above description reflects a flawed understanding of how the physical body works.

The brain sends *direct* signals to those body parts it seeks to control through the peripheral nervous system. Consequently, the head controls all of the body's parts *immediately* and *directly* through the nerves. It doesn't pass its impulses through a chain-of-command schema invoking other body parts.

Thus the head doesn't command the arm to tell the hand what to do. Instead, the head is connected to the entire body through the nervous system. For this reason, the proper application of the body metaphor preserves the unvarnished truth that there is only one source of authority in the church—Jesus Christ. And all members are connected by His life and placed under His direct control.

In this regard, the Bible is crystal clear in its teaching that Jesus Christ is the *only* mediator between God and man (1 Tim. 2:5). While the old economy had human mediators, the new covenant knows no such thing. As participants of the new covenant, we need no mediator to tell us to know the Lord. All who are under this covenant may know Him directly—"from the least of them to the greatest" (Heb. 8:6–11). Mutual subjection, not hierarchical submission, is what engenders the proper coordination of the body of Christ.

14. *Every physical body has a head. Therefore, every local body of believers needs a head. If it doesn't have one, it will be chaotic. Pastors are the heads of local churches. They are little heads under Christ's headship.*

This idea is born out of the imaginations of fallen humans. There is not a shred of biblical support for such an idea. The Bible *never* refers to a human being as a "head" of a church. This title exclusively belongs to Jesus Christ. He is the *only* Head of each local assembly. The church has no head under His own. Therefore, those who claim to be heads of churches supplant the executive headship of Christ.

15. *Don't John 5:30; John 14:28, 31; and 1 Corinthians 11:3 teach a hierarchical relationship within the Trinity?*

No, they do not. These passages don't have in view the Son's eternal relationship with His Father in the Godhead. They instead refer to His temporal relationship as a human being who voluntarily submitted Himself to His Father's will. In the Godhead, the Father and the Son experience communality and mutual submission through the Spirit.

Kevin Giles accurately says, "Nothing in Scripture indicates that the Father-Son-Spirit are eternally hierarchically ordered in being, work/function, or authority."[10]

For this reason, historic orthodoxy rejects the eternal subordination of the Son of God. It instead accepts the temporal subordination of the Son in His incarnation.[11] Christ's subordination to the Father was temporal, voluntary, and limited to the time of His incarnation (Phil. 2:4–11). Gilbert Belzikian explains,

> *It is impossible within the confines of orthodoxy to derive a model for an order of hierarchy among humans from the ontological structure of the Trinity, since all three persons are equal in essence. Moreover, because Christ's functional subjection is not an eternal condition but a task-driven, temporary phase of ministry, it is presented in Scripture as a model of servanthood and mutual submission for all believers (Phil 2:5–11).[12]*

Kevin Giles adds, "Historic orthodoxy has never accepted hierarchical ordering in the Trinity."[13] To paraphrase the Athanasian Creed, the Son is only inferior to the Father in relation to His manhood; He is equal with the Father in relation to the Godhead.[14] Scripture confirms this in many places. One example is when the writer of Hebrews says that Jesus "learned obedience"—not as the Eternal Son, but in His incarnate state (Heb. 5:8).

Therefore, the New Testament never supports a hierarchical structure or chain-of-command relationship in the Godhead. The Trinity is a communion of coequal persons (Matt. 28:18; John 5:18; 10:30; 14:9; Phil. 2:6). And the fellowship of the Godhead is egalitarian and nonhierarchical.

Again, Kevin Giles isolates the point, saying, "When a doctrine of the church builds on trinitarian thinking, there is no room for hierarchical ordering."[15] Miroslav Volf insightfully adds, "A hierarchical notion of the Trinity ends up underwriting an authoritarian practice in the church."[16]

Objections from Other New Testament Documents

1. Doesn't Hebrews 13:17 command us to obey and submit to our leaders, implying that church leaders possess official authority?

Again, a look at the Greek text proves useful here. The word translated "obey" in Hebrews 13:17 is not the garden-variety Greek word (*hupakouo*) that's usually employed in the New Testament for obedience. Rather, it's the word *peitho*. *Peitho* means to persuade or to win over. Because this word appears in the middle-passive form in Hebrews 13:17, the text ought to be translated "Allow yourselves to be persuaded by your leaders."

This text appears to be an exhortation to give weight to the instruction of local overseers (and possibly apostolic workers). It's not an exhortation to obey them mindlessly. It implies persuasive power to convince and to win over rather than to coerce, force, or browbeat into submission. In the words of Greek scholar W. E. Vine, "The obedience suggested [in Hebrews 13:17] is not by submission to authority, but resulting from persuasion."[17]

Likewise, the verb translated "submit" in this passage is the word *hupeiko*. It carries the idea of yielding, retiring, or withdrawing, as in surrendering after battle. Those who occupy themselves with spiritual oversight don't demand submission. By virtue of their wisdom and spiritual maturity, they are to be accorded with respect. Christians are encouraged to be uncommonly biased toward what they say. Not because of an external office they hold, but because of their godly character, spiritual stature, and sacrificial service to the people of God.

In the words of Hebrews 13:7, we are to "imitate their faith" as we "consider the outcome of their life." By so doing, we make their God-called task of spiritual oversight far easier to carry out (v. 17).

2. *The Bible teaches that those who watch over the souls of the church will have to give an account to God. Doesn't this mean that these people have authority over others?*

Hebrews 13:17 says that those who provide oversight are accountable *to God* for this task. But there's nothing in this text that warrants that they have special authority over other Christians.

Being accountable to God is not the equivalent of having authority. *All* believers are accountable to God (Matt. 12:36; 18:23; Luke 16:2; Rom. 3:19; 14:12; Heb. 4:13; 13:17; 1 Peter 4:5). But this doesn't mean that they have authority over others. (Incidentally, desiring dominion over others is carnal. It's not an outworking of God's grace, but of fallen flesh.)

3. *Didn't Jesus endorse official authority when He commanded His disciples to obey the scribes and Pharisees because they sat in "Moses' seat"?*

Not at all. What Jesus said about the scribes and Pharisees was a rebuke to their practice of *assuming* instructional authority when they possessed none. Matthew 23:2 says, "The scribes and the Pharisees *have seated themselves* in the chair of Moses" (NASB).

Our Lord was merely exposing the fact that the scribes and Pharisees were self-appointed teachers. And they usurped authority over the people (Matt. 23:5–7; Luke 20:46). His statement was an observation, not an endorsement.

The Lord made it unmistakably plain that despite their pretense before men, the scribes and Pharisees didn't have any authority (Matt. 23:11–33). They taught the Law of Moses, but they didn't obey it (23:3b, 23).

In this light, the verse that follows, which says "therefore *all* that they tell you, do and observe" (v. 3a NASB) cannot be understood as a blanket endorsement of Pharisaical authority. This interpretation utterly contradicts the next verse (v. 4). It also contradicts those passages where we find Jesus resolutely breaking Pharisaical teaching—and commanding His disciples to do the same (Matt. 5:33–37; 12:1–4; 15:1–20; 16:6–12; 19:3–9; etc.).

Instead, this phrase must be interpreted by our Lord's reference to Moses' seat. Moses' seat is a literal reference to a special chair set aside in each synagogue from which the Old Testament Scriptures were read.[18]

Whenever the scribes and Pharisees were seated in "Moses' chair," they read straight out of Scripture. Because Scripture has authority, what they read from this seat was binding (regardless of the hypocrisy of the readers). This is the essence of Jesus' statement. The lesson is that even if a self-styled, hypocritical teacher reads from the Bible, what he says *from the Bible* has authority.

Therefore, to project an endorsement of offici-authority onto the lips of the Savior in Matthew 23:2–3 is an example of Jesus co-opted by Roman Papalism. As such, it fails to keep pace with the historic context of the passage, and it reflects nothing of the Gospels themselves.

4. Doesn't the Greek New Testament support the idea that the church includes clergy and laity?

The clergy/laity dichotomy is a tragic fault line that runs throughout the history of Christendom. Yet despite the fact that multitudes have taken the low road of dogmatism to defend it, this dichotomy is without biblical warrant.

The word "laity" is derived from the Greek word *laos*. It simply means "the people." *Laos* includes *all* Christians—including elders. The word appears three times in 1 Peter 2:9–10, where Peter refers to "the people [*laos*] of God." Never in the New Testament does it refer to only a portion of the assembly. It didn't take on this meaning until the third century.

The term "clergy" finds its roots in the Greek word *kleros*. It means "a lot or an inheritance." The word is used in 1 Peter 5:3, where Peter instructs the elders against being "lords over God's heritage [*kleros*]" (KJV). Significantly, the word is never used to refer to church leaders. Like *laos*, it refers to God's people—for they are His heritage.

According to the New Testament, then, all Christians are "clergy" (*kleros*) and all are "laity" (*laos*). We are the Lord's heritage and the Lord's people. To frame it another way, the New Testament doesn't dispose of clergy. It makes *all* believers clergy.

Therefore, the clergy/laity dichotomy is a postbiblical concept that's devoid of any scriptural warrant. It's also a bothersome menace to what God has called the church to be—a functioning body. There's no hint of the clergy/laity or minister/layman schema in the history, teaching, or vocabulary of the New Testament. This schema is a religious artifact that stems from the postapostolic disjunction of secular and spiritual.[19]

In the secular/spiritual dichotomy, faith, prayer, and ministry are deemed the exclusive properties of an inner, sacrosanct world. A world that is detached from the whole fabric of life. But this disjunction is completely foreign to the New Testament ethos where all things are to bring glory to God—even the stuff of everyday life (1 Cor. 10:31).

5. *Don't the seven angels of the seven churches in the book of Revelation represent the presence of a single pastor in each local church?*

The first three chapters of Revelation constitute a flimsy basis upon which to construct the doctrine of "single pastor." First, the reference to the angels of these churches is cryptic. John doesn't give us any clues about their identity. Scholars are not sure what they symbolize. (Some believe they point to literal angels. Others believe they are human messengers.)

Second, there's no analog for the idea of a "solo pastor" anywhere in the New Testament. Nor is there any text that likens pastors unto angels.

Third, the idea that the seven angels refer to the "pastors" of the seven churches is in direct conflict with other New Testament texts. For instance, Acts 20:17 and 20:28 tell us that the church of Ephesus had multiple shepherds (pastors), not one. This is true for all first-century churches that had elders. They were always plural (see chapter 9).

Therefore, to hang the "sola pastora" doctrine on one obscure passage in Revelation is sloppy and careless exegesis. The fact is, there is no support for the modern pastor in Revelation or in any other New Testament document.

Objections from the Old Testament

1. *In Exodus 18, Moses set up a hierarchy of rulers under him to help lead God's people. Isn't this a biblical pattern for hierarchical leadership?*

If we read this account carefully, we'll discover that it was Moses' heathen father-in-law, Jethro, who conceived this idea (Ex. 18:14–27). There is no biblical evidence to suggest that God endorsed it. In fact, Jethro himself admitted that he wasn't sure if God would support it (Ex. 18:23).

Later in Israel's journeys, the Lord directed Moses to take a different course of action regarding the problem of oversight. God commanded Moses to commission elders to help bear the weight of responsibility. Accordingly, Moses selected those men who were *already* elder-ing (Num. 11:16).

This strategy was organic and functional. In this way, it was markedly different from Jethro's notion of a multilayered hierarchy of rulers.

2. *Don't the Old Testament figures of Moses, Joshua, David, Solomon, etc. show that God's perfect will is to have a single leader over His people?*

No, they don't. As previously stated, Moses and every other single leader in the Old Testament were shadows of the Lord Jesus Christ. They were not types of the modern-day single pastorate that was invented during the Reformation.

By contrast, God's will was to instill a theocracy in Israel. (A theocracy is a government where God is the sole King.) Regrettably, the people clamored for a human king, and the Lord gave them their fleshly desire to be like the other nations. But this was never His perfect will (1 Sam. 8:5–9).

Granted, the Lord still worked with His people under a human kingship. But they suffered dire consequences as a result. In like manner, God still works through man-made systems today. Yet they always limit His full blessing. Unfortunately, many Christians still assume that they must have a visible leader to rule over them.

In sum, the Lord's perfect will was for His people to live and serve under His direct reign (Ex. 15:18; Num. 23:21; Deut. 33:5; 1 Sam. 8:7). Israel was called to be a "kingdom of priests" (Ex. 19:6). And she was to confer with the older, wiser men (elders) in times of crisis (Deut. 22:15–18; 25:7–9).

But what Israel lost in her disobedience, the church gained (1 Peter 2:5, 9; Rev. 1:6). Tragically, however, many Christians have opted to return to the old covenant system of religious government—even though God dismantled it long ago.

It should be noted that it's only because of an indwelling Spirit that God's idea of leadership and authority can be observed today. Since the indwelling Spirit was not experienced during Old Testament days, God condescended to the limitations of His people.

When we come to the New Testament era, we discover that the indwelling Christ is the portion of all of God's children. And it is that portion that causes the church to rise to the supernatural level of the "priesthood of all believers." A level where hierarchical, titular, and official leadership styles turn obsolete and counterproductive.

3. *In Psalm 105:15, the Lord says, "Touch not mine anointed, and do my prophets no harm" (KJV). Doesn't this verse teach that some Christians (e.g., pastors) have unquestioned authority?*

Under the old covenant, God specially anointed prophets to be His oracles on the earth. Thus to speak against them was to speak against the Lord. But under the new covenant, the Spirit has been poured out upon *all* God's people. All who have received Christ (the Anointed One) are anointed by the Holy Spirit (1 John 2:27); therefore, all may prophesy (Acts 2:17–18; 1 Cor. 14:24, 31).

In this way, the prayer of Moses that all of God's people would receive the Spirit and prophesy has been fulfilled since Pentecost (Num. 11:29; Acts 2:16–18). Regrettably, Psalm 105:15 has been abused and misapplied by clergy leaders and self-proclaiming "prophets" to control God's people and to deflect criticism.

But here's the truth. Under the new covenant, "touch not God's anointed" is the equivalent of "submit to *one another* out of reverence for Christ" (Eph. 5:21). For the Spirit's anointing has come upon all who have believed on the Messiah.

Therefore, "touch not God's anointed" applies to *every* Christian today. To deny this is to deny that all Christians have the anointing (1 John 2:20, 27).

The Problem of Mistranslation

In view of the foregoing points, some may wonder why the KJV obscures so many texts that have to do with ministry and oversight. Why does the KJV repeatedly insert hierarchical/institutional terms (like "office") that are absent from the original documents?

The answer stems from the fact that the Anglican Church of the seventeenth century issued the KJV. That church rigidly espoused the wedding of the church and the state, and it possessed a mind-set that merged officialdom with Christianity.

King James VI of Scotland ordered the translation that bears his name (the King James Version). In so doing, the king acted in the capacity of the head of the Anglican Church—the state church of England. He then directed the fifty-four scholars who authored the translation not to depart from "traditional terminology" throughout the project.[20]

For this reason, the KJV naturally reflects Anglicanism's hierarchical/institutional presuppositions. Words like *ekklesia, episkopos,* and *diakonos* were not accurately translated from the Greek. Instead, they were translated into the Anglican ecclesiastical jargon of the day: *Ekklesia* was translated into "church;" *episkopos* was translated into "bishop;" *diakonos* was translated into "minister.;" *praxis* was translated into "office;" *proistemi* was translated into "rule;" etc. The original KJV of 1611 went through four revisions up until 1769. Yet these errors were never corrected.

Thankfully, some modern translations have sought to rectify this problem. They have de-Anglicized many of the ecclesiastical terms found in the KJV. They have also accurately translated the Greek words that stand behind them. For example, *ekklesia* has been translated "assembly;" *episkopos* has been translated "overseer;" *diakonos* has been translated "servant;" *praxis* has been translated "function;" and *proistemi* has been translated "guard."

The Mess We Find Ourselves in Today

The primary reason why our ideas on church leadership have strayed so far from God's will can be traced to our tendency to project Western political notions of government onto the biblical writers—reading them back into the text. When we read words like "pastor," "overseer," and "elder," we immediately think in terms of governmental offices like "president," "senator," and "chairman."

So we regard elders, pastors, and overseers as sociological constructs (offices). We view them as vacant slots that possess a reality independent of the persons who populate them. We then ascribe mere men with unquestioned authority simply because they "hold office."

The New Testament notion of leadership is markedly different. As previously stated, there's no biblical warrant for the idea that church leadership is official. Neither is there any scriptural backing for the notion that some believers have authority over other believers. The only authority that exists in the church is Jesus Christ. Humans have no authority in themselves. Divine authority is vested only in the Head and expressed through the body.

Good leadership, therefore, is never authoritarian. It only displays authority when it's expressing the mind of Jesus Christ. The basic tasks of biblical leadership are facilitation, nurture, guidance, and service. To the degree that a member is modeling the will of God in one of those areas, to that degree he or she is leading.

It's no wonder that Paul never chose to use any of the forty-plus common Greek words for "office" and "authority" when discussing leaders. Again, Paul's favorite word for describing leadership is the opposite of what natural minds would suspect. It's *diakonos*, which means a "servant."

BIBLIOGRAPHY

The following bibliography includes the principal publications quoted in this book as well as a number of other related titles.

Part One: Community and Gatherings

Austin-Sparks, T. *God's Spiritual House*. Shippensburg, PA: Destiny Image, 2001.

_____. *The Stewardship of the Mystery*. Shippensburg, PA: Destiny Image, 2002.

_____. *Words of Wisdom and Revelation*. Corinna, ME: Three Brothers, 2000.

Banks, Robert. *Going to Church in the First Century*. Beaumont, TX: Christian Books, 1980.

_____. *Paul's Idea of Community*. Peabody, MA: Hendrickson, 1994.

Banks, Robert, and Julia Banks. *The Church Comes Home*. Peabody, MA: Hendrickson, 1998.

Bilezikian, Gilbert. *Community 101*. Grand Rapids, MI: Zondervan, 1997.

Boff, Leonardo. *Trinity and Society*. Maryknoll, NY: Orbis Books, 1986.

Bonhoeffer, Dietrich. *Life Together*. New York: Harper & Row, 1954.

Bruce, F. F. *A Mind for What Matters*. Grand Rapids, MI: Eerdmans, 1990.

Brunner, Emil. *The Misunderstanding of the Church*. London: Lutterworth Press, 1952.

Cunningham, David. *These Three are One: The Practice of Trinitarian Theology*. Oxford: Blackwell, 1998.

Erickson, Millard. *God in Three Persons*. Grand Rapids, MI: Baker Books, 1995.

Fromke, DeVern. *Ultimate Intention*. Indianapolis: Sure Foundation, 1963.

Giles, Kevin. *What on Earth is the Church? An Exploration in New Testament Theology*. Downers Grove, IL: InterVarsity Press, 1995.

Girard, Robert C. *Brethren, Hang Loose*. Grand Rapids, MI: Zondervan, 1972.

_____. *Brethren, Hang Together*. Grand Rapids, MI: Zondervan, 1979.

Gish, Arthur. *Living in Christian Community*. Scottdale, PA: Herald Press, 1979.

Grenz, Stanley. *Created for Community*. Grand Rapids, MI: Baker Books, 1998.

_____. *Redisovering the Triune God*. Minneapolis: Fortress Press, 2004.

_____. *Theology for the Community of God*. Grand Rapids, MI: Eerdmans, 1994.

Haller, Manfred. *The Mystery of God: Christ All and in All*. Delta: The Rebuilders, 2004.

Hay, Alexander R. *New Testament Order for Church and Missionary*. Audubon, NJ: New Testament Missionary Union, 1947.

Kennedy, John W. *Secret of His Purpose*. Bombay: Gospel Literature Service, 1963.

Kokichi, Kurosaki. *Let's Return to Christian Unity*. Beaumont, TX: Christian Books, 1991.

Kraus, Norman C. *The Community of the Spirit: How the Church is in the World*. Scottdale, PA: Herald Press, 1993.

LaCunga, Catherine. *God for Us: The Trinity and the Christian Life*. San Francisco: HarperSan-Francisco, 1991.

Lang, G. H. *The Churches of God*. Miami Springs, FL: Conleyand Schoettle Publishing, 1985.

Leupp, Roderick. *Knowing the Name of God: A Trinitarian Tapestry of Grace, Faith and Community*. Downers Grove, IL: InterVarsity Press, 1996.

Lewis, C. S. *Mere Christianity*. New York: HarperCollins, 2001.

Lohfink, Gerhard. *Jesus and Community*. Philadelphia: Fortress Press, 1982.

Loosely, Ernest. *When the Church Was Young*. Sargent, GA: SeedSowers, 1988.

Miller, Hal. *Biblical Community: Biblical or Optional?* Ann Arbor, MI: Servant Books, 1979.

Moltmann, Jürgen. *History and the Triune God*. New York: Crossroad, 1992.

_____. *The Trinity and the Kingdom of God*. London: SCM Press, 1981.

Nee, Watchman. *The Normal Christian Church Life*. Anaheim, CA: Living Stream Ministry, 1980.

_____. *The Body of Christ: A Reality*. Richmond, VA: Christian Fellowship Publishers, 1978.

Niebuhr, H. Richard. *The Social Sources of Denominationalism*. New York: Meridian, 1957.

Peters, Ted. *God as Trinity*. Louisville, KY: Westminster Press, 1993.

Schweizer, Eduard. *The Church as the Body of Christ*. Richmond, VA: John Knox Press, 1964.

Smith, Christian. *Going to the Root: Nine Proposals for Radical Church Renewal*. Scottdale, PA: Herald Press, 1992.

Snyder, Howard A. *Decoding the Church: Mapping the DNA of Christ's Body*. Grand Rapids, MI: Baker Books, 2002.

_____. *Radical Renewal: The Problem of Wineskins Today*. Houston: Touch Publications, 1996.

_____. *The Community of the King*. Downers Grove, IL: InterVarsity Press, 1977.

_____. *Why House Churches Today?* (Audio Tape). Fuller Theological Seminary, Feb. 24, 1996.

Svendsen, Eric. *The Table of the Lord*. Atlanta: New Testament Restoration Foundation, 1996.

Thornton, L.S. *The Common Life in the Body of Christ*. London: Dacre Press, 1950.

Torrance, Thomas F. *The Christian Doctrine of God: One Being, Three Persons.* Edinburgh: T & T Clark, 1996.

_____. *The Trinitarian Faith.* Edinburgh: T & T Clark, 1988.

Trueblood, Elton. *The Company of the Committed.* New York: Harper & Row, 1961.

_____. *The Incendiary Fellowship.* New York: HarperSanFrancisco, 1978.

Viola, Frank. *Bethany: The Lord's Desire for His Church.* Gainesville, FL: Present Testimony Ministry, 2007.

_____. *The Untold Story of the New Testament Church.* Shippensburg, PA: Destiny Image, 2004.

Viola, Frank, and George Barna. *Pagan Christianity.* Carol Stream, IL: Tyndale House, 2008.

Volf, Miroslav. *After Our Likeness: The Church as the Image of the Trinity.* Grand Rapids, MI: Eerdmans, 1998.

Wallis, Arthur. *The Radical Christian.* Columbia, MO: Cityhill Publishing, 1987.

Yoder, John Howard. *The Royal Priesthood: Essays Ecclesiastical and Ecumenical.* Scottdale, PA: Herald Press, 1988.

Part Two: Leadership and Accountability

Allen, Roland. *Missionary Methods: St. Paul's or Ours?* Grand Rapids, MI: Eerdmans, 1962.

Banks, Robert. "Church Order and Government" in *Dictionary of Paul and His Letters: A Compendium of Contemporary Biblical Scholarship.* Downers Grove, IL: InterVarsity Press, 1993.

Barrs, Jerram. *Shepherds and Sheep: A Biblical View of Leading and Following.* Downers Grove, IL: InterVarsity Press, 1983.

Best, Ernest. *Paul and His Converts.* Edinburgh: T & T Clark, 1988.

Bruce, F. F. *1 and 2 Thessalonians.* Waco, TX: Word Books, 1982.

_____. *The Epistle to the Hebrews.* Grand Rapids, MI: Eerdmans, 1990.

Burks, Ron, and Viki Burks. *Damaged Disciples: Casualties of Authoritarian Churches and the Shepherding Movement.* Grand Rapids, MI: Zondervan, 1992.

Campbell, R. A. *The Elders: Seniority in Earliest Christianity.* Edinburgh: T & T Clark, 1994.

Campenhausen, Hans von. *Ecclesiastical Authority and Spiritual Power in the Church of the First Three Centuries.* Stanford, CA: Stanford University Press, 1969.

Dunn, James D. G., and John P. Mackey. *New Testament Theology in Dialogue.* Louisville, KY, Westminster Press, 1988.

Fee, Gordon D. *The First Epistle to the Corinthians.* Grand Rapids: Eerdmans, 1987.

Frame, John. *Evangelical Reunion: Denominations and the Body of Christ.* Grand Rapids: Baker Books, 1991.

Giles, Kevin. *Jesus and the Father*. Grand Rapids, MI: Zondervan, 2006.

_____. *The Trinity and Subordinationism*. Downers Grove, IL: InterVarsity Press, 2002.

Ketcherside, W. Carl. *The Twisted Scriptures*. DeFuniak Springs, FL: Diversity Press, 1992.

Miller, Hal. "Leadership in the Church: Ten Propositions." *Searching Together* 11 (1982):3.

Miller, Paul. *Leading the Family of God*. Scottdale, PA: Herald Press, 1981.

Quebedeaux, Richard. *By What Authority: The Rise of Personality Cults in American Christianity*. New York: Harper & Row, 1982.

Ray, Rudy. "Authority in the Local Church." *Searching Together 13 (1984):1*.

Schütz, John H. *Paul and the Anatomy of Apostolic Authority*. New York: Cambridge University Press, 1975.

Smith, Christian. "Church Without Clergy." *Voices in the Wilderness,* (November–December 1988).

Stabbert, Bruce. *The Team Concept*. Tacoma, WA: Hegg Brothers Printing, 1982.

Viola, Frank. *Straight Talk to Pastors*. Gainesville FL: Present Testimony Ministry, 2006.

White, John, and Ken Blue. *Healing the Wounded: The Costly Love of Church Discipline*. Downers Grove, IL: InterVarsity Press, 1985.

Yoder, John Howard. "Binding and Loosing." *Concern*, no. 14 (February 1967).

_____. "The Fullness of Christ, Perspectives on Ministries in Renewal." *Concern*, no. 17 (February 1969).

Zens, Jon. "Building Up the Body: One Man or One Another?" *Searching Together* 10 (1981):2.

_____. "Four Tragic Shifts in the Visible Church." *Searching Together*, 21 (1993):1–4.

_____. "The 'Clergy/Laity' Distinction: A Help or a Hindrance to the Body of Christ?" *Searching Together* 23 (1995):4.

_____. *The Pastor*. St. Croix Falls: Searching Together, 1981.

_____. "Wrestling With Local Church Issues: Perpetuating Biblical Truth or Tradition?" *Searching Together* 33 (2005):3–4; 34 (2006):1.

NOTES

Introduction: Toward a New Kind of Church

1. See George Barna, *Revolution* (Carol Stream: Tyndale, 2005), 9, 39, 65, 107–108.

2. Copernicus's publication, "On the Revolutions of the Celestial Spheres," is often understood to mark the beginning of the scientific revolution.

3. T. Austin-Sparks, *Words of Wisdom and Revelation* (Corinna, ME: Three Brothers, 2000), 49.

4. Adapted from Martin Luther King Jr's famous "I Have a Dream" speech delivered in Washington, DC, on August 28, 1963.

Chapter 1: Reimagining the Church as an Organism

1. Those who are not informed about the Trinity should read James R. White, *The Forgotten Trinity* (Minneapolis: Bethany House, 1998). According to the doctrinal statement of the Evangelical Theological Society, "God is a Trinity, Father, Son, and Spirit, each an uncreated person, one in essence, equal in power and glory."

2. Stanley Grenz, *Created for Community* (Grand Rapids, MI: Baker Books, 1998), 52.

3. John P. Whalen and Jaroslav Pelikan bemoaned the deplorable state of Christian theology, saying that many within the church regard the Trinity to be a "museum piece, with little or no relevance to the critical problems of contemporary life and thought" (Edmund J. Fortman, *The Triune God: A Historical Study of the Doctrine of the Trinity* [Philadelphia: Westminster Press, 1972], xiii).

4. Eugene Peterson, *Christ Plays in Ten Thousand Places* (Grand Rapids, MI: Eerdmans, 2005), 45.

5. Quoted in Ted Peters, *God is Trinity* (Louisville, KY: Westminster Press, 1993), 122.

6. Miroslav Volf, *God's Life in Trinity* (Minneapolis: Fortress Press, 2006), xiv. Today, there is a strong consensus among many evangelical and mainstream theologians on the centrality of the Trinity in the Christian life. See the bibliography, which lists many of their works.

7. For a great discussion on Trinitarian ecclesiology, see Kevin Giles, *What on Earth is the Church?* (London: SPCK, 1995), 212–29.

8. Stanley Grenz, *Theology for the Community of God* (Grand Rapids, MI: Eerdmans, 1994), 482.

9. Kevin Giles, *What on Earth Is the Church?* (London: SPCK, 1995), 222.

10. Quoted in Kevin Giles, *The Trinity and Subordinationism* (Downers Grove: InterVarsity Press, 2002), 103.

11. John 5:30, 14:28, 31, and Corinthians 11:3 do not contradict this principle. These texts have in view the voluntary subjection of Jesus Christ, the man, to God the Father. When Jesus was on earth, He subjected Himself to the Father as a human being, modeling for all human beings what it means to be subject to God. These passages don't support a hierarchical structure or chain-of-command relationship in the Godhead. For this reason, theologians have repudiated the concept of subordination within the Trinity. As Gilbert Bilezekian has said in his book, *Community 101,* "The Church has generally rejected the subordination proposal as a pagan infiltration" (p. 201). For details see Kevin Giles, *The Trinity & Subordinationism* (Downers Grove: InterVarsity Press, 2002); *Jesus and the Father* (Grand Rapids: Zondervan, 2006); Gilbert Bilezekian, *Community 101* (Grand Rapids: Zondervan, 1997), Appendix; and Miroslav Volf, *After Our Likeness: The Church as the Image of Trinity* (Grand Rapids: Eerdmans, 1998).

12. See Frank Viola and George Barna, *Pagan Christianity: Exploring the Roots of Our Church Practices* (Carol Stream: Tyndale, 2008).

13. "Biblical blueprintism" is best embodied in a doctrine known as "the silence of Scripture" and another called "the regulative principle." To my mind, both are highly legalistic and unlivable doctrines. Thus they miss the mark by a considerable distance. The New Testament was never given to us as a law to follow. As Paul said, "The letter kills, but the Spirit gives life" (2 Cor. 3:6).

14. F. F. Bruce, *A Mind for What Matters* (Grand Rapids, MI: Eerdmans, 1990), 263.

15. F. F. Bruce, *The Message of the New Testament* (Grand Rapids: Eerdmans, 1972), 98.

16. From the translator's preface to *Letters to Young Churches* by J. B. Phillips.

17. I agree with those scholars who argue that the word for "head" in reference to Christ being the Head of His body refers to the idea of authority as well as source. See F. F. Bruce, *The Epistles to the Colossians, to Philemon, and to the Ephesians* (Grand Rapids: Eerdmans, 1984), 68–69, 274–75; Francis Foulkes, *Ephesians* (Grand Rapids: Eerdmans, 1989), 73–74.

18. F. F. Bruce, *A Mind for What Matters,* (Grand Rapids, MI: Eerdmans, 1990), 238.

19. Emil Brunner, *The Misunderstanding of the Church* (London: Lutterworth Press, 1952), 54.

20. Interestingly, the noun form of the word *pastor* only appears once in the New Testament (Eph. 4:11), and it is plural ("pastors").

21. To read the story of how the New Testament was arranged nonchronologically and broken up into chapters and verses, see Frank Viola and George Barna, *Pagan Christianity: Exploring the Roots of Our Church Practices* (Carol Stream: Tyndale, 2008), Chapter 11.

22. David King, ed. *The Bible Advocate and Precursor of Unity* (London: A. Hall & Co, 1848), 126.

23. George R. Hunsberger and Craig Van Gelder, ed, *The Church Between Gospel and Culture* (Grand Rapids, MI: Eerdmans, 1996), 149.

24. This isn't magic. The reason has to do with the different pH levels in the various soils.

Chapter 2: Reimagining the Church Meeting

1. For a book that traces this pattern, see Frank Viola, *The Untold Story of the New Testament Church* (Shippensburg, PA: Destiny Image Publishers, 2005).

2. Some have suggested that 1 Corinthians 14:26 is stating a problem. But this interpretation is faulty. Most top-drawer exegetes (F. F. Bruce, Ben Witherington, and Gordon Fee being among them) show clearly that this text is referring to what should be the norm. It's an exhortation and a "description of what should be happening" in Corinth's gatherings (as Gordon Fee puts it). Later in chapter 14, Paul reels in some of the chaos in the church meetings without removing their open-participatory nature.

3. Some examples are Philippians 2:6–11; Colossians 1:15–20; Ephesians 5:14; and 1 Timothy 3:16.

4. As noted earlier, apostolic meetings are led by an apostle. But again, these meetings are temporary, and they are designed to equip the church so that it may function when the apostle isn't present.

5. John Howard Yoder, excerpted from "The Fullness of Christ: Perspectives on Ministries in Renewal," *Concern*, no. 17 (February 1969).

6. For a thorough discussion on the so-called limiting passages (1 Cor. 14:33–34 and 1 Tim. 2:11–14), see my articles "Now Concerning a Woman's Role in the Church" (www.ptmin.org/role.htm) and "God's View of a Woman" (www.ptmin.org/view.htm).

7. George Barna, *Revolution* (Carol Stream, IL: Tyndale, 2005), 51–67, 118.

8. John Howard Yoder, excerpted from "The Fullness of Christ: Perspectives on Ministries in Renewal," *Concern*, no. 17 (February 1969).

9. Taken from an audio message titled "Who Are We?" by Stephen Kaung, April 14, 1995, in Richmond, VA.

Chapter 3: Reimagining the Lord's Supper

1. For the history of how the Lord's Supper devolved from a full meal to what it is today, see Frank Viola and George Barna, *Pagan Christianity* (Carol Stream, IL: Tyndale, 2008), chapter 9.

2. Eduard Schweizer, *The Church as the Body of Christ* (Richmond, VA: John Knox Press, 1964), 37.

3. The Davidic Psalms often refer to God as "the Lord, my portion." Interestingly, David was a shadow of Jesus Christ. Therefore, his repeated statement that the Lord was his portion was a reflection of the Son's eternal relationship with His Father.

4. Stanley Grenz, *Theology of the Community of God* (Grand Rapids, MI: Eerdmans, 1994), 485.

5. Since wine is a natural disinfectant, it's safe for a group to drink it from the same glass.

Chapter 4: Reimagining the Gathering Place

1. Graydon F. Snyder, *Ante Pacem: Archaeological Evidence of Church Life Before Constantine* (Macon, GA: Mercer University Press/Seedsowers, 1985), 67; Graydon F. Snyder, *First Corinthi-*

ans: A Faith Community Commentary (Macon, GA: Mercer University Press, 1991), 3.

2. See chapter 9, pages 186–187.

3. Rodney Stark, *For the Glory of God* (Princeton: Princeton University Press, 2003), 33–34.

4. See chapter 5 of *Pagan Christianity* for a discussion on where the secular/spiritual disconnect came from.

5. Kevin Giles, *What on Earth is the Church?* (Downers Grove, IL: InterVarsity Press, 1995), 219.

6. See chapter 2 of *Pagan Christianity* for the story of where church buildings came from.

7. Taken from a lecture titled "Why House Churches Today?" presented at Fuller Theological Seminary, February 24, 1996.

Chapter 5: Reimagining the Family of God

1. Gilbert Bilezikian, *Community 101* (Grand Rapids, MI: Zondervan, 1997), 182.

2. Miroslav Volf, *After Our Likeness* (Grand Rapids, MI: Eerdmans, 1998), 129.

3. Frederick Buechner, *Listening to Your Life* (San Franciso: HarperSanFrancisco, 1992), 331–32.

Chapter 6: Reimagining Church Unity

1. See Matthew 18:15–18; Rom. 16:17; 1 Cor. 5:1–13; 2 Thess. 3:6. The following texts have in view false doctrines held by professing Christians that distort the person and work of Christ: Gal. 1:8–9; 2 Tim. 4:3; 1 John 4:3; 2 John 1:10. Christians are to reject such doctrines. In addition, texts like Romans 16:17 and Titus 3:9–11 refer to people who use doctrine to polarize and embroil the church. They use their own doctrinal beliefs to divide God's people.

2. The evolution of the clergy system was in large part the result of trying to curb false teaching. But it was a bad solution that created more problems. See *Pagan Christianity,* chapter 5.

3. See Andrew Miller, *Miller's Church History* (Addison: Bible Truth Publishers, 1980).

4. John M. Frame, *Evangelical Reunion: Denominations and the Body of Christ* (Grand Rapids, MI: Baker, 1991), 31.

5. Ibid. In the same vein, H. Richard Niebuhr spoke of the "evil of denominationalism," calling it the ultimate expression of the "moral failure of Christianity." H. Richard Niebuhr, *The Social Sources of Denominationalism* (New York: Meridian, 1957), 21, 25.

6. John W. Kennedy, *Secret of His Purpose* (Bombay: Gospel Literature Service, 1963), 48.

7. Kevin Giles, *What on Earth is the Church?* (Downers Grove, IL: InterVarsity Press, 1995), 202.

Chapter 7: Church Practice and God's Eternal Purpose

1. Some translations say "the purpose of the ages." See also Rom. 8:28; Eph. 1:11; and 2 Tim.1:9.

2. See Frank Viola, *From Eternity to Here* (forthcoming from David C. Cook, early 2009).

3. DeVern Fromke, *Ultimate Intention* (Indianapolis: Sure Foundation, 1963), 24–25.

4. See Frank Viola, *From Eternity to Here* (forthcoming from David C. Cook, early 2009).

5. Stanley Grenz, *Created for Community* (Grand Rapids, MI: Baker Books, 1998), 216.

6. The Lord's Prayer in Matthew 6:10 captures the divine dream: "Your kingdom [rule] come, your will be done on earth as it is in heaven."

7. Miroslav Volf, *After Our Likeness* (Grand Rapids, MI: Eerdmans, 1998), x.

8. Quoted in John McNeil "'Denatured' Church Facing Extinction." ASSIST News Services, February 19, 2006.

9. See Frank Viola, *Bethany* (Gainesville, FL: Present Testimony Ministry, 2007), free eBook at www.ptmin.org/bethany.pdf.

Chapter 8: Reimagining Leadership

1. See Frank Viola and George Barna, *Pagan Christianity* (Carol Stream, IL: Tyndale, 2008), 137–40.

2. Christian Smith, "Church Without Clergy" Voices in the Wilderness, Nov/Dec 1988.

3. Ibid.

4. Kevin Giles, *What on Earth is the Church?* (London: SPCK, 1995), 225.

5. James D. G. Dunn and John P. Mackey, *New Testament Theology in Dialogue* (Philadelphia: Westminster Press, 1987), 126–29.

6. James D. G. Dunn, *Unity and Diversity in the New Testament* (Philadelphia: Westminster Press, 1977), 351.

Chapter 9: Reimagining Oversight

1. See Robert Banks, *Paul's Idea of Community* (Peabody, MA: Hendrickson, 1994), 131–33.

2. Acts 11:29–30; 15:2–6, 22–40; 20:17; 21:17–18; Eph. 4:11; 1 Thess. 5:12–13; 1 Tim. 4:14; 5:17–19; Titus 1:5; Heb. 13:7, 17, 24; 1 Peter 5:1–2.

3. For information on the chronology used, see Frank Viola, *The Untold Story of the New Testament Church* (Shippensburg: Destiny Image, 2004).

4. See Frank Viola and George Barna, *Pagan Christianity* (Carol Stream: Tyndale, 2008), chapter 5, for the history of modern ordination.

5. Regrettably, I've watched contemporary elders do just that. See Frank Viola, *Straight Talk to Pastors* (Gainesville, FL: Present Testimony Ministry, 2006), www.ptmin.org/straight.pdf.

6. See 2 Thessalonians 3:7–9 for the same principle.

7. In 1 Corinthians 9, Paul uses this same analogy. In that text, however, Paul is speaking of apostolic workers (not elders), and he makes clear that finances are in view (not honor).

8. For some powerful insights on the relationship between apostolic work and finances, see Roland

Allen, *Missionary Methods* (Grand Rapids, MI: Eerdmans, 1962), chapter 6, and Watchman Nee, *The Normal Christian Church Life* (Anaheim, CA: Living Stream Ministry, 1980), chapter 8.

9. Note that the "Pastoral Epistles"—1 Timothy, 2 Timothy, and Titus—were written to Paul's apostolic coworkers, not to pastors or churches.

Chapter 10: Reimagining Decision-Making

1. Israel's worship of the golden calf (Ex. 32), their refusal to possess the Promised Land (Num. 13—26), their desire to have an earthly king (1 Sam. 8), and the church in Corinth's approval of an immoral man (1 Cor. 5) are just some examples.

2. Christian Smith, *Going to the Root: Nine Proposals for Radical Church Renewal* (Scottdale, PA: Herald Press, 1992), 72–73.

Chapter 12: Reimagining Authority and Submission

1. Thayer's Greek Lexicon, #5293.

2. This explains why Peter and James, as well as Paul and Barnabas, fluctuated with respect to the measure of spiritual authority they exerted (Acts 1:15; 2:14; 12:17, 25; 13:2, 7, 13ff.; 15:2, 7, 13, 22).

3. Miroslav Volf, *After Our Likeness: The Church as the Image of the Trinity* (Grand Rapids, MI: Eerdmans, 1998), 236.

4. John Howard Yoder, *The Royal Priesthood: Essays Ecclesiastical and Ecumenical* (Scottdale, PA: Herald Press, 1988), 324.

Chapter 13: Reimagining Denominational Covering

1. Just a personal note: I have never been hurt by anyone in the institutional church, so I have no personal axe to grind. All the pastors I have known have been dear friends of mine. Our differing views on ecclesiology never affected our friendship.

2. See David B. Barrett, George T. Kurian, and Todd M. Johnson *World Christian Encyclopedia* (Oxford: Oxford University Press, 2001), 16.

3. The Watchtower Society, the Way International, the Unification Church, the Church of Jesus Christ of Latter-Day Saints are just some examples.

4. An earlier version of the same idea was put forth by Vincent of Lerins in these words: "Christianity is what has been held always, everywhere, and by all."

Chapter 14: Reimagining the Apostolic Tradition

1. John W. Kennedy, *Secret of His Purpose* (Bombay: Gospel Literature Service, 1963), 26.

2. The tradition of the apostles is contained within Scripture. Therefore, the notion held by some Catholic and Orthodox theologians that there exists a body of authoritative and infallible tradition outside of the Bible is untenable.

3. F. F. Bruce, *A Mind for What Matters* (Grand Rapids, MI: Eerdmans, 1990), 239.

4. Howard Snyder, *The Community of the King* (Downers Grove, IL: InterVarsity Press, 1977), 138.

5. See Frank Viola and George Barna, *Pagan Christianity* (Carol Stream: Tyndale, 2008).

6. Note that I have not dealt with these aspects of church life in this volume because this book would end up being far too long.

7. For a detailed discussion on the Tabernacle of David, see Frank Viola, "The Tabernacle of David" audio CD (Gainesville, FL: Present Testimony Ministry, 2002), www.ptmin.org/audiocd.htm.

Chapter 15: Where Do We Go from Here?

1. Greg Hawkins and Cally Parkinson, *Reveal: Who Are You?* (South Barrington, IL: Willow Creek Association), 2007.

2. This definition comes from http://en.wikipedia.org/wiki/Emerging_church. Some people draw a distinction between "emergents" and "emerging Christians." Others do not. I'm using them as synonyms in this chapter.

3. See http://ptmin.org/emergingchurch.htm for details.

4. See Brian McLaren, *A Generous Orthodoxy* (Grand Rapids, MI: Zondervan, 2004).

5. For further reflections on the emerging church conversation, see Frank Viola, *Will the Emerging Church Fully Emerge?* (Gainesville, FL: Present Testimony Ministry, 2005), www.ptmin.org/fullyemerge.htm.

6. T. Austin-Sparks, *Explanation of the Nature and History of "This Ministry"* (Tulsa: Emmanuel Church, 1998), 18.

7. Arthur Wallis, *The Radical Christian* (Columbia, MO: Cityhill Publishing, 1987), 87–88.

8. For more on this principle, see my article "Finding Organic Church" at www.ptmin.org/findingchurch.pdf.

9. The purpose of this book is not to offer a "5-step program" for transitioning an organized church into an organic church. No such program exists. Every congregation is different. And an endless number of factors make this a highly complex endeavor. I would be happy to dialogue with those pastors who are serious about making such a transition. However, let me warn you ahead of time: The process is not like getting a facial; it's reconstructive surgery!

10. If you are a pastor who is reading this and thinking, *I agree with your argument, but if I leave my present job, how will I support my family?* then I invite you to go to www.HouseChurchResource.org and visit the ex-pastors page. That page includes an Ex-Pastors Survival Guide that you may find helpful.

11. Frederick Buechner, *Listening to Your Life* (San Francisco: HarperSanFrancisco, 1992), 331.

Appendix: Objections and Responses about Leadership

1. J. N. Darby, *The Holy Scriptures: A New Translation From the Original Languages* (Wembley: Kingston Bible Trust, 1991), 1435.

2. Gerald F. Hawthorne and Ralph P. Martin, *Dictionary of Paul and His Letters* (Downers Grove, IL: InterVarsity Press, 1993), 658–66.

3. I agree with those scholars who accept the Pauline authorship of the "Pastoral Epistles."

4. F. F. Bruce, *The Epistle to the Hebrews* (Grand Rapids, MI: Eerdmans, 1990), 374, 385, 391.

5. F. F. Bruce, *1 and 2 Thessalonians* (Waco, TX: Word Books, 1982), 118–20; Robert Banks, *Paul's Idea of Community* (Peabody, MA: Hendrickson, 1994), 141, 144.

6. Ibid, F. F. Bruce.

7. For details on the history of modern ordination, see Frank Viola and George Barna, *Pagan Christianity* (Carol Stream, IL: Tyndale, 2008), chapter 5.

8. Not all churches in the first century had elders. For instance, it doesn't appear that there were elders in Corinth or Antioch of Syria. Consequently, present-day workers may acknowledge elders in some churches and not in others. The method of endorsement may also vary from church to church, depending on the circumstances and the Lord's guidance.

9. Gordon D. Fee, *The First Epistle to the Corinthians* (Grand Rapids, MI: Eerdmans, 1987), 622.

10. Kevin Giles, *Jesus and the Father* (Grand Rapids, MI: Zondervan, 2006), 127. Gilbert Bilezikian echoes the point in *Community 101* (Grand Rapids, MI: Zondervan, 1997), 200, saying, "The notion of such a relationship of subordination in the Godhead is completely foreign to Scripture. Indeed, its content teaches exactly the opposite."

11. Kevin Giles, *Jesus and the Father* (Grand Rapids, MI: Zondervan, 2006), 9, 38–39.

12. Gilbert Bilezekian, *Community 101* (Grand Rapids, MI: Zondervan, 1997), 192.

13. Kevin Giles, *Jesus and the Father* (Grand Rapids, MI: Zondervan, 2006), 13.

14. The following books successfully refute the idea that the Trinity is hierarchical: Kevin Giles, *The Trinity and Subordinationism* (Downers Grove, IL: InterVarsity Press, 2002); *Jesus and the Father* (Grand Rapids, MI: Zondervan, 2006); Gilbert Bilezekian, *Community 101* (Grand Rapids, MI: Zondervan, 1997), appendix; Miroslav Volf, *After Our Likeness: The Church as the Image of Trinity* (Grand Rapids, MI: Eerdmans, 1998).

15. Kevin Giles, *What on The Earth is the Church?* (Downers Grove, IL: InterVarsity, 1995), 224.

16. Miroslav Volf, *After Our Likeness* (Grand Rapids, MI: Eerdmans, 1998), 4.

17. *Vine's Expository Dictionary of New Testament Words* (Mclean: Macdonald Publishing Company), 806.

18. E. L. Sukenik, *Ancient Synagogues in Palestine and Greece* (Oxford: Oxford University Press, 1934).

19. For details, see Frank Viola and George Barna, *Pagan Christianity* (Carol Stream, IL: Tyndale, 2008), chapter 5.

20. *The Christian Baptist*, vol. 1 (Nashville: The Gospel Advocate, 1955), 319–24.

MANY CHRISTIANS take for granted that their church's practices are rooted in Scripture. Yet are they—and what difference does it make anyway?

Pagan Christianity? (Tyndale) leads us on a fascinating tour through history that examines the origins of present-day church practices and explains why Viola and Barna believe many of these practices actually hinder spiritual transformation.

The authors' aim: that every believer would settle for nothing less than an authentic, life-transforming church experience that lives out Christ's vision for His church.

PaganChristianity.org